Travel to the edge of America and you end up in San Diego, wedged between th
Anza-Borrego Desert, the **Mexican border**, the **Pacific Ocean**, and the Orang
County–Los Angeles sprawl. The nation's eighth-largest city is tucked so far dow
in the southwest corner of the map it often escapes attention and is rarely men
tioned in the national news, almost as if it exists only as a backdrop for majc
events.

San Diegans hosted the **2003 Super Bowl**, showing off palm trees and tans t
football fans on the East Coast huddled between their fireplaces and TV sets. Eac
time the city shows up on TV, the population rises. Visitors love San Diego, an
with good reason. The city is so mellow, pretty, and laid-back that stress jus
melts away. There's never been an earthquake as intense as those in Los Angele
and San Francisco—just a few tremors to remind locals of their faults. Whe
something horrid does happen, like the 2003 and 2007 wildfires that destroye
neighborhoods, it seems everyone pitches in to help. For the most part, life is caln
here, which drives some of San Diego County's 2.9 million residents to distrac
tion. But it drives others to create great science, art, theater, and literature
There's a reason Dr. Seuss and Dr. Salk both took up residence here.

San Diego's history is lightly buried under its modern façade. The beachfron
lawns, cascades of bougainvillea, and sky-high palms all came from elsewher
The region's original Kumeyaay residents lived in a brown landscape of rocks
chaparral, and sand. In 1769 Spanish explorers and missionaries chose San Di
ego's **Presidio Hill** for their first fort and Franciscan mission in what was the
known as **Alta California**. The early settlers built their first homes and shops a
the base of the hill in what is now called **Old Town**. The developers of the mid
1800s moved their centers of commerce to the shores of San Diego Bay, laying th
foundation for today's downtown. By the late 1800s, San Diego's first buildin
boom was on, to be followed every few decades by another.

San Diego's first big national attention-getter was the **1915–1916 Panama
California Exposition**, designed to celebrate the opening of the Panama Cana
The exposition's greatest effect on the city was an architectural one. Several c
San Diego's most significant buildings were built during that era, from th
Spanish-Moorish palaces in **Balboa Park** to the Spanish-Colonial–style **Santa F
Depot** downtown. Stroll through the park on a Sunday morning, or better yet o
a weekday in late afternoon, and enjoy the sights; it's one of the city's greates
attractions. But ultimately, San Diego's heart is at the beach. Grab a pair of in
line skates and cruise the **Mission Beach Boardwalk**, or sip a cappuccino by L
Jolla Cove. Build a bonfire on **Coronado's Silver Strand**; ride the waves on
boogie board in **Ocean Beach**. Once the sand gets between your toes, you'll b
hooked.

For culture and culinary thrills, visit the village of **La Jolla**'s tony gallerie
and trendy cafés. Do as the locals do and order a glass of white wine and seare
ahi at **George's at the Cove** overlooking the water, or cruise **Prospect Street** in
limo. For more exciting nightlife, head downtown, where the white sails of th
San Diego Convention Center glow against a neon-laced skyline. Take you
chances on getting a table at one of the trendy restaurants in the **Gaslamp Quar
ter**, where shops and cafés stay open past midnight.

ACCESS
SAN DIEGO

Orientation	4
Balboa Park	12
Downtown/Little Italy/Gaslamp Quarter	32
Coronado	62
Uptown	76
Old Town and Mission Valley	90
Point Loma/Harbor Island/Shelter Island	102
Mission Bay and Beaches	114
La Jolla	138
Day Trips	160
Tijuana	168
Gay San Diego	184
History	193
Index	197

SAN DIEGO

Pacific Ocean

La Jolla Blvd.

Turquoise St.

La Jolla Blvd.

Grand Ave.

Kate O. Sessions Memorial Park

Balboa Ave.

Ingraham St.

Mission Bay Dr.

Sail Bay

Mission Bay

Fiesta Island

Mission Blvd.

W Mission Bay Dr.

Mission Beach Park

Mission Bay Park

■ Sea World

San Diego Fwy.

Mission Bay Dr.

Sea World Dr.

Friars Rd.

Ocean Beach Fwy.

Pt. Loma Blvd.

Midway Dr.

Sports Arena Blvd.

Sunset Cliffs Blvd.

Nimitz Blvd.

Barnett Ave.

✈ Lindbergh Field San Diego Int'l Airport

Pt. Loma Ave.

Chatsworth Blvd.

Rosecrans St.

N Harbor Dr.

Catalina Blvd.

Sunset Cliffs Park

North San Diego Bay

Cabrillo Memorial Dr.

US Naval Air Station

Navy Sea 'n Air Golf Course

Alameda Blvd.

4th

CORONADO

Ocean Blvd.

Cabrillo National Monument

N

Got a few more days? Drive to the **Cleveland National Forest** and ride mountain bikes through **Julian**. Pose beside a blossoming ocotillo cactus in the Anza-Borrego Desert; go sleigh-riding on **Mount Laguna**. Just leave plenty of time for the beach.

Area code 619 unless otherwise noted.

Getting to San Diego Airport

Lindbergh Field is on the shores of **San Diego Bay**, 3 miles northwest of downtown. The wisdom of having a major international airport so close to the city has been debated for decades, but it certainly is convenient for visitors, who have a 5-minute cab ride to downtown hotels. Taxis to other destinations are another story—you can easily run up a hefty fare heading north or east (see below). The airport has three terminals: **Terminal 1** (the East Terminal); **Terminal 2** (the West Terminal); and **Commuter** terminal, with transportation between provided by the Red Bus Shuttle. Be forewarned that you cannot walk to the Commuter terminal from the main airport. Ask which terminal your flight is leaving from before heading to the airport. www.san.org

AIRPORT SERVICES (AREA CODE 619)

Currency Exchange....295.1501 (Terminal 1); 681.1941 (Terminal 2)	
Customs	557.5370
Ground Transportation	231.7361
Harbor Police Emergency	223.1133
Harbor Police Nonemergency	686.6272
Information Recording	400.2404
Lost and Found	400.2140
Operations Supervisor	400.2710
Paging	400.2900
Parking	291.2087
Traveler's Aid	231.7361 (Terminal 1); 231.5230 (Terminal 2)

AIRLINES

Aeroméxico	238.2093, 800/237.6639
Air Canada	888/247.2262
Airtran Airways	800/247.8726
Alaska Airlines	800/252.7522
Aloha Airlines	800/367.5250
America West	800/235.9292
American Airlines	800/433.7300
Continental Airlines	800/252.0280
Delta Airlines	800/221.1212
Expressjet Airlines	888/958.9538
Frontier Airlines	800/432.1359
Hawaiian Airlines	800/367.5320
JetBlue	800/538.2583
Midwest Airlines	800/452.2022
Northwest Airlines	800/225.2525
SkyBus Airlines	www.skybus.com
Southwest Airlines	800/435.9792
Sun Country	800/359.6786
United Airlines	800/864.8331
US Air	800/428.4322
WestJet	888/937.5838

Getting to and from Lindbergh Field

BY BUS

San Diego Transit's bus 992 "The Flyer" (685.4900, 233.3004, 800/262.7837, 800/COMMUTE) runs between all of the airport's terminals and downtown approximately every 10 minutes between around 5:00AM and midnight. There is an excellent web site at www.sdcommute.com that details bus routes and times.

BY SHUTTLE

Shuttles can be found at the transportation plazas across from Terminals 1 and 2. Companies that provide door-to-door shuttle service from the San Diego airport are A Blue Shuttle (466.6885, 800/719.3499), Coronado Livery (435.6310), EZ Ride (800/777.0585), Seatop Shuttle (222.2744), Xpress Shuttle (591.0303, 800/900.7433), Cloud 9 Shuttle (800/974.8885), Access Shuttle (282.1515, 800/690.9090), and Sea Breeze Shuttle (297.7463, 800/777.0585).

BY LIMOUSINE

Limousines are not commonly used for airport transportation in San Diego. A limo from the airport to La Jolla is a very expensive option. Companies providing limousine service are listed below.

La Costa Limousine	888/299.5466
Paul the Greek's Limo	287.6888, 440.5555
Presidential Limousine	702.7737, 888/267.7080

BY CAR

From the airport, take **Harbor Drive** to downtown and to **Interstate 5** (**I-5**) north, which goes to Old Town and La Jolla and connects with **Interstate 8** (**I-8**) to the beaches and **Mission Valley**. To get to the airport from downtown, take Harbor Drive; from other areas, take I-5 to the airport exit and follow the signs through a convoluted series of right turns to Harbor Drive and the

How to Read This Guide

ACCESS® SAN DIEGO is arranged by neighborhood so you can see at a glance where you are and what is around you. The numbers next to the entries in the following chapters correspond to the numbers on the maps. The text is color coded according to the kind of place described:

Restaurants/Clubs: Red

Hotels: Purple | Shops: Orange

P Parks/Outdoors: Green | Sights/Culture: Blue

♿ Wheelchair accessible

Wheelchair Accessibility

An establishment (except a restaurant) is considered wheelchair accessible when a person in a wheelchair can easily enter a building (i.e., no steps, a ramp, a wide-enough door) without assistance. Restaurants are deemed wheelchair accessible *only* if the above applies *and* if the restrooms are on the same floor as the dining area and their entrances and stalls are wide enough to accommodate a wheelchair.

Rating the Restaurants and Hotels

The restaurant star ratings take into account the quality, service, atmosphere, and uniqueness of the restaurant. An expensive restaurant doesn't necessarily ensure an enjoyable evening, whereas a small, relatively unknown spot could have good food, professional service, and a lovely atmosphere. Therefore, on a purely subjective basis, stars are used to judge the overall dining value (see the star ratings at right). Keep in mind that chefs and owners often change, which sometimes drastically affects the quality of a restaurant. The ratings in this guidebook are based on information available at press time.

The price ratings, as categorized at right, apply to restaurants and hotels. These figures describe general

price-range relationships among other restaurants and hotels in the area. The restaurant price ratings are based on the average cost of an entrée for one person, excluding tax and tip. Hotel price ratings reflect the base price of a standard room for two people for one night during the peak season.

Restaurants

★	Good
★★	Very Good
★★★	Excellent
★★★★	Extraordinary Experience
$	The Price Is Right (less than $10)
$$	Reasonable ($10–$15)
$$$	Expensive ($16–$20)
$$$$	Big Bucks ($21 and up)

Hotels

$	The Price Is Right (less than $100)
$$	Reasonable ($100–$175)
$$$	Expensive ($175–$250)
$$$$	Big Bucks ($250 and up)

MAP KEY

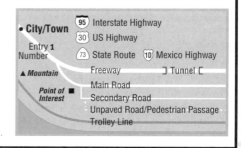

airport entrance. Ask in advance which terminal your airline is in so you can take the proper entrance to the airport. Entrances are clearly marked.

RENTAL CARS

Some car-rental companies have counters at the airport, while others have courtesy phones at baggage claim and shuttle transport to their facilities. They're generally open between 5:30AM and midnight. Car rental return for most companies is located by the Commuter terminal.

Advantage 858.3730, 800/777.5500

Alamo 297.0311, 800/462.5266

Avis 688.5000, 800/331.1212

Budget 254.8686, 800/527.0700

Dollar 866/434.2226

Hertz 220.5222, 800/654.3131

National 497.6777, 800/227.7368

Payless 296.4966, 800/729.5377

Rent4Less 233.6277, 866/614.7368

BY TAXI

Taxis line up at the transportation plaza and the fares are the same for all cab companies. The fare to downtown is usually between $10 and $12; to Mission Valley and the beaches, it's about $20 to $25. But if you're headed for La Jolla and other outlying communities, the shuttles are a better deal.

BUS STATION (LONG-DISTANCE)

Buses are not as popular here in autoland as they are on the East Coast, and bus travel seems popular primarily among those who simply can't afford to get around any other way. The **Greyhound Lines** terminal is downtown (120 W Broadway, at First Ave; 515.1000, 800/231.2222; baggage, 515.1103). Taxis are available at the bus station.

PERSONAL SAFETY

Pedestrians from other cities might be shocked by how San Diegans obey crossing signs. The police actually do cite people for jaywalking and crossing against the light. The most common crimes tourists deal with are car theft and robberies; keep all your belongings stashed out of sight and your doors locked.

PUBLICATIONS

San Diego's one major daily newspaper, the *San Diego Union-Tribune*, covers the arts, entertainment, and restaurants. Its Thursday *Night & Day* section has listings of events in San Diego and Baja. The *Reader* is distributed free on Thursdays at restaurants and shops and contains information on dining and entertainment. *Riviera*, distributed in hip restaurants and clubs, has the best coverage of new trends and happenings.

RESTAURANTS

Restaurants in San Diego are generally casual, with few requiring jackets and ties for men. Waits can be long, especially in downtown's **Gaslamp Quarter** and in **La Jolla;** reservations are strongly advised for weekend dinners. Most establishments accept credit cards.

SHOPPING

Galleries and boutiques abound in the **Gaslamp Quarter, Old Town, Hillcrest, Seaport Village, Fashion Valley, Mission Valley,** and **La Jolla.**

SMOKING

Smoking is prohibited in public buildings, stores, restaurants, bars, and even at the stadium. There is a county-wide ban on smoking in all state parks and there are city-wide bans in San Diego, Del Mar, and Solana Beach that forbid smoking in public parks and on beaches. Be aware that in health-conscious California, you're likely to offend someone even when you're lighting up outdoors.

STREET PLAN

The ocean provides a perfect geographical landmark to the west; if it's on your left, you're heading north. Most attractions are located near the coast.

TAXES

San Diego's sales tax is 7.75% on all purchases except groceries. The hotel tax is 10.5%.

TICKETS

Ticketmaster (Charge-By-Phone, 220.8497) is a computerized ticket center for concerts and sports events; there are several outlets around town, or you can charge your tickets by phone.

The **San Diego Performing Arts League's Arts Tix** (28 Horton Plaza, downtown; 497.5000, 238.0700) sells half-price, day-of-performance tickets on a first-come, first-served basis. They are also a Ticketmaster outlet.

TIME ZONES

San Diego is on Pacific Time, 3 hours earlier than New York and 3 hours later than Hawaii.

TIPPING

A 15% tip is standard in restaurants and taxis, and $1 per bag is expected by hotel porters. Concierges anticipate tips based on the extent and quality of their services. Hotel housekeepers appreciate $1 for each night's stay.

VISITORS' INFORMATION CENTERS

The excellent **International Visitor Information Center** (1040⅓ W Broadway at Harbor Dr; 236.1212) is open June, July, and August seven days a week from 9AM to 5PM. From Labor Day (Sept) thru Memorial Day (May) it is open daily from 9AM to 4PM. The **San Diego Convention and Visitors Bureau** will send brochures and a good visitor's guide magazine on request. Write them at 2215 India Street, San Diego, CA 92101; call 232.3101; or go to their web site at www.sandiego.org. The **San Diego Visitor Information Center** (2688 E Mission Bay Dr, off I-5, Mission Bay; 276.8200) is open Monday through Saturday between 9AM and 5PM and on Sunday between 9:30AM-4:30PM and is filled with brochures; clerks can help you make hotel reservations. For travelers with disabilities, **Accessible San Diego** (P.O. Box 124526, San Diego, CA 92112-4526; 858/279.0704; www.accessandiego.com) operates an information hotline with complete info on access to tours, hotels, attractions, and businesses.

BALBOA PARK

In a wise and prescient move, San Diego's early developers reserved 1,200 acres
rugged canyons and hilltops just outside downtown for a community park (an
made the smart decision to hire the city's premier horticulturist, Kate Sessions,
design the landscape). Actually, they also had commerce in mind. **Balboa Park**
first Spanish-Colonial buildings were constructed for the **1915–1916 Panama
California Exposition.** Several of the exhibition's structures are still in use, includ
ing the **Cabrillo Bridge,** the **California Building** (topped by the tiled **Californ
Tower**), the **Administration Building,** and the **Chapel of St. Francis,** all part of to
day's **Museum of Man.** Fairgoers entered the park via the Cabrillo Bridge over th

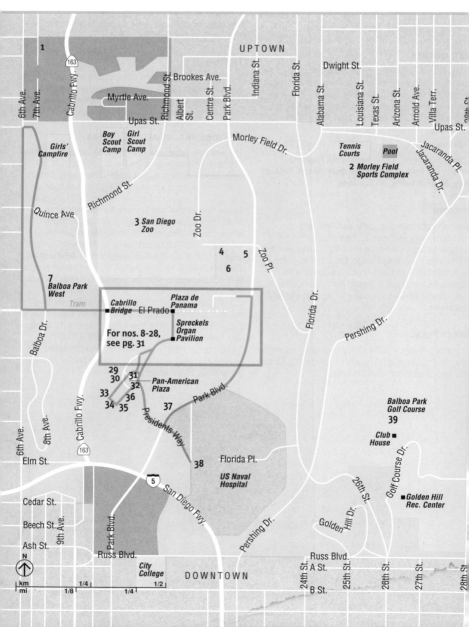

FREE TUESDAYS

A thorough tour of **Balboa Park** can be expensive, as most museums charge an entry fee. A good way to save money is by purchasing a Passport to Balboa Park, available at the **Balboa Park Visitors Center** in front of the **Timken Art Gallery**. The $30 passport covers admission to 13 of the museums and is valid for a week. Alternatively, visit the park on a Tuesday—most museums have free admission one Tuesday of each month, as follows:

1st Tuesday
Natural History Museum

San Diego Model Railroad Museum

Reuben H. Fleet Science Center (fee charged for Space Theater)

Centro Cultural de la Raza

2nd Tuesday
Museum of Photographic Arts

Museum of San Diego History

Veterans Museum and Memorial Center

3rd Tuesday
San Diego Museum of Art

San Diego Museum of Man

Japanese Friendship Garden

Mingei International Museum

San Diego Art Institute

4th Tuesday
San Diego Air & Space Museum

San Diego Automotive Museum

San Diego Hall of Champions

House of Pacific Relations International Cottages

In 1978 **Balboa Park** was struck by its second arson fire in just a few months, and the entire Globe complex was destroyed. By December 1979 ground had been broken for a new and better complex that was still modeled after the first. In 1982 the new **Old Globe Theatre** became the centerpiece of three stages, which also included the **Cassius Carter Centre Stage** and the outdoor **Lowell Davies Festival Theatre**, where summer-night performances of plays like *The Night of the Iguana* are enhanced by animal cries from the zoo next door. The Globe is scheduled for a major renovation starting in the summer of 2008 (projected to run into 2010) and will completely rebuild the smallest of its three theaters to create the Cassius Carter Centre Stage for the new **Sheryl and Harvey White Theater**. A new education center is planned for a second story above the existing pub. Over the years, scores of famous actors and actresses have begun or advanced their careers here under the direction of Executive Director Craig Noel and Artistic Director Jack O'Brien (winner of several Tonys for his work on Broadway and elsewhere). Both Dennis Hopper and Hal Holbrook starred in *Merchant of Venice*; Neil Simon premiered two of his works at the Globe. *Into the Woods*, *Play On!* and *The Full Monty* all went on to Broadway after successful runs here.

The Tony award–winning Globe Theatres produce over a dozen plays annually. The complex includes an excellent gift shop with puppets, T-shirts, books and videos on theater topics, and even Cliff's Notes for those not quite familiar with Shakespeare. **Lady Carolyn's Pub** serves salads, sandwiches, desserts, and coffee drinks 90 minutes before performances. ◆ Theater tours Sa, Su, 10:30AM. Tour fee. El Prado (between the Museum of Man and the San Diego Museum of Art). 23-GLOBE, tour info, 231.1941. ↻ www.theoldglobe.org

SAN DIEGO MUSEUM OF ART

9 SAN DIEGO MUSEUM OF ART

Above this museum's ornate entryway are the coats of arms of San Diego, California, Spain, and America; statues of Spanish painters Murillo, Zurbarán, and Velázquez; and a giant curved seashell, representing the shell that carried St. James to the coast of Spain. The façade, designed in stages by **William Templeton Johnson** and **Robert W. Snyder** between 1924 and 1926, was meant to resemble the buildings of the 16th-century Spanish Renaissance. It was decorated in the Plateresque style, derived from the Spanish word *platero* (silversmith),

Restaurants/Clubs: Red | Hotels: Purple | Shops: Orange | Outdoors/Parks: Green | Sights/Culture: Blue

SAN DIEGO MUSEUM OF ART

Upper Level

The Gluck Collection
Elevator
South Asian Art
Contemporary Art
European Old Master Paintings
Rest Rooms

Ground Level

Asian Art
Asian Art
Asian Art
Restrooms
Image Gallery
Elevator
American Art
Special Exhibition
European Art
Rotunda
Museum Store
Docent Desk
Phone
Coat Check
Information
Main Entrance
Special Exhibitions

Auditorium

Sculpture Garden
Sculpture Court & Café
Library

because the intricate ornamentation resembles the refinements of the silver-smith's art.

The museum was known as the **Fine Arts Gallery of San Diego** until 1978, when curators found that visitors assumed the museum's collection was for sale. The name was then changed, though the membership is still called the Fine Arts Society. Between the 1920s and the 1940s, much of the gallery's internationally acclaimed collection of Italian Renaissance and Spanish Baroque paintings was donated by Anne R. and Amy Putnam, two

On seeing the grounds of the 1935 Exposition, retiree Joseph E. Dryer said, "Truly, this is heaven on earth." In 1940 he started the Heaven on Earth Club, an early-day tourism bureau aiming to perpetuate the civic impetus from the fair and promote San Diego.

The Park is nearly square. It is one and 1/2 miles across. The skyline to the north is outlined by chains of mountains 10,000 feet high. To the southwest, the Coronado Islands are weird, fantastic forms in the unlimited space of ocean. To the northwest is Point Loma. Beyond are glimpses of the Pacific, and below the beautiful San Diego Bay covering twenty-two square miles in this wonderful land.

—the *New York Evening Post*, 1902

sisters who devoted their lives and estates to collecting important paintings. During World War II, the paintings were loaned to several other US museums, and the gallery became a 423-bed military hospital. When the patients moved out, William Templeton Johnson was commissioned and paid $5 a day to get the galleries back in shape.

Thanks to the largesse of several San Diegans, the museum's permanent collection has continued to grow. Spanish Baroque paintings, 19th- and 20th-century European paintings, and works by contemporary California artists comprise the bulk of the museum's holdings. Architects **Robert Mosher** and **Roy Drew** designed the **West** and **East Wings**, in 1966 and 1970, respectively, for Asian arts and sculpture. The **May S. Marcy Sculpture Garden** was designed in 1972 by **Marie Wimmer** and **Joseph Yamada** to provide needed space to update the museum's growing sculpture collection, including works by Henry Moore and Louise Nevelson.

The museum presents exciting and unusual traveling exhibits; recent ones have included a fascinating display of picture frames from 1860 to 1960. One popular exhibit displayed psychedelic rock posters; another covered the works of Grandma Moses. Each spring, the museum presents **Art Alive**, with floral designers, artists, and gardeners creating arrangements of flowers and greenery to express their interpretations of the museum's artworks. The exhibit draws enormous crowds; proceeds benefit the museum's educational programs. Jazz, chamber music, classical guitar, and other concerts are held at the museum frequently, along with various lecture series.

Harking back to its role as a landscaped plaza at the 1915 exposition, the parking lot in front of the museum is called the **Plaza de Panama**. The museum marks the northern side of the plaza; the **Spreckels Organ Pavilion** is at its south end. ♦ Admission. Tu-Su, 10AM-6PM; Th, 10AM-9PM. 232.7931. ♿ www.sdmart.org

Within the San Diego Museum of Art:

Waters Café

★$ Waters Fine Catering operates the café in the museum's Sculpture Court and serves gourmet salads, sandwiches, and tempting desserts amid the bronzes. ♦ Tu-F, 11AM-2:30PM; Sa, Su, 11:30AM-3:30PM. 237.0675

10 Botanical Building and Lily Pond

Designed by **Carleton Winslow** and **Gerald Wellington**, this structure and pond (originally called **La Laguna**) were built as a garden display for the 1915 fair. The building was closed during and after World War I; it reopened for a short time in the 1930s, when hundreds of yellow canaries were caged beside floral displays inside the building. The edifice was closed again during World War II and remained so until it was restored in 1957. At that time, new redwood lathing was used to strengthen the structure, which measures 250 feet long, 75 feet wide, and 60 feet high. The building was closed for several months in early 2002 while 12 miles (or 70,000 linear feet) of redwood lath was replaced. Inside, sunlight streams over towering tree ferns; waterfalls and fountains are covered with moss and delicate orchids; and in spring, tulips and lilies abound. The plants are clearly labeled, giving local gardeners a chance to explore new treasures for their plots at home.

Pastel yellow, pink, and blue lotuses and lilies bloom in the 193-foot-long pond, also known as the Reflecting Pool, that stretches from El Prado to the **Botanical Building**. During World War II, the pond was a swimming pool for patients of the **Naval Hospital**; during the summer of 1945, over 22,000 San Diego children also made this their swimming hole. Today artists, musicians, magicians, and mimes set up shop on weekends for the crowds beside the pond. A truly beautiful spot, the lawns surrounding the pond are popular with loungers, sunbathers, and locals who come here to relax and read the Sunday newspapers. ♦ Free; closed on Th. Between the Casa del Prado and the Timken Art Gallery. 235.1100

11 Village Grill

★$ Located beneath shade trees near the **Spanish Village,** this small grill serves hotdogs, hamburgers, soups, and other fast food. The tile-decorated tables under umbrellas are in big demand on sunny days; you can also find a seat to eat your lunch under the shade of the Moreton Bay fig tree across the street. ♦ Old Globe Way (at Village Place). Daily, 9AM-4PM, 5PM in summer. 702.2428

12 Casa del Prado

This edifice was the inspiration of Bea Evenson, who founded the Committee of 100 in 1967 to preserve **Balboa Park**'s architecture. Originally erected in 1914 as the fair's **Food and Beverage** building (another **Carleton Winslow** design), it was used by the navy during both world wars and as offices for civic groups in between. The building became temporary headquarters for the **San Diego Public Library** between 1952 and 1954. Like many of the park's structures, it fell into disrepair over the years. The city could barely keep up with maintenance and restoration of the many buildings left from the two expositions, and this was one of those to fall by the wayside. The civic groups using the building's offices gradually found more modern space, and the edifice was virtually abandoned in the 1960s.

The structure was declared unsafe and closed after a moderate earthquake in 1968. Before it was sold to a wrecking company for $25, members of the Committee of 100 carefully removed much of the statuary from the original building and had it recast for what is standing here today. Architect **Richard George Wheeler** was already familiar with the park's buildings from the 1915 exposition—he had sketched them as a child—when he designed the current structure.

Like its forerunner, this edifice combines copies of various Mexican and Spanish buildings, including chapels from the Catedral Metropolitana in Mexico City and a patio in Querétaro, Mexico. The ornaments and embellishments on the façade include the face of Neptune, the figures of St. Jerome and Queen Isabella, and a veritable covey of cherubs.

A 680-seat auditorium houses the **Junior Theatre** and other performing-arts

organizations. The San Diego Floral Association sponsors garden shows in the building on most weekends throughout the year, with some impressive displays of orchids, bonsai, and cacti. ♦ Between the Natural History Museum and the Lily Pond. Junior Theatre box office, 239.8355. &
www.juniortheatre.com

13 NATURAL HISTORY MUSEUM

The San Diego Society of Natural History was founded in 1874 but didn't have a permanent setting for its collection until Ellen Browning Scripps donated $125,000 for a museum in 1931. **William Templeton Johnson** designed the structure, which was completed in 1933. For many decades, the museum housed displays on the region's minerals, endangered and extinct animals, and desert and seashore life. In 1991, the museum's leaders adapted a new approach to their mission, focusing on the binational region of San Diego and Baja California, Mexico. It contributed to the making of the IMAX film *Ocean Oasis* about the Sea of Cortez, and established the Biodiversity Research Center of the Californias.

At the same time, the museum embarked on a building campaign, which resulted in a renovation and addition that more than doubled the size of the building. The new wing, which opened in 2001, was designed by the **Bundy and Thompson** architectural firm of San Diego. Its most striking feature is a soaring glass-fronted entrance and atrium with balconies and vast display areas. Exhibits include **Fossil Mysteries**, an interactive exhibit that explores evolution, extinction, ecology, and Earth processes, and a **Kid's Habitat** with interactive games. In 2007, the museum presented a comprehensive exhibit of Dead Sea Scrolls and antiquities that drew worldwide attention.

The museum's society also offers biological expeditions throughout the county, as well as walks through the park's canyons and

educational whale-watching boat trips. The north entrance atrium sits beside a Moreton Bay fig tree that is said to be over 150 years old. A fence surrounds the tree's rambling roots. ♦ Admission. Daily, 10AM-5PM. Between Park Blvd and the Casa del Prado. 232.3821, 255.0271. & www.sdnhm.org

Within the San Diego Natural History Museum:

DINOSAUR CAFÉ

★$ A cool respite in the atrium of the museum, the café serves coffee drinks, sandwiches, salads, and pastries. ♦ Tu-Sa, 10AM-3PM. 255.0317

14 CABRILLO BRIDGE

Designed by **Thomas B. Hunter** as a dramatic entrance to the 1915 fair, this cantilevered bridge is a truly heartwarming sight at Christmastime when it is strung with colored lights. The first passenger to cross the bridge was Franklin D. Roosevelt, then secretary of the navy. At that time, it spanned a barren canyon that was transformed from the city pound into a glassy pond reflecting the **California Tower**. The pond is now a freeway, and the bridge is busy with cars, bicycles, in-line skaters, and pedestrians vying for space. Though the way across is hardly as serene as it once was, the view—from the shrouded canyon walls to the Coronado Bridge—is still impressive. The bridge caught fire in June 2004, but luckily no serious damage was done. ♦ From Sixth Ave to the California Quadrangle

15 MUSEUM OF MAN

Located in the original entryway to the park, this gallery—originally called the **San Diego Museum**—was established in 1915 to continue the archaeological and anthropological work that was begun for the fair. The museum's main exhibits are housed in the **California Building**, designed by **Bertram Goodhue** and **Carleton Winslow** for the 1915 exposition. The building, one of the most architecturally impressive in the park, is topped by the 200-foot-high **California Tower**, where the Westminster Chimes continue to sound the quarter-hour on the carillon. The elaborate façade includes full-size sculpted figures of Father Junípero Serra, Sebastián Vizcaíno, and Father Luis Jaime—California's first Christian martyr. Much of the rest of the park has been built to carry on the ornamental Spanish-Colonial theme that Goodhue created with this building back in 1915.

Bull Hewitt, the museum's first director, had convinced the Smithsonian Institution and the School of American Archaeology to support a $100,000 comprehensive exhibit called *The Story of Man through the Ages* for the 1915–1916 exposition. Archaeologists, physical anthropologists, and ethnologists were dispatched to Peru, Central America, Africa, Central Europe, Siberia, the Philippines, and the Southwest US to collect the 5,000 specimens of ethnological importance that still comprise the core of the museum's permanent collection. Under the museum's sky blue dome is a cast replica of the grand stela (carved pillar) at the Maya ruins in Quirigua, Guatemala. The museum's original stela was remolded in 1999 by local artist Tony Neff. It took him 2 years to replicate the intricate Mayan symbols on the 21-foot-tall monument, which was moved ever so gingerly back to the museum in 2001. Its carvings of Maya gods and legends are more distinct than on the original stela, which suffered from being exposed to the jungle's elements.

In early 2002, the museum completed the $2 million renovation of its west wing, which now houses an anthropology exhibit, *Footsteps Through Time: Four Million Years of Human Evolution*. The exhibit covers 7,000 square feet and features five galleries filled with more than 100 touchable replicas of early humans, primates, and futuristic cyborgs (part human, part machine).

Among the permanent collection is an exhibit on the Kumeyaay Indians, San Diego's original residents. *Lifecycles and Ceremonies* includes a hands-on, high-tech lesson in biology and reproduction. There are also exhibits on the costumes and rituals of San Diego's many ethnic communities, and one focusing on the sun gods and mummies of ancient Egypt, complete with a real human mummy. The Children's Discovery Center features *Discover Egypt*, an interactive learning experience for kids. The exhibit highlights the role of archaeologists and anthropologists in interpreting ancient Egyptian culture. Children can listen to a description of mummification as told by the Egyptian god Anubis or decipher a message written in hieroglyphics. ♦ Admission. Daily, 10AM–4:30PM. 1350 El Prado (between Plaza de Panama and Cabrillo Bridge). 239.2001. & www.museumofman.org

Within the Museum of Man:

CHAPEL OF ST. FRANCIS

Built in Spanish-Colonial style for the 1915 fair, this chapel was used for weddings and as a military chapel during World War II, but was never consecrated. The centerpiece above the altar echoes the fanciful façade of the museum, with sculptures of *Our Lady and Child* and *St. Francis Xavier*.

ADMINISTRATION BUILDING

Located adjacent to the **California Building**, this was the welcoming point for the 1915 exposition. **Irving Gill**, San Diego's premier architect at the time, began designing the building in 1911. Midway through Gill's work, the park's overseers shifted their focus from a modernistic, minimalist style to the more ornate design of New York architects **Bertram Goodhue** and **Carleton Winslow**, who added Beaux Arts balconies and filled the structure with intricate Baroque ornamentation. The grand lobbies and spacious offices were used for international receptions during the fair and as a military hospital during World War II. In 1978 the city planned to demolish the building, which had been vacant for years. The state intervened, saying it was included with **Balboa Park**'s other architectural treasures in the National Register of Historic Places and could not be destroyed. A mid-1990 restoration opened up more gallery space for displaying the museum's collection.

16 TIMKEN ART GALLERY

Mrs. Appleton (Timken) Bridges and her husband were major benefactors of the **Fine Arts Gallery** (now the **San Diego Museum of Art**) from 1925 through the 1940s. When Mrs. Bridges died, Anne R. and Amy Putnam took over the major support of the museum, donating works by old masters from their collection. In the 1950s, the sisters founded the Putnam Foundation under the direction of their attorney Walter Ames (who had been Mrs. Bridges's lawyer in the 1920s). Sometime later, either the sisters or their lawyer had a falling out with the Fine Arts Gallery, and Ames convinced the Timken family to create a foundation, build a museum, and move the remarkable Putnam collection to the new space. The result was this small, unobtrusive building designed by **Frank Hope** in 1965. Be sure to stop in the **American Room** to see *Cho-looke, the Yosemite Fall*, a painting by Albert Bierstadt. The **European Rooms** display priceless

---

paintings from the 14th to 19th centuries, including works by Rembrandt, Rubens, Pisarro, and Cézanne. But the gallery's real treasures are to be found among the *Russian Icons*—elaborate altar screens and small panels used to section off a space for private religious devotions in the home. ♦ Free. Closed Monday and the month of September. 1500 El Prado (between the Lily Pond and Plaza de Panama). 239.5548. www.timkenmuseum.org

17 ALCAZAR GARDEN

Depending on the season, snapdragons, zinnias, and calendula splash color through the beds of this hidden garden, one of the prettiest resting spots in the park. Designers Requa & Perry patterned the gardens after those surrounding the Alcazar Castle in Seville, Spain. Moorish-style fountains are inlaid with turquoise, yellow, and green tiles, and the cement benches near the flowerbeds are perfect for reading and relaxation. ♦ Behind the House of Charm (south side of El Prado)

18 HOUSE OF CHARM

During the first exposition, this Mission-style building—designed by **Carleton Winslow** in 1915—housed displays of American Indian arts; during the second, it held souvenir stands. It fell into disrepair and was saved from the wrecking ball by the Committee of 100. Restoration began in 1994 with workers making meticulous plaster casts of the exterior ornamentation so they could faithfully reproduce Winslow's original design. New tenants set up operation in the building in 1996 and have made it one of the most gorgeous structures in the park. ♦ 1439 El Prado (next to the Alcazar Garden)

Within the House of Charm:

MINGEI
INTERNATIONAL
MUSEUM

MINGEI INTERNATIONAL MUSEUM

Once housed in a shopping mall, this museum of world folk art, craft, and design never ceases to enthrall its fans with fascinating exhibits. The permanent collection includes works by many of Mexico's most famous folk artists, along with 16,400 art objects from 100 countries. Exhibit themes range from American Shaker arts to hand-carved and painted carousel horses to Indonesian and Chinese textiles.

The museum has produced several books and videos on various subjects, including kites as art and the Japanese arts of daily life. As might be expected, the shop is packed with irresistible finds. Admission. Tu-Su, 10AM-4PM. 239.0003. ♦ 1439 El Prado (next to the Alcazar Garden). www.mingei.org

19 EL CID

Anna Hyatt Huntington's 23-foot-tall sculpture of Rodrigo Díaz de Vivar (known as El Cid)—the chivalrous Castilian who drove the Moors from Spain in the 11th century—was donated to the **Fine Arts Gallery** in 1927. **William Templeton Johnson** designed a limestone pedestal for it, and in 1930, *El Cid* took up residence between the gallery and the **Spreckels Organ Pavilion**. A smaller Huntington sculpture of *Diana* stands by the entrance to the **San Diego Museum of Art**. ♦ El Prado (near the House of Hospitality)

20 HOUSE OF HOSPITALITY

The prettiest part of this elaborate complex—said to resemble the Hospital of Santa Cruz in Toledo, Spain—is the courtyard's tiled fountain, wherein sits *La Tehuana de Tehuantepec, Mexico*. This serene señorita, pouring water from her rounded jar, was created from a 1,200-pound block of limestone by sculptor Donal Hord for the 1935 fair. Her visage has been photographed unceasingly ever since. The structure, designed in 1915 by **Bertram Goodhue** and **Carleton Winslow**, was first used as the **Foreign Arts Building**, then as headquarters for the Women's Executive Committee. It was restored and refurbished in 1935 by **Sam Hamill** and used for community organizations, banquets, receptions, and dances, except during World War II, when its cavernous dining rooms and hallways served as dorms for 600 military nurses. In 1995 the building underwent a $15 million, 2-year reconstruction, keeping

In 1950 fences were built on both sides of the Cabrillo Bridge to prevent the despondent from jumping to their deaths; at least 50 people had been successful by that time, causing a local cynic to post a sign on the road below the bridge reading "Beware of falling bodies."

—Florence Christman,
The Romance of Balboa Park

Zoo leaders have always been creative in their quest for new occupants. In 1938, San Diego Zoo director Belle Benchley sent a weekly jar of fleas from the dog pound to a flea circus in New Jersey in exchange for several rare snakes.

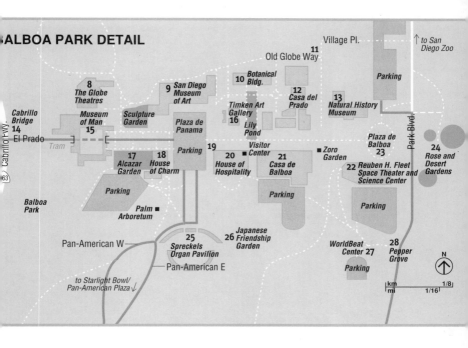

BALBOA PARK DETAIL

Village Pl.

↑ to San Diego Zoo

Old Globe Way 11

Botanical 10 Bldg.

Parking

8 The Globe Theatres

9 San Diego Museum of Art

12 Casa del Prado

13 Natural History Museum

Cabrillo Bridge 14

Museum of Man 15

Sculpture Garden

Plaza de Panama

Timken Art Gallery 16 Lily Pond

El Prado

Tram

19 Parking

Visitor Center 20

Zoro Garden

Plaza de Balboa 23

Park Blvd

24 Rose and Desert Gardens

63

17 Alcazar Garden

18 House of Charm

20 House of Hospitality

21 Casa de Balboa

22 Reuben H. Fleet Space Theater and Science Center

Parking

Balboa Park

Parking

Palm ■ Arboretum

Parking

Parking

Pan-American W

25 Spreckels Organ Pavilion

26 Japanese Friendship Garden

WorldBeat Center 27

28 Pepper Grove

Pan-American E

Parking

N

to Starlight Bowl/ Pan-American Plaza ↓

km mi

1/8 1/16

veteran and active-duty military activities. Donation. ♦ Tu-Sa, 9:30AM-3PM. 2115 Park Blvd (at Presidents Way) 239.2300. www.veteranmuseum.org

BALBOA PARK MANAGEMENT CENTER

The San Diego Department of Parks and Recreation is responsible for the hands-on supervision, maintenance, and planning that keeps the park a pleasurable public space. The office staff handles questions about the park's facilities and permits. ♦ M-F. 235.1100

BALBOA PARK ACTIVITY CENTER

Opened in 1999, the activity center is the newest building at Balboa Park in over 3 decades. Designed by local architect **Rob Wellington Quigley**, the center is a 38,000-square-foot multipurpose gymnasium built to accommodate table tennis, volleyball, and badminton. Tournaments on the state and national level are held here. The Sports Information Office for the City of San Diego Parks and Recreation Department is located at the center. ♦ Daily; call for hours. 2145 Park Blvd (at Presidents Way). 858/581.7100

39 BALBOA PARK GOLF COURSE

Golfers had staked their claim in the park in 1915—even before the first exposition— behind what is now the **Natural History Museum**. They used sheep to keep the chaparral from covering their dirt course, until the poundmaster (an early-day animal control officer) raised a fuss. The powers behind the fair convinced the golfers to move southeast, where they doggedly cleared a 9-hole course (and created a duffer's nightmare called the **Rockpile**) in time for the fair. In 1920, the course was upgraded and extended to 18 holes; in 1934 a local work relief project and the Work Progress Administration built a clubhouse and resodded the course, which is still very much in use today. You'll find a fascinating cross-section of San Diegans here, and great views of the park and downtown. ♦ Greens fee. Daily, dawn to dusk. Golf Course Dr (at Pershing Dr). Pro shop: 239.1660; computer reservations, 570.1234

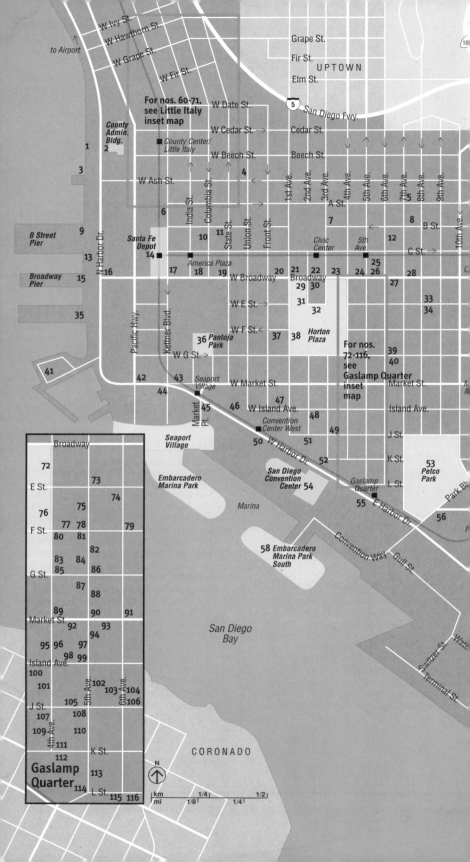

Downtown/Little Italy/ Gaslamp Quarter

Park Blvd.

US Navy Hospital

Pershing Dr.

Balboa Park

Golden Hill Dr.

ss Blvd.

Russ Blvd.

A St.

■ City College

B St.

C St.

Broadway

E St.

F St.

94

25th St.

19th St.

21st St.

22nd St.

23rd St.

24th St.

19th St.

Market St.

Island Ave.

14th St.

15th St.

16th St.

17th St.

San Diego Fwy.

5

J St.

K St.

21st St.

22nd St.

24th St.

25th St.

26th St.

27th St.

29th St.

Imperial Ave.

Imperial Ave.

25th & Commercial

Commercial St.

Logan Ave.

Julian Ave.

Crosby St.

Franklin Ave.

Everett St.

Webster Ave.

16th St.

National Ave.

Kearney Ave.

Ocean View Blvd.

Clay Ave.

Newton Ave.

Dewey St.

Irving Ave.

Harrison Ave.

Franklin Ave.

Sigsbee St.

Main St.

Evans St.

Sampson St.

Ocean View Blvd.

Beardsley St.

59

Chicano Park

5

Sicard St.

28th St.

Barrio Logan

John J. Montgomery Fwy.

Logan Ave.

Marcy Ave.

National Ave.

Logan Ave.

Crosby St.

Barrio Logan

Main St.

Newton Ave.

26th St.

National Ave.

75

Harbor Dr.

Newton Ave.

San Diego- Coronado Bay Bridge

Little Italy

60

W Ivy St.

W Hawthorn St.

62

63

61

W Grape St.

5

64

65

W Fir St.

66

67

W Date St.

68

69

W Cedar St.

County Center/ Little Italy

→ 70 ←

India St.

Columbia St.

State St.

W Beech St.

Pacific Hwy.

W Ash St.

Kettner Blvd.

71

W A St.

Grant Hill Park

DOWNTOWN/LITTLE ITALY/ GASLAMP QUARTER

After decades of intense development and restoration, downtown San Diego ha emerged as a vibrant neighborhood with attractions that last long after ban ing hours. The city center is now a magnet for travelers, conventioneers, and loca who once abhorred the thought of leaving their safe, secure neighborhoods ar venturing into the evil Big City. Few can resist the magnificent **San Diego Conver tion Center** on the waterfront, and **Horton Plaza**, the Disneyesque shopping cente Streets are filled with pedestrians long into the night, thanks to the proliferation trendy cafés and nightclubs in the historic **Gaslamp Quarter**. Cruise ships, sai boats, and US Navy aircraft carriers fill **San Diego Bay**, facing a shimmering sk line of windows dedicated to the view.

The bay has served as San Diego's focal point since the first Spanish conquero disturbed the peaceful camps of the Kumeyaay Indians along the fertile coastlin Portuguese explorer Juan Rodríguez Cabrillo, sailing under the Spanish flag, di covered San Diego Bay on 28 September 1542 and named it San Miguel. Sebastiá Vizcaíno rediscovered the bay on 10 November 1602 and renamed it San Diego honor of the Spanish saint San Diego de Acalá, whose feast day is celebrated on November. When Spain's first explorers and missionaries settled in San Diego 1769, they bypassed the harbor and built their mission and fort on a hill overlool ing what is now called Old Town. For nearly a century, the bay was a rustic landir station for San Diego's pioneers. But in 1850 an ambitious financier, William Hea Davis, envisioned a great seaport that could someday rival San Francisco as th queen city of the Pacific Coast. He convinced the army to build a supply depot ar began raising prefabricated houses along the new dirt streets of downtown. Unfo tunately, his fortunes ran out long before his city could become established, and th few wooden structures by the bay became known as **Davis's Folly**.

Davis's dream wouldn't die, however. In 1867 Alonzo Erastus Horton bought 9€ acres of mudflats and sagebrush and called the area **New Town**. Within 2 years, th city had an infrastructure of sorts, free lots for churches, free whitewash f homeowners, and **Horton's Wharf**, **Horton's Bank Block**, and the luxurious Horto **House Hotel**. Alonzo E. Horton had built himself a city that belied the naysayer label of **Horton's Folly**.

Today, as in Horton's day, the bay is what first captivates visitors to downtown. Th area that stretches along **Harbor Drive** from the international airport at **Lindberg Field** to the mock sails atop the San Diego Convention Center has been the focus considerable development since the early 1980s. Along the waterfront, high-rise h tels and high-price condos pierce the sky between parks. An overhead sign at the fo of **Fifth Avenue** by the San Diego Convention Center marks the entrance to th **Gaslamp Quarter**. Here in downtown's first center is a cluster of renovated histor buildings housing some of the city's best restaurants and clubs. Central downtown marked by **Horton Plaza**, the fantastical shopping center surrounding the origin park and fountain of the plaza of old, dedicated to the city's father in 1909 with plaque that reads "Fountain for the People of Broadway." Downtown's main boulevar since the late 1800s, **Broadway** is losing its tattoo parlors and dive bars to hote modern business centers, and a courthouse. North of Broadway, business goes on a usual in established offices and banks as the red **San Diego Trolley** whooshes by.

Development continues in downtown, at an amazing pace. City planners have mapped out seven development districts within an area that only a few decades ago seemed like a ghost town, except during office hours. Each district is undergoing massive change, with everything from public parks to exclusive condos under construction. The **East Village** is now the site of a new baseball stadium and several large hotel and residential complexes. Little Italy, a neighborhood formed by Italian immigrants northwest of downtown, is undergoing a complete face-lift and has become an exciting dining and entertainment area. And the Gaslamp Quarter, where Horton first plotted his folly, is now a wildly successful model of urban renewal. It seems there's no shortage of visionaries in downtown, and no end to its possibilities.

DOWNTOWN

1 SAN DIEGO BAY AND THE EMBARCADERO

If you drive from the airport into downtown, you'll be riding beside San Diego Bay, where aircraft carriers, cruise ships, sailboats, ferries, and water taxis jockey for space. On clear, sunny Saturdays the horizon is nearly obliterated by billowing sails; at night, the murky dark water reflects the skyscrapers' lights. A pathway popular with joggers and strollers runs beside the bay and its many attractions, winding from the pier where the historic ship *Star of India* is docked, south to **Embarcadero Marina Park**. An ambitious redevelopment project along the waterfront will result in a bayfront esplanade with large park areas, new shops and restaurants, and a pedestrian bridge spanning North Harbor Drive. The project is still in the early development stages. N Harbor Dr

2 SAN DIEGO COUNTY ADMINISTRATION BUILDING

Few downtown towers are as graceful and elegant as this Spanish Colonial–Beaux Arts complex, especially when it's flooded with columns of light at night. At the west entrance, Donal Hord's sculpture *Guardian of the Water* portrays a pioneer woman carrying a water jug on her shoulder—perhaps the only public art beloved by all San Diegans. The motto "The Noblest Motive Is the Public Good" is inscribed over the west entrance, with its floor of gold and azure tiles; "Good Government Demands the Intelligent Interest of Every Citizen," reads the mosaic in the foyer floor. Designed by architect **Sam Hamill**, the 13-story administrative center was built on 18 acres of prime waterfront land during the Depression with $1 million from the Works Progress Administration; President Franklin Delano Roosevelt dedicated the building in 1938. If you are in the mood to get married, there is a gazebo on the west side of the building with a lovely view of the water where the county performs civil ceremonies. ♦ 1600 Pacific Hwy (between W Ash and W Grape Sts). County administration offices, 531.5880

3 MARITIME MUSEUM

Volunteers have been staffing this organization since 1958, when a group of enthusiastic volunteers calling themselves the 40 Thieves set to work on the *Star of India*, now the cornerstone of the museum's collection of historic vessels, navigational tools, scale models, and a replica of Cabrillo's vessel. The group is headquartered on the *Berkeley* ferry. ♦ Admission. Daily, 9AM-8PM. 1492 N Harbor Dr (at W Ash St). 234.9153. www.sdmaritime.org

At the Maritime Museum:

STAR OF INDIA

Built in 1863, this is the oldest iron merchant ship afloat in the world. It is the undisputed masterpiece of the bay, and easily the most popular attraction. The main mast soars 127 feet into the blue sky, the 205-foot-long hull is built of more than 1,000 tons of Swedish iron, and 15,000 square yards of white canvas unfurl into her sails. Christened the *Enterpe* at the Isle of Man, the vessel made 21 trips around the world and served as a ferry for immigrants from England to Australia and as a courier on the East Indian trade route. In 1906 the ship was registered in the US as the *Star of India* and used as a cannery tender, shuttling Asian laborers from San Francisco to Alaskan canneries. It made its last journey to Bristol Bay, Alaska, in 1923, and was retired to float and disintegrate in San Diego Bay in 1927. In 1959, an enthusiastic group of volunteers set to work stripping the deck, polishing the figurehead, and restoring its

THE BEST

Chef Bernard Guillas
Marine Room, La Jolla

On a date, sipping champagne at the **Marine Room** during summer high tides.

Fishing on a local lake and never catching anything.

Going to a *true* jazz club at **Anthology** in Little Italy

Picking your own strawberries in **Carlsbad** and eating them while walking through the **Flower Fields**.

Shopping for live Santa Barbara prawns at **99 Ranch Market**.

Enjoying the change of seasons in **Julian** while eating fresh apple pie.

Playing golf at **Torrey Pines** and looking over the 13th fairway to **La Jolla Cove**.

Walking through **Balboa Park**, enjoying the museums.

Morning at the zoo, sharing my newspaper with the monkeys.

Cruising the **Gaslamp Quarter** in my '67 Buick with Brian Malarkey, the chef of **Oceanaire.**

Summer jazz concerts at **Thornton Winery** in **Temecula**.

Going on safari at the **Wild Animal Park** and kissing the giraffe.

Jewel Ball at the **La Jolla Beach & Tennis Club** is a blast.

Hot-air balloon ride over the **Del Mar Fairgrounds**.

A day with the ponies, always betting on the donkey.

Visiting local farmers in the morning mist.

Building my own castle at **Legoland** with the kids.

Cocktails at **Addison** watching the sun set over the lush greens.

Riding the carousel at **Seaport Village** and taking the ferryboat to **Coronado Island**.

---

dignity. The vessel's sails captured the wind on 4 July 1976 for its first journey in 50 years; it sails approximately once a year now with a crew of 60 volunteers on deck and in the rigging.

THE *BERKELEY*

An 1898 propeller-driven ferry as ornate as any riverboat on the Mississippi, this was the **Southern Pacific Railway**'s only misguided attempt at building a ship of this type. The unwieldy 289-foot-long boat could carry 1,709 passengers but had a difficult time maneuvering between the San Francisco and Oakland piers on its daily route. The ferry's moment of glory arrived when it carried shiploads of refugees from the 1906 earthquake and fire in San Francisco to the relative safety of Oakland. The **Maritime Museum**'s offices are located on the ship's main deck, with carved wood paneling, plate glass mirrors, and stained-glass windows in the clerestory. Also on board are a maritime research library, workshop, model shop, and the museum store.

THE *MEDEA*

Captain MacAllister Hall of Torrisdale Castle, Scotland, commissioned this iron-hulled, steam-powered yacht in 1904 for his grouse and deer hunting soirées off the Scottish isles. Members of Parliament and other such British gentry have owned it from time to time, and the boat patrolled the English Channel for submarines during World War I. In 1969, Paul and Olive Whittier spotted the

ship covered with snow and ice off the coast of Sweden. Enchanted, they bought it, had it restored in Canada, and in 1973 donated the yacht to the **Maritime Museum**.

HMS *SURPRISE*

Star of the hit film *Master & Commander: The Far Side of the World*, this replica of an 18th century British warship received a permanent home at the museum in 2004. On board, guests can view displays of period artifacts, costumes, and props from the award-winning film.

4 EXTRAORDINARY DESSERTS

★★★★$ Baker Karen Krasne has become a San Diego star. Her small dessert shop in Hillcrest is a favorite stop for sugar connoisseurs who pay big bucks for just a slice of her lemon cake. Chocolate, hazelnut, whatever your fave, Krasne can create a masterpiece to be photographed and savored with lingering nibbles. Her success has spawned the hippest eatery on the border between downtown and Little Italy. The entryway is awesome, from the cactus plantings outside the heavy glass doors to the display cases of cakes topped with violets and fruit. Krasne's treats now include homemade granola, panini, and other munchies that serve as fine appetizers before the big event. Dessert can be as simple as a shortbread cookie or as over-the-top as a white chocolate linzer torte topped with fresh flowers. The Asian-inspired shopping area carries homemade exotic jams, honeys and syrups, cookie dough, and an eclectic display of books, teapots, and other delightful splurges. ◆ M-Th, 8:30AM-11PM; F, 8:30AM-midnight; Sa, 10AM-midnight; Su, 10AM-11PM. 1430 Union St (between Ash and Beech Sts). 294.7001. Also at 2929 Fifth Ave (between Palm and Quince Sts), 294.2132 (M-Th, 8:30AM-11PM; F, 8:30AM-midnight; Sa, 10AM-midnight; Su, 10AM-11PM). www.extraordinarydesserts.com

5 SHERATON SUITES SAN DIEGO

$$$$ The hotel's lobby is on the 12th floor, so entering can be a bit disconcerting until a bellhop comes to your rescue and takes you up in the elevator. Classical music befitting **Copley Symphony Hall** plays throughout the pink-and-green marble lobby and atrium-like lounge connecting the office tower with the hotel. The rooms aren't overly lavish, but they're ideal for business travelers who like having a handsome wood desk to work on (with a convenient view of the television, a telephone, and French doors to separate it from the bedroom). All 264 rooms are suites; some have conference tables in the living room area, and all have refrigerators and coffeemakers. The **Renditions** restaurant serves breakfast, lunch, and dinner daily. ◆ 701 A St (between Eighth and Seventh Aves). 696.9800, 888/625.4988; fax 696.1555. www.starwoodhotels.com

6 RAINWATER'S ON KETTNER

★★★$$$$ A popular spot with the power-lunch crowd for its classic American chop-house fare, this restaurant has spacious private booths and freestanding tables in the middle of it all. This is one of the best places in town for stick-to-your-ribs, soul-satisfying steaks, chops, and fish. A midday repast in the old style might include dry martinis, oysters, and a perfect filet mignon or meat loaf. Dinner would be steamed asparagus, a massive Caesar salad, and Rainwater's "famous" pepper fillet. Killer desserts like Southern-style pecan pie should follow all meals for the full (and filling) experience. And best of all, the waitstaff greets strangers with the same graciousness given the politicos and business honchos who consider Rainwater's their private club. ◆ American ◆ M-F, lunch and dinner; Sa, Su, dinner. Reservations recommended. 1202 Kettner Blvd (between West B and West A Sts). 233.5757. www.rainwaters.com

7 4TH & B

Downtown's well-established hipster concert venue attracts top-notch musicians of every breed, from jazz to hip-hop to Latin rock. There are several bars, lounges, and concert halls in the converted bank building. ◆ 345 B St (between Fourth and Third Aves). 231.4343. www.4thandb.com

7 DOWNTOWN JOHNNY BROWN'S

★$ Office workers cram into this casual bar for after-work beers, pool games, and burgers. The walls and ceilings are covered with memorabilia from local sports teams. The best burger, topped with avocado, Ortega chiles, and jack cheese, is named for the San Diego State University's Aztec football team. Stop here for a cheap meal before a concert or play at the **Civic Theatre**. ◆ American ◆ 1220 Third Ave (between B and A Sts). 232.8414

8 SYMPHONY TOWERS

Copley Symphony Hall sits at the base of these twin glass and red-granite towers designed by **Skidmore, Owings & Merrill** in 1989. The lobby for the **Sheraton** hotel is on the 12th floor; other giants have moved in above; and the **University Club**, one of the oldest private clubs in downtown, is on top. ◆ 750 B St (between Eighth and Seventh Aves). 234.5200

Within Symphony Towers:

COPLEY SYMPHONY HALL

The **San Diego Symphony** has the distinction of owning this performance hall set in a magnificently restored theater. The original Rococo–Spanish Renaissance **Fox Theatre** (designed by **Weeks & Day**) opened in 1929 with the talkie *They Had to See Paris* to a celebrity crowd including Buster Keaton, Jackie Coogan, George Jessel, and the film's star, Will Rogers. Walt Disney loved the theater so much he opened all his movies here. Like most of downtown's old theaters, it steadily disintegrated over the decades and seemed destined for destruction until a developer bought the entire block in 1984 and sold this building to the **San Diego Symphony**. The **Deems/Lewis** architectural firm was hired to handle the renovation. The 12-foot-wide chandelier—which held eight chorus girls and the accordion-playing orchestra conductor on opening night—and the 26,000-pipe organ were also restored, giving longtime San Diegans a jolt of nostalgia for the Fox. The symphony performs from October through May at this

---

2,252-seat theater. It also hosts a SummerPops series. ◆ Box office, 235.0804. &. www.sandiegosymphony.com

9 B STREET CRUISE SHIP TERMINAL

San Diego has become a major cruise port, with over 190 ships coming to call annually. Round-trip cruises to Mexico, Hawaii, Alaska, and the Panama Canal depart from the terminal on the downtown waterfront. Up to four ships dock at the foot of B Street in a day, disgorging thousands of passengers on shore excursions. The terminal itself is off-limits to nonpassengers, and several large parking lots serve those leaving their cars for a week or more. ◆ 1140 N Harbor Dr (between W Broadway and W Ash St). 686.6200. www.portofsandiego.org

10 KARL STRAUSS' BREWERY & RESTAURANT

★★$$ The late brewmaster Karl Strauss, who perfected his skills for 44 years at the Pabst brewery, made San Diego's first participant in the microbrewery craze a winner. The stainless-steel tanks are visible from the long bar; the smell of malt and hops fills the air. Homemade brews, ranging from pale ale to amber lager, are available on tap in small sampler glasses, 12-ounce glasses, pints, and 23-ounce schooners. Accompaniments include great Cajun-spiced fries, the brewpub club, and andouille sausages with garlic mashed potatoes and spicy mustard sauce. ◆ Eclectic ◆ Daily, lunch and dinner. 1157 Columbia St (between West C and West B Sts). 234.2739. Also located in La Jolla, 1044 Wall St. 858/551.2739. www.karlstrauss.com

11 W HOTEL

$$$$ Although newer hotels have raised downtown's hip quotient, the W is still très chic among visitors seeking a vibe with their room. The best feature is the rooftop beach, with sand around the swimming pool. The lobby-level bar is popular with after-work martini drinkers. Lighting could be improved in the hallways, but the 261 rooms are bright and so very modern, with flat-screen TVs and see-through showers. ◆ 421 West B St (at State St). 398.3100,

When the San Diego Trust and Savings' downtown headquarters closed, some longtime clients were allowed to keep the doors to their safe-deposit boxes. The vault holding those boxes is now a meeting room in the Mariott Courtyard hotel.

877/946.8357; fax 231.5779. www.starwoodhotels.com/whotels

12 CAFÉ CERISE

★★$$ Jason Seibert had enough faith in the neighborhood to create his bright café with bubble-like cherries bouncing about the walls on a somewhat seedy block. His menu combines Mediterranean comfort food like a charcuterie plate and grilled Tuscan sausage with more daring daily specials like an almond-crusted Idaho trout and arugula crepe. The exceptional list of wines by the glass and very reasonable prices have made the café a favorite with downtown denizens, workers, and frequent visitors. ◆ Café ◆ M-F lunch; Tu-Sa, dinner. 1125 Sixth Ave (between C and B Sts). 595.0153. www.cafecerise.com

13 SAN DIEGO HARBOR EXCURSION

This company offers 1- and 2-hour harbor cruises throughout the day, as well as dinner cruises on summer weekend nights. Whale-watching excursions are conducted by trained naturalists twice daily during January, February, and March. Call the recorded info line for times. ◆ Fee. 1050 N Harbor Dr (between the Broadway and B St Piers). 234.4111. 800/44-CRUISE. www.sdhe.com

13 HORNBLOWER DINING YACHTS

Come aboard one of the yachts in this fleet for a dinner cruise of the harbor with dance music, or a Sunday brunch cruise with a lavish spread of fruits, salads, meats, and pastries. Call ahead to find out which boat will be sailing; the yachts are available for private parties as well. ◆ Fee. 1066 N Harbor Dr (between the Broadway and B St Piers). 686.8700. www.hornblower.com

13 SAN DIEGO BAY FERRY

When the arching blue Coronado Bridge opened in 1969, the venerable ferry to Coronado stopped running until 1987. Now the *Silvergate* and the *Cabrillo* ferry passengers a mile across the bay from downtown to Coronado's east shore, where restaurants, shops, bike rentals, and trolley tours are available at the **Ferry Landing Marketplace**. ◆ From downtown daily on the hour; Su-Th, 9AM-9PM; F, Sa, 9AM-10PM; from Coronado daily on the half hour. Fee. 1050 N Harbor Dr (at W Broadway). 234.4111

14 SANTA FE DEPOT

The 1915–1916 exposition's most lasting contribution to downtown is **John R.**

Blakewell's Spanish-Colonial–style train station, with its blue, yellow, and white glaze-tile dome echoing the vision of **Balboa Park**'s landmark **California Tower**. There was an earlier train depot at the site, considered to be the best of its kind in the 1880s, but it wasn't up to par with the exposition's grand schemes. Fortunately, this 1915 depot is on the National Register of Historic Places, and plans in the late 1960s to replace it with a high-rise were thwarted. The depot was refurbished in 1982 by **Tucker Sadler**, and is considered so spectacular that celebrity balls and special events are held in the spanking-clean station with its polished wood benches, tiled wainscoting, and polychrome wood beams. The **Coaster** commuter rail line runs from the depot up the coast eight stops to Oceanside, and **Amtrak** operates trains to Orange County and Los Angeles (with nationwide connections in LA) from the depot. ♦ 1050 Kettner Blvd (between W Broadway and West C St). Amtrak reservations, 800/872.7245; Coaster, 800/262.7837; information, 685.4900

15 BROADWAY PIER

This World War II pier was renovated as a berthing area for visiting naval vessels and is now used as an annex to the cruise ship pier. ♦ W Broadway and N Harbor Dr

16 INTERNATIONAL VISITOR INFORMATION CENTER

An excellent resource for travelers and locals, this center is staffed by volunteers who speak several languages (other translators can be contacted by phone). In addition to offering basic tourist information in an extremely helpful manner, the staff provides informative literature from the San Diego Convention and Visitors Bureau, including a great selection of brochures from budget hotels. Tickets for the Old Town Trolley Tours (see Orientation chapter) and area attractions are available here. ♦ Daily, 9AM-5PM June, July, Aug; 9AM-4PM Labor Day through Memorial Day. 1040⅓ W Broadway (at N Harbor Dr). 236.1212

17 ONE AMERICA PLAZA

Three architectural firms collaborated on this 500-foot-high office tower spearing the sky with what looks to some like the business end of a Phillips screwdriver. A crescent-shaped glass-and-steel canopy covers the trolley tracks that run along the base of the tower from the **San Diego Convention Center** through downtown. There's plenty of underground parking, and the **Amtrak** depot is right across the street. ♦ 600 W Broadway (between India St and Kettner Blvd) &

17 MUSEUM OF CONTEMPORARY ART SAN DIEGO (DOWNTOWN)

The original branch of this fine museum is in La Jolla, but since 1993, MCASD Downtown has provided a second venue for temporary exhibitions. The museum has two floors of galleries, with exhibitions focusing on young regional artists on the cutting edge, as well as outdoor plazas for sculpture. **Helmut Jahn** designed the original building as part of the **One America Plaza** complex, while the interiors were the result of collaboration by artists Robert Irwin and Richard Fleischner working with architect David Raphael Singer. There is also a first-rate selection of art books, posters, gifts, and cards in the MCASD Downtown store.

The museum grew dramatically in 2007, when new facilities opened at the **Santa Fe Depot** across the street from the original downtown location. MCASD Downtown is now a two-building campus (with more exhibition space than in La Jolla). Architect **Richard Gluckman** renovated the historic 1915 warehouse adjacent to the train station. The new **Joan and Irwin Jacobs Building** has large and spacious exhibition spaces, a gallery devoted to multimedia and video, permanent outdoor sculpture installations, and the adjacent three-story **David C. Copley Building** with a lecture hall for programs and films. ♦ F-M, W 11AM-5PM; Th 11AM-7PM; closed Tu. 1100 and 1001 Kettner Blvd (between W Broadway and C St). 234.1001. www.mcasd.org

18 500 WEST

$ Built in 1924, the historic **Armed Services YMCA Building** has been remodeled into a budget hotel for culturally savvy, value-oriented travelers. A living room—style lobby leads to 259 guest rooms with state-of-the-art technology, including high-speed wireless Internet and flat-screen televisions. The amenities are astonishing given the low room rate. Beds have pillow-top mattresses and writing desks; hair dryers, irons, and other extras are available on request. Guests have use of the Y's fitness center and pool. ♦ 500 W Broadway (at Columbia St). 234.5252. www.500westhotel.com

19 WESTIN SAN DIEGO

$$$$ The latest incarnation for lower Broadway's iconic Emerald Plaza is a serene,

---

Restaurants/Clubs: Red | **Hotels: Purple** | Shops: Orange | **Outdoors/Parks: Green** | Sights/Culture: Blue urban Westin hotel with 436 rooms. Emerald-green neon rings cap the three hexagonal towers designed by **C. W. Kim** in 1990. Quite controversial when it opened, the building incorporated as-yet trendy feng shui principles. The 100-foot-high lobby atrium is striking and a tad intimidating, and certainly not your typical San Diego hotel entrance. You can see Coronado and the entire bay from the upper floors (25 stories in all); all guest rooms feature the delightful Westin heavenly bed and the sensible layout and work spaces that make the chain popular with business travelers. A **Reebok** fitness center is open 24 hours, and the **400 West** restaurant has a comfy bistro feel. ♦ 400 W Broadway (between Columbia and State Sts). 239.4500; fax 239.3274. www.starwoodhotels.com

20 SOFIA HOTEL

$$ In the old days (before the recent turn of the century), this block of Broadway was about as seedy as Manhattan's 42nd Street used to be. The Pickwick Hotel was in the heart of it all, providing cheap rooms between the train and bus stations. These days lower Broadway is nearly as happening as the rest of downtown and Little Italy. After a $16.3 million remodel and renovation, the Pickwick's become the budget boutique Sofia, with 212 sleek rooms, an efficient business center, a yoga and fitness center, and added services like pet care. ♦ 150 W Broadway (between Front St and First Ave). 800/826.0009. www.thesofiahotel.com

21 THE BRISTOL

$$ You certainly won't have any trouble waking up in one of these bright, cheery

rooms with red walls, yellow and orange bedspreads, and pop art. Somehow, it all comes together, and the 102 rooms are a pleasant change from standard hotel décor. The rates are great and the location is a bit quieter than at other downtown hotels. Try to sneak a peek at the top-floor Starlight Ballroom with its retractable roof. It's used for private parties. California cuisine is served in the **Daisies Bistro**. ♦ 1055 First Ave (between Broadway and C St). 232.6141, 800/662.4477. www.thebristolsandiego.com

21 SUSHI DELI TWO

★★$ The setting of this Japanese eatery is like a no-frills diner where clients belly up to the counter or squeeze into an empty seat and recite their orders with accuracy and speed. The best deals are the platters, which all include rice, salad, and a couple of entrées—like ahi sashimi and teriyaki chicken. The sesame chicken and mixed tempura plate are great, as are the California rolls—if you don't mind artificial crab. ♦ Japanese ♦ Lunch and dinner. 135 Broadway (between Second and First Aves). 233.3072

22 WESTGATE

$$$$ The lobby of this hotel is a re-creation of the anteroom of Versailles, where French nobility awaited the attention of King Louis XV. Baccarat crystal chandeliers, Kerman Persian carpets, and 18th-century chairs and desks fill the public spaces, whereas the 223 guest rooms are furnished with European antiques from the Louis XV, Louis XVI, Georgian, and English Regency periods. Guests are fittingly treated like royalty, and you almost expect a curtsy or bow whenever you enter a room.

This property was the crowning jewel of financier C. Arnholt Smith's dynasty, though he ended up losing money on it. Smith hired architects **Fujimoto & Fish** in 1970 and spent $14.5 million on the structure while his wife toured Europe collecting $2.4 million in period antiques. Smith sold the complex for $14.7 million in 1974. Today the hotel is popular with European and Latin American travelers accustomed to gracious accommodations and impeccable service. It's a good location for a special night at the theater or symphony. The main restaurant, **Le Fontainebleau**, is a study in gracious propriety and gourmet cuisine. Make reservations way in advance for the Friday-night seafood soirée or Sunday champagne brunch. Afternoon tea, accompanied by harp music, is served daily. ♦ 1055 Second Ave (between Broadway and C St). 238.1818, 800/221.3802; fax 557.3737. www.westgatehotel.com

A linear park called Tweet Street is in the works for the edge of Cortez Hill at the edge of Interstate 5. The city is creating pathways lined with birdhouses to encourage humans and their winged friends to enjoy downtown's natural attributes.

C. Arnholt Smith built the Westgate Hotel in 1970 after prominent Republicans told him San Diego did not have the proper hotels to host the Republican National Convention.

23 U.S. GRANT HOTEL

$$$$ This hotel offers grandiose nostalgia at its best, with crystal chandeliers dripping with sparkling lights, marble gleaming with the luster of age, and a gentrified, refined air. If you dine in the venerable **Grant Grill** and entertain acquaintances in the ever-so-elegant lounge, you'll be following the tradition of former guests Charles Lindbergh, Albert Einstein, and Harry S. Truman.

The history of this landmark goes back to Ulysses S. Grant Jr., a young man with a dream of creating a monument to his father's memory that would also glorify the son. To do so, Junior razed the original structure on the site, the massive **Horton House**, and hired **Harrison Albright** to create this masterpiece dedicated on 15 October 1910 to President Ulysses S. Grant. Albright gave full rein to his fantasies of an Italian-Renaissance palace, fashioning it from marble, steel, and cement, with a nine-story tower, two seven-story wings, 400 rooms, 200 baths, a saltwater swimming pool, and a ladies' billiard room.

Over the decades, the hotel has been both a fantastic monument and a financier's nightmare. The structure's quirks and limitations have haunted all of its owners—and there have been quite a few over the years. The Sycuan Band of the Kumeyaay Nation purchased the U.S. Grant in 2003 and soon after shut its doors for an extensive renovation. After 21 months and a $52 million face-lift, the hotel reopened in October 2006 as part of the Starwood Luxury Collection. Various features were restored to their original opulence, including the gold-leaf pillars, crystal chandeliers, and white marble grand staircase. Several artists were commissioned to create paintings and sculptures with Native American influences. Though the historical aspects of the hotel were preserved, the Kumeyaay incorporated designs and artwork to reflect the tribe's pride in reclaiming a significant part of downtown. The thoroughly modernized rooms have fabulous beds with original art serving as the headboards, and Wi-Fi, gourmet coffee machines, and Italian linens. Some rooms are still very small, with tiny baths sans tubs. The larger suites are big enough

to host a party. ♦ 326 Broadway (between Fourth and Third Aves). 232.3121, 866/837.4270; fax 239.9517. www.usgrant.net

Within the U.S. Grant Hotel:

GRANT GRILL

★★★$$$$ Beginning in the 1940s, this posh pub with cushy booths displayed a sign reading "Gentlemen only until 3 o'clock." This tradition held firm until 1969, when seven women insisted on being seated for lunch. They reached their desired goal of integration three years later, when a $1 million lawsuit charging violations of the Federal Civil Rights Act was filed. Today the grill honors the seven intrepid interlopers with a plaque.

Along with the hotel's renovation, the grill was remodeled and updated with a white-on-tan décor that lightens the room considerably. The bar's dramatic lanterns drop down in a high arc, and the tables have extravagant floral arrangements. The dining room remains comfortably genteel, with leather booths and courtly waiters clad in tuxedo jackets. An updated menu segues from classic meat dishes (sautéed beef filet) into contemporary seafood sashimi and scallops. Breakfast is a leisurely delight. A serene, courtly manner prevails, though the dress code is no longer in effect. The Grant's lounge is an ideal spot for a quiet after-work martini. The grill hosts afternoon tea and 'tinis from Thursday through Sunday, with both traditional and modern SoCal touches. ♦ American ♦ Daily, lunch and dinner. Reservations recommended. 744.2077

24 RA SUSHI

★★$$$ Splurge on "signature sushi" in a happening space. Soaring ceilings amplify the chatter and loud music, making conversation next to impossible. The food and service are above par (though you can find less expensive good sushi downtown). ♦ Asian ♦ Daily, 11AM-11PM, lunch and dinner. 474 Broadway (between Fourth and Fifth Aves). 321.0021. ♿ www.rasushi.com

25 HOUSE OF BLUES

Part bar/restaurant, part concert venue, San Diego's HOB is one of a few tourist attractions bringing sightseers north of Broadway. Go for the famed gospel brunch, which is fun and filling, or for the music. Name acts appear in various underground spaces. Teens are entranced by the witchy décor. ♦ 1055 Fifth Ave (between Broadway and C St). 299.2583. www.hob.com

THE BEST

Hugh M. Davies

David C. Copley Director, Museum of Contemporary Art San Diego

Fort Rosecrans National Cemetery for the spectacular view and sense of serenity. A great place to watch the whale migration in January.

Centro Cultural Tijuana (CECUT), an impressive cultural center with a marvelous multimedia display of the history of the Californias. Fine café, IMAX theater, state-of-the-art concert and lecture hall. Easy to reach over the border.

Border Field State Park for a true sense of what it feels like to live on the border between the US and Mexico. A simple fence—*la linea*—runs all the way to the ocean, separating the two countries. Also, there is a beautiful bird sanctuary there and a festive, convivial atmosphere.

Top of **Mount Soledad** in La Jolla for the 360-degree view of San Diego.

Timken Art Gallery in Balboa Park, a jewel box of a museum with a great repository of European old masters, Russian icons, and historical American paintings.

Roppongi Restaurant and Sushi Bar in La Jolla for its wonderful hamachi appetizer—served in a most inventive fashion on four upright forks.

Salk Institute—Louis Kahn's architectural masterpiece—for the magnificent vista of the sea framed by a timeless building.

The truly challenging and visually splendid south course at **Torrey Pines Golf Course**.

First white corn in July from **Chino's** in Rancho Santa Fe.

Exploring the tide pools in La Jolla on a Sunday afternoon.

Guy Fleming Trail at Torrey Pines State Park.

Strawberry-banana gelati from **Gelato Vero** in Mission Hills.

Going to see the Neville Brothers at the **Belly Up Tavern** in Solana Beach.

Playing darts and eating Scotch eggs and chips at the **Princess Pub and Grille** on India Street.

26 COURTYARD BY MARRIOTT

$$$$ Blessed be the investor group that purchased downtown's grandest historic bank and turned it into a one-of-a-kind hotel. The original San Diego Trust and Savings Bank was designed by **William Templeton Johnson** in 1927. Originally there was a shooting gallery on the 14th floor with a steel backstop, soundproof walls, and FBI offices. San Diego's first aviation beacon flashed from the building's cupola.

Many of the bank's Italian Romanesque Revival details have been restored, and the sweeping marble lobby with painted coffer ceilings and bronze teller cages separating customers from clerks is essentially intact. A restaurant occupies much of the lobby, whereas the boardroom and original vault are now meeting rooms. The hotel has 245 rooms that echo the building's design with deep red carpets and heavy drapes while providing up-to-date amenities for business travelers. ♦ 530 Broadway (between Sixth and Fifth Aves). 446.3000, 800/321.2211; fax 446-3010. www.courtyard.com/sancd

Downtown's artists and gallery owners band together each spring to present the annual Artwalk, with special gallery shows, performance art, and a street fair. It usually takes place during a weekend in April.

27 ON BROADWAY

High rollers hobnob with visiting celebrities at this classy nightclub in one of downtown's oldest high-rise bank buildings. The Renaissance-Revival building from the 1920s seems well suited to its latest incarnation. The gleaming marble floors and gold inlaid ceilings create a mood of opulence enhanced by the well-dressed patrons who must pass inspection by the doorman before forking over the cover charge. Reserve a table at the club's **Zen Café** to avoid the lines and defer the cover charge. The two-story club is separated into eight rooms, from quiet lounges to a billiard hall to a disco dance floor. Expect long lines unless you're a VIP. ♦ Cover. F, Sa. 615 Broadway (at Sixth Ave). 231.0011. www.onbroadwayeventcenter.com

28 WAHRENBROCK'S BOOK HOUSE

Books pack shelves on three stories in this shop specializing in rare, used, and antiquarian books. A dreadful fire hit the shop in 2006, inspiring tributes and support from longtime fans. The shop isn't like any chain bookstore you've ever seen; the stock is much more eclectic and absorbing. Bibliophiles beware—you could lose the better part of a day here. ♦ M-Sa, 9:30AM-5:30PM. 726 Broadway (between Eighth and Seventh Aves). 232.0132

29 DOBSON'S

★★$$$$ The official watering hole of downtown's bigwigs, this place even has brass plaques over the booths for regulars. Owner Paul Dobson—who is also a skilled matador—has created an elegant, cozy pub resplendent with beveled glass and lustrous mahogany. The best seats are at the edge of the upstairs balcony overlooking the bar; the best meal is the exceptional broiled salmon. If you're on a budget, sit at the bar and order a California Chardonnay and the mussel bisque *en croûte* (thick mussel soup with a pastry crust on top), a puffy, fragrant bowlful of culinary ecstasy. ◆ French ◆ M-F, lunch and dinner; Sa, dinner. Reservations recommended. 956 Broadway Cir (at Broadway). 231.6771. www.dobsonsrestaurant.com

29 SPRECKELS THEATRE

Harrison Albright was commissioned by John D. Spreckels to design this Chicago School-style neo-Baroque theater to commemorate the opening of the Panama Canal and the **1915–1916 Panama-California Exposition**. The theater originally had 1,915 seats in honor of the exposition; subsequent remodeling reduced the capacity to 1,450. It still has outstanding acoustics and is one of the best concert venues in town, though not popular with the big names seeking massive crowds. ◆ 121 Broadway (between Second and First Aves). 235.9500. www.spreckels.net

30 NBC

The local NBC affiliate took over the **Home Savings Tower** on Broadway in 2002, creating a center for public excitement with their street-level studio. Locals now gather in front of the building in San Diego's version of the *Today Show* crowd, and crews often tape news segments amid the crowds. 225 Broadway (at Second Ave). 231.3939

Within the NBC Building:

DOWNTOWN INFORMATION CENTER

Information on downtown developments and housing is available at this office in the **NBC Building**. The large model of downtown with labels for current and upcoming development projects is immensely informative and helps newcomers figure out the lay of the land. Visitors and locals can join the tours of the downtown redevelopment district that the center offers on the first and third Saturdays of each month. ◆ M-Sa.

Reservations required for tours. 225 Broadway (at Second Ave). 235.2222

31 WESTIN HORTON PLAZA

$$$$ If shopping is a major activity when you travel, then this is the hotel to drop your bags in. Set smack up against **Horton Plaza**, this place is low on frills and high on volume. There are 450 rooms decorated in pastels, a fitness center, small pool, two rooftop tennis courts, and a restaurant. Tour buses and taxis fill the driveway roundabout, which features a weird obelisk sculpture and fountain with water spurting out of plaster pelicans. ◆ 910 Broadway Cir (between Broadway and G St). 239.2200, 888/625.5144; fax 239.0509. ♿ www.starwoodshotel.com

32 LYCEUM THEATRE

In San Diego's thriving theater scene, the **San Diego Repertory Theatre** company stands out for its innovative, imaginative productions, iconoclastic humor, and cast of longtime supporters and participants. The troupe was founded by artistic director Douglas Jacobs and producing director Sam Woodhouse in 1976 at the **Sixth Avenue Playhouse**, a cold, uncomfortable former church where crowds gathered to witness such delights as *Rap Master Ronnie*, an irreverent look at the Reagan years. In 1986, the **Rep** became the resident managers of this venue, which offers two separate stages—the 545-seat **Lyceum Stage** and the 260-seat **Space**. Eight productions a year are performed at the **Lyceum Theatre**, either by the Rep itself or by visiting companies. Sometimes too experimental for San Diegans' tastes, the Rep has come close to demise a couple of times. But philanthropic forces always manage to rescue this worthy cause. In 1996 the Rep launched a bilingual, binational program commissioning works that speak about this community. Its 2007 program included *Ain't Misbehavin'*, a tribute to Fats Waller, and *Sweet Fifteen*, the story of a Mexican girl's *quinceañera*, or 15th birthday party. ◆ Admission. 79 Horton Plaza (on Broadway Cir). Administrative office, 231.3586; box office, 544.1000. ♿

Adjacent to Horton Plaza:

ARTS TIX

Purchase same-day half-price tickets for concerts, symphony performances, and plays at this small booth outside **Horton Plaza**. Discounts are also available on tickets to most major attractions and tours.

Restaurants/Clubs: Red | Hotels: Purple | Shops: Orange | Outdoors/Parks: Green | Sights/Culture: Blue

♦ Daily. 28 Horton Plaza (on Broadway Cir, between Fourth and Third Aves). 497.5000. www.sandieoperform.com

33 SAN DIEGO PUBLIC LIBRARY

This main library is San Diego's greatest civic embarrassment, a pitifully under-funded, outmoded structure that librarians knew would soon become outdated even as it opened in 1954. There was little money in architect **William Templeton Johnson**'s budget for ornamentation on the reinforced concrete façade, except for two cast concrete bas-reliefs picturing the cultural heritage of East and West as sculpted by Donal Hord. The building has only five stories, no parking, and no room to grow. Its warmth and wealth of tables and chairs are attractive to the many homeless living on nearby streets, and library users and staff have grown accustomed to having their heartstrings and wallets tugged constantly. Years of debate and delay have stalled repeated attempts at construction of a new library. A piece of city-owned land at Twelfth and J near Petco Park is reserved for Library Circle and future construction on a 366,000-square-foot building. The project is still in the development stages and is slated for completion in 2010. Architects **Rob Wellington Quigley** and **Tucker Sadler & Associates** have come up with a design that has drawn raves, and it looks like San Diego's bibliophiles might someday have a library worthy of their devotion. ♦ Su, 1PM-5PM; M, W, noon-8PM; Tu, Th-Sa, 9:30AM-5:30PM. 820 E St (between Ninth and Eighth Aves). 236.5800. & www.sannet.gov/public-library

34 SAN DIEGO POST OFFICE

Designed in 1936 by **William Templeton Johnson** as San Diego's postal service headquarters, today this Art Moderne post office is a large branch serving the downtown area. ♦ M-F. 815 E St (between Ninth and Eighth Aves). 233.0610

35 SAN DIEGO AIRCRAFT CARRIER MUSEUM

The gray USS *Midway* somehow blends into its surroundings at the Navy Pier beside the cruise ship terminal. Touring the ship, where more than 200,000 sailors lived during the Vietnam and Persian Gulf wars (and other crises), involves a lot of walking and stair climbing. Intruder, Corsair, and Hawkeye aircraft are parked on the flight deck, and the gift shop is stocked with intriguing curiosities. ♦ Admission. Daily, 10AM-5PM. 910 N Harbor Dr (between Market St and W Broadway). 544.9600. & www.midway.org

36 PANTOJA PARK

The oldest park in downtown San Diego, this pretty spot near the bay was originally dedicated in 1850 as the **Plaza de Pantoja y Arriaga**. A central plaza in William Heath Davis's ill-fated plan to turn the settlement of San Diego into a flourishing city, it was named for the pilot of a 1782 expedition that charted San Diego Harbor. The view of the bay is now blocked by buildings, and the park is surrounded on three sides by condo and office towers. There are large trees and perfectly manicured lawns, but no park benches or picnic tables. A statue of Benito Juárez, a gift from Mexico, was erected in 1981. ♦ West G St (between Kettner Blvd and State St)

37 ATHENS MARKET TAVERNA

★★★$$ Mary Pappas and her Greek kitchen crew were downtown denizens of a small taverna long before the influx of beyond-hip restaurants drove rents sky high. They subsequently moved to this place—filled with sunlight, chatter, and the same captivating smells—that looks onto a small park by the **Federal Building**. A perfect, if somewhat unbalanced, meal for four would include creamy *taramosalata* (a whipped caviar dip), Greek salad heavy on the feta and olives, *loukanikos* (savory sausage from a Pappas family recipe), luscious leg of lamb, and if you still have room, some honey-drenched baklava and thick Greek coffee. ♦ Greek ♦ M-F, lunch and dinner; Sa, dinner. 109 West F St (between First Ave and Front St). 234.1955. & www.athensmarkettaverna.co

38 WESTFIELD SHOPPINGTOWN HORTON PLAZA

A bit tired after more than two decades as the heart of downtown's early redevelopment efforts, this shopping center lacks the cachet of malls that have been revamped more recently. Dedicated to Alonzo Horton in 1910, the original Horton Plaza was a small park on Broadway across the street from the **U.S. Grant Hotel**. It had a fountain designed by **Irving Gill** that boasted colored lights, flowing water, and three plaques on its base commemorating Juan Rodríguez Cabrillo, Padre Junípero Serra, and Alonzo Horton. Today, the park and fountain front this complex, which fulfilled shopping mall magnate Ernie Hahn's dream of an urban amusement park for well-heeled adults—filled with shopping, entertainment, and dining thrills. Architect **Jon Jerde** took Hahn's concept and turned it into a multitiered fantasyland of arches, cupolas, and gargoyles. Designer Deborah Sussman, using a palette of dusty rose, sky blue, vivid yellow, and muted rust, created an explosion of color that set tongues wagging. Traditionalists were horrified by this Disneyland plunked into the center of their city.

But shortly after it opened in 1985, suburbanites and travelers started flocking to downtown like never before. The plaza became a six-block-square, five-story-high neighborhood—a self-contained community with shops, restaurants, the **Westin Hotel**, galleries, movie theaters, street vendors, and close to 2,200 parking spaces.

If you park at the plaza, be sure to memorize the floor you're on (e.g., avocado, pepper, or onion) and take note of the shops closest to your car. The plaza and parking lot have an extremely confusing layout, with the floors staggered in uneven levels; you can see where you want to go, but getting there is a whole different matter. Parking is free for 4 hours with validation from the movie theaters or the **Lyceum Theatre**, and for 3 hours with proof from the shops and dining spots.

Restaurants and a 14-theater complex are on the top floor; the major department stores (**Nordstrom** and **Macy's**) have entrances on the streets bordering the plaza—Broadway, G Street, and Fourth and First Avenues. Apartments, shops, and restaurants line the Fourth Avenue side of the plaza at street level, integrating this massive development with businesses in the **Gaslamp Quarter**.

There are over 130 small shops selling everything from kites to cutlery. Considerable dining options including full-service restaurants are on the plaza's top floor overlooking the harbor. Take-out stands line the south side, where tables and chairs are clustered along the banisters. **Wonder Sushi** has the healthiest selection of quick snacks among the kiosks serving Japanese, Greek, Italian, and Mexican fare, along with all-American corn dogs and cheese-covered french fries. ♦ Daily. Bounded by Fourth and First Aves and by G St and Broadway. 239.8180. ♿ www.westfield.com/hortonplaza

39 Comfort Inn Gaslamp

$$ A good place to set up housekeeping if you're in town for several days, the Comfort Inn has 103 rooms with microwaves, small refrigerators, and coffeemakers. There's a laundry room on the property, but no restaurant or pool. Continental breakfast is included in the rate. ♦ 660 G St (between Seventh and Sixth Aves). 877.424.6423, 800/598.1810; fax 238.5310. ♿ www.comfortinngaslamp.com

40 Pannikin

Former owners Bob and Gay Sinclair turned this 1909 redbrick and timber Davidson furniture warehouse (designed by **D.S. Harbison**) into the headquarters for their coffee importing business in 1976. A former employee now owns this venerable shop and coffeehouse with its delightful assortment of imported curiosities, many with a coffee theme. Up front is a cluster of comfy couches for coffee sippers and a huge selection of blends from around the world available by the pound for home brewers. ♦ Daily. 675 G St (between Seventh and Sixth Aves). 239.7891

41 Tuna Harbor

Tuna fishing was a lucrative industry in San Diego between the 1940s and the 1960s, and Portuguese and Italian fisherfolk unloaded their catches here at what was then called the **G Street Mole**. The tuna fleet is now nearly extinct, and today this is home to an enormous two-restaurant complex with one of the biggest parking lots in downtown. Both dining spots offer a smashing view of the bay, and on warm days the bayside patio bar is a great place to soak up the sun. ♦ 750 N Harbor Dr (between W Market St and W Broadway). 232.3474

Within Tuna Harbor:

The Fish Market

★★$$ This downstairs eatery has bustling oyster and sushi bars and several sections of tables and booths, many with a view of the water. You can't go wrong with any of the grilled fresh fish or pasta dishes. ♦ Seafood ♦ Daily, lunch and dinner. 232.3474. ♿ www.thefishmarket.com

Top of the Market

★★$$$ White linen tablecloths, roses in bud vases, and glistening crystal make this upstairs dining room far more elegant and refined than its downstairs sister. Most tables have at least a glimpse of the waterfront—the best seats are on the deck and worth reserving in advance. Seafood is imported from all over the world, and diners can choose Maine or Australian lobster, New Zealand or Washington oysters, Holland Dover sole, Mississippi catfish, and a variety of caviar. The smoked tuna, ahi, and dorado are moist and flavorful. A few nonseafood choices are available as well, including homemade pastas. The extensive wine list includes champagnes by the glass and a wide variety of after-dinner drinks. ♦ Seafood ♦ Daily, lunch and dinner; Su, brunch. Reservations recommended. 234.4867. ら

42 EMBASSY SUITES

$$$$ This is one of the best deals near the **San Diego Convention Center** for those who like spacious rooms. All 337 suites have separate living rooms, mini-kitchens, and work areas. The neon bull's-eye atop the 12-story neoclassical Mediterranean tower ensures you won't lose your bearings at night. All rooms open onto an atrium filled with palm trees, koi ponds, and fountains. The best breakfast bargain in town is in the hotel's atrium restaurant, where hotel guests are served a complimentary cooked-to-order breakfast. ◆ 601 Pacific Hwy (at W Harbor Dr). 239.2400, 800/EMBASSY; fax 239.1520. ら www.embassysuites.com

43 KANSAS CITY BARBEQUE

★$ It doesn't get any funkier than this—a rattletrap shack beside the railroad tracks, made famous as a flyboy hangout in the movie *Top Gun*. Be prepared for a heavy dose of spice and grease in the barbecued ribs, chicken, and hot links served with slices of Wonder bread and onion rings. The food does not inspire rave reviews, but the décor is still popular with Tom Cruise fans. ◆ Barbecue ◆ Daily, lunch and dinner. 610 W Market St (at Kettner Blvd). 231.9680. www.kcbbq.net

44 SEAPORT VILLAGE

A farsighted developer staked out 14 acres of prime waterfront land in 1980 and hired architect **Norbert W. Pieper** to create this theme-park shopping and dining complex with tropical landscaping by Wimmer, Yamada & Associates. A shingled replica of the Mukiltea Lighthouse in Everett, Washington, and the 1895 hand-carved Broadway Flying Horses Carousel give a historic feeling to the village. There's enough variety in the 54 shops and sufficient dining options to occupy most folks' attention; mimes, jugglers, balloon sculptors, magicians, and fire painters offer further entertainment. A long grassy jetty thrusts from the boardwalk shopping zone into the bay; picnickers, kite flyers, bicyclists, and strollers while away the day here. Others come here for concerts, fireworks displays, and other scheduled celebrations. In addition to a few restaurants, there are food stands serving Mexican, Chinese, Italian, deli sandwiches, burgers, and hot dogs. Tables are scattered near the carousel and waterfront.

Most city tours include a stop at the village, and the **Orange Line** of the San Diego Trolley connects it with the **San**

Diego Convention Center and C Street downtown. ◆ 849 W Harbor Dr (at Pacific Hwy). Offices, 235.4014. ら www.seaportvillage.com

Within Seaport Village:

EMBARCADERO MARINA PARK

At the beginning of this wide sweep of grass out over the bay is the *Morning Statue*, Donal Hord's sculpture of a fisherman. Magicians and musicians perform nearby, and the lawns here are a good spot to escape the crowds at the village and relax over a peaceful picnic. Concerts and fireworks displays are held here on holidays.

UPSTART CROW AND COMPANY

Great books, fragrant espresso, and reading areas with comfortable chairs are the draws at this wonderful place to escape to when it's not crowded. ◆ Daily, 9AM-9PM. 232.4855. www.upstartcrowtrading.com

SWINGS N' THINGS

Hang out on high-quality hammocks and swinging chairs from the Yucatán and Brazil while the others are shopping. ◆ Daily, 9:30AM-9PM. 234.8995. www.swingsandthingssd.com

GREEK ISLAND CAFE

★★$ This is the best informal dining spot in the village. Enjoy well-prepared Greek roasted chicken, salads, and gyros while seated at bright blue picnic tables on the boardwalk by the bay. ◆ Greek ◆ Daily, lunch and dinner. 239.5216. www.greekislandcafe.com

45 MANCHESTER GRAND HYATT SAN DIEGO

$$$$ The slim, cream-colored towers of this hotel rise above the waterfront like a sleek obelisk, standing tall against neighboring mirrored spires. City leaders and the **Skidmore, Owings & Merrill** architectural group planned the space specifically to be pedestrian-friendly—a 2-acre park and a parking lot covered with trellises and vines were incorporated into the hotel's design. The 1,625 rooms and suites are much like those in other members of this worldwide chain, but the third-story pool has a great view of San Diego Bay, and the **Top of the Hyatt** bar also boasts a spectacular vista. There's also a fitness center, several nice shops, and three restaurants. ◆ One Market Pl (at Harbor Dr). 232.1234, 888/591.1234; fax 233.6464. ら www.manchestergrand.hyatt.com

Within the Grand Hyatt San Diego:

65 INDIA INK PAPERS

Fabulous paper, cards, stationery, ribbons, pens, and other writerly accoutrements are artfully displayed in this little shop, a good place to find a houseguest gift. ♦ 1907 Columbia St (at W Fir St). 233.4203. www.indiainkpapers.com

66 CAFÉ ZUCCHERO

★★$$ Skip the sidewalk tables and narrow dining room and head for the backyard, where tables are set amidst clotheslines draped with shirts and vines as if at grandma's house. Joe and Lisa Busalacchi, of a longtime local restaurant family, created this Italian café where pannini and pastas please diners escaping work at lunch or looking for a peaceful, satisfying dinner. The pastries and gelato keep sweet teeth satisfied. ♦ Café ♦ Daily. 1731 India St (between W Date and W Fir Sts). 531.1731. www.cafezucchero.com

66 FILIPPI'S PIZZA GROTTO

★★$ San Diego's original pizzeria (ca. 1950) is still one of the most popular pizza parlors in the city. The aromas of garlic and olive oil pervade the crowded dining quarters decorated with giant salamis dangling from the ceiling, red-checkered tablecloths, a few phony grape arbors, and dim lighting to hide the flaws of age. Although spaghetti, ravioli, fettuccine, and the like are on the menu, for a true experience, order a jug of Chianti and a thick-crusted pizza with extra cheese, anchovies, ripe olives, and pepperoni (though you can choose a tamer combo if you like). Everything on the menu—plus deli meats, cheese, virgin olive oil, and fresh-baked Italian cookies—is available at the front take-out counter. ♦ Italian ♦ Daily, lunch and dinner. 1747 India St (between W Date and W Fir Sts). 232.5094. www.realcheesepizza.com

67 LA PENSIONE HOTEL

$ Budget travelers who don't mind being away from the beach are in luck at this stylish hotel in the heart of Little Italy. The 75 rooms, remodeled in 2003, are so tiny some guests call them "shoe boxes." Earplugs come in handy to block street noise. Each guest room has a queen-size bed, cable television, and a kitchenette with microwave, sink, and refrigerator. The shady courtyard adjacent to the lobby is secluded and peaceful. Several great Italian restaurants in the neighborhood will fill all your dining needs. Downtown is within easy walking distance, and there is a trolley stop nearby. ♦ 606 W Date St (at India St).

236.8000, 800/232.4683; fax 236.8088. & www.lapensionehotel.com

68 PRINCESS PUB AND GRILLE

★★$ A great watering hole for mugs of Guinness or Black-and-Tans, or Scotch eggs and chips. Old photos of Princess Di are featured prominently on the walls; regulars play darts, watch golf on TV, or belly up to the shiny wood bar with brass beer taps. Traditional pub décor is lightened by open front windows and swirling ceiling fans. Patrons must walk through a gauntlet of smokers relegated to the sidewalk thanks to California's no-smoking ordinance. ♦ Pub ♦ Daily, lunch and dinner. 1665 India St (between W Cedar and W Date Sts). 702.3021. www.princesspub.com

68 SOLUNTO BAKING COMPANY

If you eat in any Italian restaurant in San Diego or just order a submarine sandwich from a deli, chances are you'll be served the crusty, melt-in-your-mouth bread made at this institution. Even the French cafés are known to buy their baguettes here. Stop by for a loaf or for one of the flaky, fruit-filled breakfast pastries, light-as-air doughnuts and crullers, or Florentine cookies coated with bittersweet chocolate. For further sustenance, consider a serving of spicy eggplant Parmesan, a sausage sandwich dripping with sauce, or a salami sub lathered in vinegar and oil. There are tables in front of the deli counter for those who can't wait, but most customers get their goodies to go. ♦ Daily. 1643 India St (between W Cedar and W Date Sts). 233.3506. &

69 OUR LADY OF THE ROSARY PARISH

Long before Little Italy became trendy, this small church was its social center. It remains so for the families who've been here for decades. Venetian painter Fausto Tasca decorated the ceiling and walls with paintings depicting the mysteries of the Rosary and the Last Judgment. Californian sculptor Carlos Romanelli contributed statues of Our Lady, St. Anne, and St. Joseph and the church, consecrated in 1925, has several beautiful stained-glass windows. ♦ 1629 Columbia St (between W Cedar and W Date Sts). 234.4820. www.olrsd.org

70 INDIGO GRILL

★★★$$$ Chef Deborah Scott could never create boring food. Her spicy multicultural cuisine borrows a bit from Mexico and a touch from the Pacific Northwest, with a generous dose of Scott's own inventive style. The full bar is stocked with fine tequilas, mescals, and rum to complement Scott's sometimes fiery creations. Try her corn pudding, blackened salmon, chili-rubbed steak salad, and anything with a Latin bent. The décor is as uplifting as the cuisine, with Inuit and Oaxacan carvings, totem poles, and water streaming down the wall behind the bar. ◆ Eclectic ◆ M-F, lunch and dinner; Sa, Su, dinner. Reservations recommended. 1536 India St (between W Beech and W Cedar Sts). 234.6802. www.cohnrestaurants.com

71 ANTHOLOGY

★★★$$$ Brand-new in the summer of 2007, this impressively cosmopolitan jazz supper club is definitely edging San Diego toward a more sophisticated stance. The three-level, $6 million, 1940s-inspired club spotlights musicians in the world of jazz and international music.

Celeb chef Bradley Ogden consulted with executive chef Jim Phillips to create a farm- and ocean-fresh local California cuisine unlike anything Downtown and Little Italy have seen. Dining tables ring the stage and 18-foot fireplace on the mezzanine level, and a spacious outdoor balcony overlooks India Street. The elegant menu covers are made from woods used in Taylor Guitars' custom guitars (the San Diego business is a longtime fave of professional guitarists worldwide). In just the first few months, Anthology hosted performances by Arturo Sandoval, Flora Purim, Chick Corea, Jessie Colin Young, and Jazz Fusion Superstars. Pricing varies with performer and nothing is inexpensive, from the excellent wine selection to the sophisticated ambience (you'll want to dress up). ◆ Californian ◆ Tu-Su. 1337 India St (between W A and W Ash Sts). 595.0300. www.anthologysd.com

GASLAMP QUARTER

An overhead sign spanning the foot of Fifth Avenue at Harbor Drive marks the entrance to the Gaslamp Quarter, downtown's most popular dining, shopping, and entertainment enclave. The Gaslamp's late 20th-century transformation from a seedy, sleazy near slum to an upscale attraction gained acclaim from dining critics and urban planners around the country. Its streets are jam-packed on weekend nights—a sight that would have made Alonzo Horton beam with pride. When Horton established his New Town in 1867, its center was along Fifth Avenue, where runaway horses galloped through dirt streets lined by saloons and brothels. As downtown prospered, the center of commerce shifted toward Broadway, and

the original buildings of Horton's frontier town fell into disrepair. The area became known as the Stingaree, a red-light district.

When city planners started focusing on downtown redevelopment in the 1970s, the Gaslamp Quarter, as the area south of Broadway around Fifth Avenue was known, looked like prime turf for rampant destruction. But San Diegans protested and formed the Gaslamp Quarter Foundation, which oversees the area and protects downtown's heritage. The quarter was designated a National Historic District in 1980 and now encompasses a 16-block area with brick sidewalks, wrought-iron benches, gas streetlamps, and street signs with distinctive brown lettering. The beautifully restored historic buildings were built between 1870 and 1930 in a variety of styles—including Frontier, Victorian, Italian Renaissance, Romanesque, Chicago Commercial, Oriental, Modern, Interna-tional, and Spanish Renaissance—and today house restaurants, offices, and shops.

The Gaslamp has become hip, trendy, and ever so cutting-edge. Its proximity to the **Convention Center** makes it the obvious evening destination for thousands of out-of-towners who can spot the brightly lit Gaslamp Quarter sign at the foot of Fifth Avenue from their convention hotels. Discerning diners have their pick of dozens of restaurants—the dining and nightlife scenes are constantly changing. Club hoppers roam from pubs to martini bars to late-night dance venues. Shops stay open until 10PM or even midnight on weekends, and limos, Hummers, taxis, and pedicabs cruise the streets. Many restaurants offer valet parking, and several parking lots are full by 9PM. A parking guide is available at www.gaslamp.org. The trolley also stops nearby, which helps ease the congestion.

Roving bands of kids with too much time and too little money are drawn to the neighbor-hood, as are transients and the homeless. Given the popularity of venues pushing large volumes of alcohol, the ambience can become edgy, especially late on weekend nights. The police presence is significant, with cops patrolling the streets on horseback, bicycles, and foot. Keep your wits about you and carry ID and only as much cash as you're willing to spend (plus a bit of plastic). You'll find an ever more intriguing selection of shops, hotels, and eateries. Several annual celebrations are held in the neighborhood, including a big Mardi Gras parade, Taste of the Gaslamp, and ShamROCK, a music festival that takes place on St. Patrick's Day. Call the Gaslamp Quarter Association, 614 Fifth Avenue, for information at 233.5227 or visit www.gaslamp.org. The area is bounded by Sixth and Fourth Avenues and by East Harbor Drive and Broadway.

72 BALBOA THEATER

Many years ago, plans were approved to rehabilitate this circa-1923 stage theater and reopen it for performances—but that's hardly news. The building was nearly razed in the flurry of redevelopment when **Horton Plaza** went in but was designated a historical landmark and protected. Various individuals and agencies have tried to restore the theater, but the cost of bringing the building up to current standards is prohibitive. The original theater, designed by **William Wheeler** in 1924, had two 20-foot-high waterfalls inside that flowed freely during intermissions. The tiled dome echoes the form of the domes on the **Santa Fe Depot** and the **California Tower**. A tile mosaic in the sidewalk at the entrance depicts Balboa discovering the Pacific Ocean. Selective demolition and reconstruction began in 2005, but was severely hampered by the constraints of a seismic retrofit. Renovation was underway in 2006 and 2007, with a reopening slated for 2007. At press time, the building is closed to the public. ♦ Fourth Ave (between E St and Broadway). www.thebalboa.org

73 DAKOTA GRILL & SPIRITS

★$$ Noisy and busy with two stories of dining areas and live piano music, this place serves good Southwestern cuisine with sauces and spices that sometimes work and sometimes don't. Try the tempura calamari, BBQ chicken pizza, and baby-back ribs. ♦ Southwestern ♦ Daily, lunch and dinner. 901 Fifth Ave (at E St). 234.5554. & www.cohnrestaurants.com

74 RAMADA INN & SUITES

$$$ The *Saint James* name still stands out in bright lights atop this 1913 hotel building. When first designed by the architectural firm of **Henry, Harms, and Preibisuis**, the hotel was elegant and entirely up to standard, according to advertisements of the day. Probably the commerce enacted therein was of a more illicit type during the Stingaree

years; later, the hotel became a flophouse. New owners renovated the hotel in the 1980s, investing $2.5 million in the lobby alone, with its crystal chandeliers and old-fashioned elevators. The hotel never quite caught on as a luxurious hostelry but has 99 rooms and suites with character at an affordable price. ♦ 830 Sixth Ave (between F and E Sts). 531.8877, 800/664-4400; fax 231.8307. www.stjameshotel.com

75 THE ONYX ROOM

Descend the stairway to this underground cocktail lounge reminiscent of the stylish 1950s. Red upholstered barrel chairs are clustered around cocktail tables where hip patrons sip pink squirrels, old-fashioneds, and other classic cocktails. The live music ranges from acid jazz to high-energy dance music. Visiting DJs spin the vinyl most nights; Tuesdays are reserved for jazz jam sessions. The dress code prohibits baseball caps, gym shoes, and other casual attire. ♦ Cover. Closed Su, M. 852 Fifth Ave (between F and E Sts). 235.6699. www.onyxroom.com

76 BANDAR

★★★$$ Behrooz Farahani moved his family from Iran to San Diego more than a decade ago and used his skills as an architect to transform one of the Gaslamp's historic structures into a fabulous contemporary restaurant. The aromas of saffron, cilantro, charbroiled onions, and simmering sauces immediately alert the taste buds as you enter the fashionable dining room. The menu offers an irresistible array of homemade yogurt and shallot appetizers, salads with feta cheese, and entrées served with lovely layers of white and gold basmati rice. Choose the Bandar special so you can sample both the chicken and lamb skewers, and have someone in your party order one of the veal stews. ♦ Persian ♦ Daily, lunch and dinner. 825 Fourth Ave (between F and E Sts). 238.0101. & www.bandarrestaurant.com

77 PATRICK'S II

Live jazz and blues are played nightly here in one of downtown's oldest bars, tucked

"Information" Anderson, aka Adolph H. Anderson, was hired by the San Diego Electric Railway Company in 1915 as a public relations gesture. From his booth at Horton Plaza, he researched and answered some 22 million questions about San Diego and transportation over a span of 33 years.

into a small space off F Street. ◆ Cover, F, Sa. Daily, 9AM-2AM. 428 F St (between Fifth and Fourth Aves). 233.3077. www.patricksii.com

77 KEATING HOTEL

$$$$ The first hotel designed by Pininfarina, the legendary Italian car-design company behind Ferrari and Maserati, was bound to make a statement—and it does. The 35 sexy rooms have no interior walls separating bathing and sleeping spaces—apparently showering is part of the overall experience. Of course the linens are high-end, the minibar is a study in self-indulgence, and the Bang & Olufsen sound systems and 37-inch HD plasma TVs are perfect playthings. Beneath the Keating is the **Minus 1** private lounge. Access is granted to hotel guests and members who pay the $2,500 annual fee. ◆ 432 F St (between Fifth and Fourth Aves). 814.5700, 877/753.2846. www.thekeating.com

78 CROCE'S RESTAURANT & JAZZ BAR

★★★$$$$ Ingrid Croce, widow of singer-songwriter Jim Croce, dedicated this restaurant and jazz club to the memory of the man who created "Bad, Bad Leroy Brown." Since she first opened it in 1985, Croce has expanded her business into every corner of the 1890 Romanesque **Keating Building** and on down the block. She's become an industry of her own, with a cookbook aptly titled *Thyme in a Bottle*. Son A.J. Croce plays the piano in a bluesy New Orleans style that has made him a recognized musician in his own right. **Croce's** was one of the first successful restaurants and clubs in the Gaslamp, and it continues to fill with loyal diners. The contemporary American menu features pasta, fish, seafood, beef, chicken, and lamb dishes, and there is an extensive wine list. Sit in the glassed-in dining room or at the sidewalk tables. Live rhythm-and-blues groups play nightly at the adjacent **Croce's Top Hat Bar & Grill**, with such national acts

as Maynard Ferguson, Rita Coolidge, and Arlo Guthrie appearing for special engagements, with or without A.J. Croce, who's on his sixth album and a steady rise to fame. Groups also appear at the **Jazz Bar**. The cover charge for acts is included in dinner entrées at the restaurant. ◆ Contemporary American ◆ Daily, breakfast, lunch, and dinner. 802 Fifth Ave (at F St). 233.4355. www.croces.com

79 IVY HOTEL

$$$$ This entry into the high-high-end super-sexy lodging scene opened with several splashes and parties that started in May 2007 and continued for months. The 159 rooms and suites are designed to absolutely thrill trendoids seeking glassed-in showers and tubs, 42-inch TVs, 24-hour butler service (need your bath drawn for you?), the latest favorite liquors, and various sensual amenities. Complimentary Cadillac Escalade service is available for a sweet ride to clubs and restaurants. On Friday and Saturday nights their multilevel dance club **Envy** is open, with cocktail waitresses in vinyl catsuits and some of Southern California's hottest DJs spinning vinyl. **Eden**, the rooftop bar, is sparsely decorated with concrete, white, and bamboo, with private cabanas for sunning and posing. It's pretty calm during the day, but heats up at night. ◆ 600 F St (between Seventh and Sixth Aves). 814.1000. www.ivyhotel.com

Within the Ivy:

QUARTER KITCHEN

★★★$$$$ The LA vibe is alive in this large see-and-be-seen space with some of the priciest food in downtown. Celeb chef Damon Gordon presents lobster in ravioli, a clever potpie, a gigantic club sandwich, and Kobe beef by the ounce. The various chefs and cooks are on view in the open kitchen and strangers mingle at the long communal kitchen. You could begin with caviar tacos for a total dinner and just hang out for the entire night (service can be leisurely). ◆ American Contemporary ◆ 814.2000. www.quarterkitchen.com

80 CAFÉ LULU

★$ Late-night revelers refuel and unwind with herbal teas, coffee drinks, veggie soups, and delightful desserts at this bohemian café. Best seats are the padded benches with pillows along the walls, where you can visit with friends as if at home. Champagne, wine, and beer are also available. ◆ Su-Th, 9:30AM-1AM; F, Sa, 9:30AM-3AM. 419 F St (between Fifth and Fourth Aves). 238.0114

The *Spirit of St. Louis*, flown by Charles Lindbergh in his 1927 New York–to–Paris flight, was built by San Diego's Ryan Airlines in 60 days.

The Jessop clock in Horton Plaza was built by clock maker Claude D. Ledger in 1906. When Ledger died in 1935, the clock stopped running. It was restarted, but it stopped again on the day of Ledger's funeral, prompting an entry in *Ripley's Believe It or Not*.

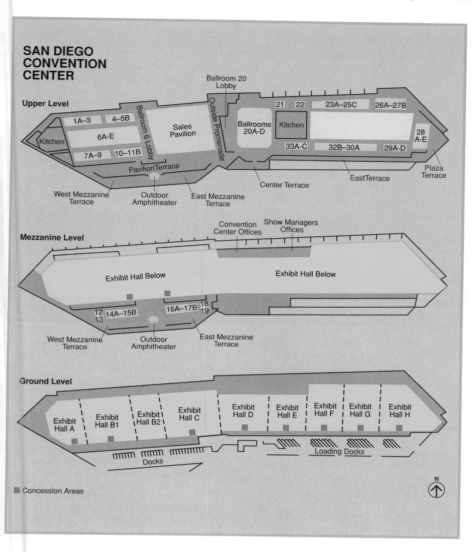

SAN DIEGO CONVENTION CENTER

81 THE BITTER END

Jeans, sandals, hiking boots, and other casual wear are forbidden in the upstairs lounge of this stylish bar. The code relaxes a bit for the main bar and the **Underground** dance club, where the music rocks and the crowd is young and exuberant. ◆ Cover, Th-Sa. 770 Fifth Ave (at F St). 338.9300. ♿ www.thebitterend.com

82 OLE MADRID CAFE

★★$$ About as hip as a tapas bar could be, this spot covers two stories and a sidewalk patio. The tapas—especially the mushroom or chicken and garlic—are good, as are the pasta and paella, but the food isn't nearly as important as whom you know and how you're dressed. Stick with black and you'll fit in fine. ◆ Tapas ◆ Daily, dinner. 755 Fifth Ave (between G and F Sts). 557.0146. www.oldmadrid.com

83 LE TRAVEL STORE

Owners Joan and Bill Keller created what may have been the first shop geared completely to travelers' needs in Pacific Beach in 1976. The business moved from Pacific Beach to Horton Plaza in 1985, then became one of the pioneers on Fifth Avenue in 1994 when

The Best

Rob Wellington Quigley and Everyone Else in the Office

Architects

Fidel's, Solana Beach—great Mexican food in a building with courtyards that ramble on forever.

Point Loma Seafoods—this bustling waterfront take-out seafood restaurant has the best fresh seafood for sale and a wonderfully crispy, fried fish sandwich served on sourdough bread. Ask for it sloppy so you get lots of tartar sauce.

Chicano Park, under the San Diego side of the **Coronado Bridge**—after the freeway bisected their community, local Chicano artists reclaimed their turf and created a park by painting the supports under the bridge in colorful murals.

Salk Institute—every architect who visits the San Diego area has to see **Louis Kahn**'s best building.

Baltic Inn (521 Sixth Avenue), **J Street Inn** (222 J Street),and **La Pensione** (India and Date)—San Diego has set an example for the country in providing housing for the lower economic levels in single-room-occupancy hotels.

La Jolla Woman's Club—Irving Gill innovated the use of tilt-slab construction on this wonderfully regional building located across the street from the **Museum of Contemporary Art, San Diego** on Prospect in **La Jolla**.

Crystal Pier (Garnet Avenue, Pacific Beach)—the little cottages on this pier are a great place to stay and be lulled to sleep by the waves. Not recommended during big storms!

163 through Balboa Park—the best inner-city freeway experience in California; a true gateway to the city. Hopefully they'll never widen this and destroy the special feeling of driving through the canyon and trees under the **Cabrillo Bridge**.

Stuart Collection, UCSD—an inspired series of site-specific sculptures scattered throughout the **UCSD** campus in an ongoing program.

---

they restored a 1907 brick building. Local travel aficionados and tourists from all over the world stop by to peruse the excellent displays of books, luggage, and the latest gadgets. The extensive line of Eagle Creek gear is enough to make you donate your old backpacks and roll-aboards. There's a travel agency in the front of the shop, and the Kellers now have a mail-order business at their web site (your purchases can also be shipped from the on-site facility). ◆ Daily. 745 Fourth Ave (between G and F Sts). 544.0005, 800/713.4260. ♿ www.letravelstore.com, www.luggage.com

84 OSTERIA PANEVINO

★★$$$ Frequent downtown diners consistently rate this trattoria among the better of the area's Italian eateries. The narrow dining room and sidewalk tables are popular in the evening when diners linger over stuffed focaccia, gnocchi, sublime spinach ravioli, and osso buco The menu and décor are meant to transport diners to Tuscany. The tables inside that are near the exposed brick walls are the best if you're seeking the European ambience. ◆ Italian ◆ Daily, lunch and dinner. Reservations recommended. 722 Fifth Ave (between G and F Sts). 595.7959. ♿ www.osteriapanevino.com

85 MONSOON

★★★$$$ Downtown's most distinctive Indian restaurant is so successful the owner (who also owns **Bombay** in Hillcrest)

has expanded the space. The lunch buffet is a standout for its price, quality, and the plain or garlic nan (bread) cooked to order. The menu is filled with treats, from a spicy tomato-and-cucumber salad to lamb with saffron and raisins. Go with a group and settle in for a feast. Waterfalls, drumming background music, and belly dancers on weekend evenings add sufficient entertainment to create a dining adventure. ◆ Indian ◆ Daily, lunch and dinner. 729 Fourth Ave (between G and F Sts). 234.5555, 800/MONSOON. www.monsoonrestaurant.com

86 PACIFIC GASLAMP STADIUM 15

Should the Gaslamp action become overwhelming, you can always step into this 15-screen movie house that dominates a corner lot. The building is way too massive for the corner it commands, and jars with the surrounding architecture. The seats are comfy, however. ◆ 701 Fifth Ave (at G St). 232.0400. ♿ www.pacifictheatres.com

87 JIMMY LOVE'S

★★$$ Dining and dancing come with a sense of style at this classy restaurant that caters to a well-dressed, over-30 crowd. There's live jazz, R&B, or disco most nights, and the menu offers a bit of everything, from gourmet pizzas to New York steak Bordelaise. The restaurant takes up two stories of the old city government building, built in 1887. ◆ American ◆ Daily, dinner. 672 Fifth

replaced in 2001 by the Bridgeworks complex, which has won several awards for its striking brick, glass, and steel architecture. ◆ 401 K Street (at Fourth Ave)

Within Bridgeworks:

HILTON SAN DIEGO
GASLAMP QUARTER

$$$$ You don't have to buy a downtown loft to feel like a sophisticated urbanite. The **Hilton's Enclave** has 30 suites and lofts with soaring ceilings, high windows that let in plenty of natural light, brick and burnished-steel accents, and original paintings by local artists. These creative spaces have a few more creature comforts than most lofts, however, including plush beds with Frette linens, whirlpool tubs, velvety couches, and chocolates on the down pillows at night. The hotel's 245 regular rooms also have a modern, artsy décor and all the right touches, including windows that open to views of the city. The **New Leaf** restaurant is an ideal place for conventioneers and Gaslamp workers to gather at the breakfast bar and buffet or on the terrace by the **King Promenade**. Drinks by the two-sided fireplace in the lounge are the perfect beginning for your evening's Gaslamp crawl. The hotel's rooms and public space offer a pleasant respite from the nearby convention hotel giants. ◆ 401 K Street (at Fourth Ave). 231.4040, 800/774.1500; fax 231.6439. ᪐ www.hilton.com

113 ARTESIA DAY SPA AND SALON

Are your feet and eyes tired from touring or working? Book a pedicure (with exfoliation and massage), a facial designed to diminish those bags and circles under your eyes, or a hot stone massage that will melt your tense muscles. The spa is light and airy yet soothing with its subdued music and lighting. A visit here may be the best lunch break you could take. ◆ Daily. 240 Fifth Ave (between L and K Sts). 338.8111. www.artesiadayspa.com

114 HARD ROCK HOTEL

$$$$ The fall 2007 opening of San Diego's first branded condo-hotel was all the buzz as we went to press. The first phase of 300 suites sold out in 9 hours, long before the building was anywhere near completion.

San Diego Mayor Jerry Sanders smashed a guitar to celebrate the construction of the 12th and final floor. The 420 rooms and suites are decked out with techie toys (42-inch HDTV, integrated video and sound system), larger suites have separate bedrooms, and the loftlike Rock Star Suites have spa-like bathrooms and outdoor decks with views of the city and bay. With a **Nobu** restaurant, Rande Gerber rooftop bar, a 24-hour Maryjane's Coffee Shop, and various event spaces, the Hard Rock is sure to totally transform the south end of Fifth Avenue. ◆ 207 Fifth Ave (at the corner of L St). 866/751.0025. www.hardrockhotelsd.com

115 TIN FISH

★★★★$ When you see beat cops and construction workers lunching at outdoor tables, you know you've stumbled across good food at reasonable prices. Order fish tacos or garlicky shrimp burritos (go for the crisscut fries) at the counter and claim an umbrella-shaded table beside an ingenious fountain with water spurting intermittently from holes in the sidewalk. ◆ Seafood/Mexican. ◆ Daily, lunch; F, Su, dinner. 170 Sixth Ave (at L St). 628.8414. www.thetinfish.net

116 OMNI SAN DIEGO

$$$ A sky bridge connects the tasteful Omni with **Petco Park,** and a nearby pedestrian crossing makes the walk from the hotel to the **Convention Center** a zip. Naturally, San Diego Padres owner John Moores has a posh home atop the hotel, above 36 private condominiums; his private collection of baseball memorabilia fills display cases in public spaces. Corner rooms on the east side have a spot-on view of the ballpark; others overlook the Convention Center and bay. The 511 rooms are sensibly and comfortably designed for both business and leisure travelers, and the outdoor pool with fireplace is the favorite hangout for cold-weather guests. A **McCormick & Schmick**'s restaurant serves decent seafood and hotel standards, and a building across the street offers some take-out food franchises. ◆ 675 L St (between Seventh and Sixth Aves). 231.6664, 800/843.6664. www.omnihotels.com

CORONADO

Though Coronado is often referred to as an island, it is really a peninsula connected to the mainland by the narrow isthmus of highway and sand called the Silver Strand. The Coronado Islands are actually offshore and to the south, in Mexican waters; this bit of land was named after that island chain. Coronadans don't refer to their hometown as an island but rather as "The Village," despite its 26,000 residents.

Coronado does seems like a village, a self-contained island community where multiple generations of old-line families live next door to each other on quiet, tree-lined streets. Within its 5.3-square-mile radius, the city has at least 18 public parks—some no larger than a good-size living room in one of the area's stately old mansions—and 28 miles of sandy beach line its shores on the **Pacific Ocean** and **San Diego** and **Glorietta Bays**. The US Navy frames Coronado to the north with the **North Island Naval Air Station** and to the south with the **Naval Amphibious Base** on the Silver Strand. Downtown San Diego is just a 5-minute ferry ride across the San Diego Bay to the east; **Point Loma** is visible to the west.

Residents speak of San Diego as a foreign entity; their city was incorporated in 1890 and has withstood outside intervention ever since. As a rule, Coronadans are faithful to tradition, respectful of local lore, and resistant to change. It's a remarkably safe and thoughtful community, steeped in a colorful and stimulating history that never ceases to fascinate newcomers and old-timers alike.

The history of Coronado begins with Elisha S. Babcock Jr. and Hampton L. Story, two hunting buddies who (as the story goes) became enamored in the 1880s of their hunting grounds on what appeared to be an island in San Diego Bay. On boat trips across the bay, they gradually began to envision a full-scale, spectacular resort where quail and jackrabbits roamed free on scruffy, barren land. Babcock and Story (with additional investors) purchased the peninsula for $110,000 in 1885; by 1887 they had sold $1 million in property, laid out streets and a pipeline to carry fresh water under the bay to the settlement, named it Coronado, and begun construction on the **Hotel Del** (as residents familiarly call the **Hotel del Coronado**). Despite booming land sales, Babcock and Story were broke by 1900, and John Diedrich Spreckels took control of the hotel. Spreckels was the son of Claus Spreckels, called the "Sugar King" for the fortunes he amassed selling Hawaiian sugar in San Francisco. J.D. Spreckels commenced to reign over Coronado's most prosperous and glamorous era, when millionaires built mansions along the waterfront and travelers from all over the world visited the hotel and the adjacent glorified summer camp called **Camp Coronado** (later **Tent City**).

Spreckels combined his many investments to create an irresistible vacation destination conveniently accessible to his railroad lines. He commissioned George T. Marsh create the formal **Japanese Garden** beside the Spreckels mansion (now the **Glorietta Bay Inn**) on Glorietta Bay. Hotel guests rode in rickshaws pulled by Japanese workers along the ocean and bay to the garden on the edge of Coronado's first golf course. The number of guests touring the garden increased considerably when construction was completed on Spreckels's most imaginative creation—Tent City. Located south of the hotel on the Silver Strand, this outdoor resort consisted of elaborate red-and-white striped tents with wooden floors, furnished in styles from barracks-basic to luxurious. Some tents had separate small cook tents; washtubs for dirty dishes and laundry were provided on every block. Over the years, Tent City grew until it encompassed Main Street, an indoor swimming pool, dance pavilion, carousel, bowling alley, and

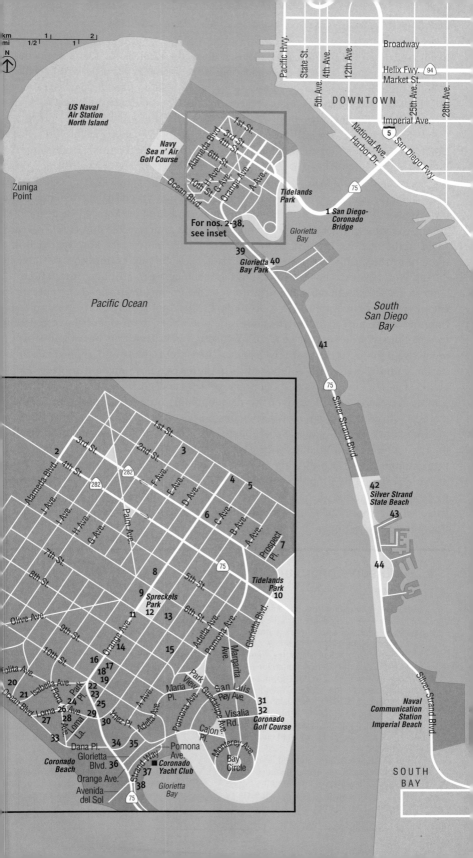

bandstand. Even Coronado residents closed down their homes for 1 or 2 weeks duri
the summer months to spend their vacations at Tent City. When J.D. Spreckels died
1926, his San Francisco–based family sold most of his Coronado properties except
the Hotel Del. Tent City was demolished in 1939. The hotel continued to be a glo
ous—though somewhat tarnished—resort, and the city kept growing.

In the meantime, the military was becoming an ever more visible presence
North Island, which was separated from Coronado by the **Spanish Bight**, a narr
body of water. In 1914 the US Marines set up their first camp on North Island. Wh
the US entered World War I in 1917, the War Department took control of the 1,2:
acre island for the army and navy. The naval air station officially began operations
8 November 1917 and has been in control of North Island ever since (the army left
1940), contributing greatly to the population and character of Coronado. The na
filled in the Spanish Bight in 1944, giving the base more space and further linki
the city to the military. Another navy base for amphibious training was establish
during World War II, thus sandwiching Coronado between military installations.

Perhaps the single most important event for Coronado in the 20th century w
the opening of the **San Diego–Coronado Bridge** in 1969. The city was no lon
immune to the horrors of traffic, pollution, and noise, but residents have continu
to tenaciously protect their peaceful paradise, restricting tour buses and traffic
much as possible. In the past few decades, the Hotel Del has undergone major rer
vations, and the city has completed an ambitious redevelopment project that
cludes a new police station, elementary school, and civic center. Several belov
landmarks have been destroyed by development; others have been lovingly
stored. Toll collectors stopped gathering dollars at the bridge in July 2002—;
another controversial move. Some locals feel the toll deters swarms of lookie-lc
on their streets. Coronadans will always have opinions about what happens
their community. Nothing gets done capriciously. Public hearings became hea
and impassioned as proposals for a new **Glorietta Bay Civic Center and Prom**
nade were discussed; debate continued even after the city hall and other stru
tures on the shores of Glorietta Bay were razed in 2003. The new City Hall a
Community Center opened to much fanfare in 2005.

1 SAN DIEGO–CORONADO BRIDGE

The views both of and from this 2.13-mile-long bridge are staggering, as is the drive across—especially when there's a strong wind. At its highest point, the bridge arches 246 feet above the San Diego Bay, framing sailboats, freighters, and submarines in the water and the skylines of both downtown and Coronado on the horizon. When the bridge opened in 1969, some islanders thought it was a horrifying blight; others, a blessing—a sign on the **Hotel del Coronado** said "At Last." But all knew it had changed their small-town lives forever. On 2 August 1969, California governor Ronald Reagan gave the dedication speech. Hundreds of runners and bicyclists inaugurated the bridge with a throbbing pulse of energy that tested its earthquake readiness. At 12:01AM on 3

August 1969, cars started rolling in, payir 60 cents each way and wiping the bridge debt clean in less than 20 years. The brid became toll-free in July 2002. Be forewar that traffic flows speedily along this aspha arch; first-time drivers will be hard-presse to get a glimpse of the side views. ◆ Hwy from downtown San Diego to Fourth St, Coronado

2 NORTH ISLAND

This area was originally an island, separat from Coronado by the Spanish Bight—a narrow body of water that in the 1940s wa filled in with sand and mud dredged from bay. Early aviators used the area as a landing strip, and it was the home of the US's first military aviation school. The US Navy took over the island shortly after Wc War I broke out, and today the **North Islar** **Naval Air Station** is an accepted neighbc the small community; many of Coronado's residents, in fact, are naval retirees. The base is closed to the public. ♦ Fourth St (at Alameda Blvd)

3 JESSOP HOUSE

One of the earliest homes on this side of the city, this house was built in 1901 for Joseph Jessop, founder of **Jessop Jewelers**, the first jewelry business in San Diego. The Colonial Revival architecture is patterned after Jessop's old family home in England. It's a private residence. ♦ 822 First St (between E and F Aves)

4 ZAZEN

Owner Kate Stromberger displays the work of talented designers who create an eclectic mix of clothing, jewelry, furniture, and folk art. She expanded her shop in late 2007 to include more display space and a venue for art events. ♦ M-Sa, 10AM-5PM. 1110 First St (between C and Orange Aves). 435.4780 ♿

4 TARTINE

★$ Roasted eggplant, red peppers, and goat cheese on panini is just one reason to stop here for lunch. Another is the brie and ham on a fresh baguette. Or perhaps you'll be tempted by the baby spinach salad with goat cheese, dried cranberries, toasted pecans, and champagne vinaigrette. The high-ceilinged dining room feels spacious and comfortable, and you can see the water from some of the sidewalk tables. ♦ European ♦ Daily, breakfast, lunch, and dinner. 1106 First St (between C and Orange Aves). 435.4323. ♿ www.tartinecoronado.com

5 FERRY LANDING MARKETPLACE

The most enjoyable way to reach Coronado from downtown is the traditional route—aboard a ferry. This modern complex, designed by **Delawie, Bretton and Wilkes**, houses not only the ferry pier but commercial enterprises as well. It looks like a Victorian-New England-Old California fishing village, with restaurants, shops, and visitor services clustered under red peaks that call to mind the profile of the **Hotel Del**. An excellent bike path runs south to the **Silver Strand** from the ferry landing under the bridge. A farmers' market is held here every Tuesday afternoon. ♦ Daily. 1201 First St (between B and C Aves). 435.8895. ♿ www.coronadoferrylanding.com

Within the Ferry Landing Marketplace:

SAN DIEGO FERRY

From the opening of the Coronado Bridge in 1969 until its debt was paid off almost two decades later, this ferry to downtown did not operate. Today it carries commuters, bicyclists, and sightseers (but no cars) back and forth across the bay. ♦ From Coronado M-Th, Su, on the half hour, 9:30AM-9:30PM; F, Sa, 9:30AM-10:30PM; from downtown M-Th, Su, on the hour, 10AM-9PM; F, Sa, 9:30AM-10:30PM. 234.4111

BIKES & BEYOND

Rent a beach cruiser, tandem bike, four-wheel quadricycle seating four, or a pair of in-line skates at this shop and peaceably cruise Coronado's back streets. Customers get a map of suggested bike routes, as well as helmets and locks. Another option is to take a bike on the ferry to downtown and cruise the waterfront there. ♦ Daily. 435.7180

PEOHE'S

★★$$$$ Though the décor resembles something out of Disneyland's Pirates of the Caribbean—lush tropical foliage, trickling waterfalls, and curved bridges—the view of the bay and downtown skyline from this dining spot is undoubtedly the best on the island. Fresh Hawaiian seafood with a tropical flair is the specialty here—try halibut with bananas and macadamia nuts, and the wok-fried whole bass. Many diners have a hard time resisting the crispy coconut shrimp, which you can order as an entrée or in the bar with the requisite mai tai. Don't miss the sinfully rich macadamia-nut ice cream with warm bittersweet-chocolate sauce. ♦ Seafood ♦ M-Sa, lunch and dinner; Su, brunch and dinner. Reservations recommended. 437.4474. ♿ www.peohes.com

IL FORNAIO

★$$$ Some say the cappuccino at this large Italian eatery is the best you can find anywhere, and the bread and pastries are always divine. The entrées—pastas, seafood, veal—are sometimes exceptional. The excellent wine list includes several Italian imports by the glass and half glass; try the Cedro liqueur, similar to limoncello. The real draw is the terrace seating with an unobstructed view of downtown across the water. You can almost imagine you're in Venice. ♦ Italian ♦ M-Sa, lunch and dinner; Su, brunch and dinner. 437.4911. ﾠ www.ilfornaio.com

6 BEST WESTERN SUITES HOTEL

$$ Chain hotels are usually verboten in Coronado, but this hostelry manages to fit in comfortably, thanks to its sloping and curved red shingled roofs à la the **Hotel Del**, convenient location at the entrance to Orange Avenue from the Coronado Bridge, and hidden enclosed parking. The color scheme is muted blue and mauve, with dormer windows acting like skylights to bring the sunshine in. All 63 rooms have refrigerators, coffeemakers, and microwaves, and an outdoor heated swimming pool is perfect any day of the year. Continental breakfast is served in the lobby, but there's no restaurant. It's a good choice for those seeking dependability, accessibility, and reasonable rates. ♦ 275 Orange Ave (at Third St). 437.1666, 800/528.1234; fax 437.0188. ﾠ www.bestwestern.com

7 CORONADO ISLAND MARRIOTT RESORT

$$$$ Designed in 1986 by **Mosher, Drew, Watson & Ferguson** and approved by Coronadans who had looked at several other models, the hotel's buildings are subtle and unobtrusive. Three-story, pale gray structures surround gorgeous lagoons and tropical gardens that meander over 16 acres along the waterfront facing downtown. Golden koi drift in peaceful streams, and the sounds of waterfalls and gurgling geysers hum in the air.

The 300 rooms (including suites and villas) have a French Provincial motif, with such luxurious amenities as soft terry robes; extra-large bathrooms (with extra-large tubs); and phones by the beds, on writing tables, and in the bathrooms. Further pampering takes place in the spa, where guests indulge in facials, massages, hydrotherapy baths, and the like. For athletic types, there's state-of-the-art fitness equipment, six tennis courts, and a 25-meter heated lap pool (in addition to two other pools). The Wired-for-Business amenity gives you free high-speed Internet access and free local and long-distance (within the US) calls for less than $10. ♦ 2000 Second St (at Prospect Pl).

435.3000, 800/228.9290; fax 435.4183. ﾠ www.marriott.com

8 CROWN CITY INN

$$ This inn stands out for its sensible, light-filled rooms equipped with writing tables, coffeemakers, microwaves, and refrigerators. The 35 guest rooms are decorated in light pastels with bleached wood furnishings; there's free parking and an in-house laundromat. The **Crown City Bistro** is decorated in pink and green, with ceiling fans reminiscent of *Casablanca*, and is open for breakfast, lunch, and dinner. Afternoon shortbread and oatmeal cookies and iced tea and hot cocoa are served daily in the lobby. ♦ 520 Orange Ave (at Fifth St). 435.3116; bistro, 435.3678, 800/422.1173; fax 435.6750. www.crowncityinn.com

9 CORONADO LIBRARY

J.D. Spreckels hit his stride around 1907, funding the construction of significant buildings in San Diego—from the **Organ Pavilion** in **Balboa Park** to the **Spreckels Theatre** downtown. The library trustees on Coronado took note of his prodigious output (including a home on Ocean Boulevard) and asked Spreckels to fund a Coronado library. He agreed and in 1909 commissioned his favored architect, **Harrison Albright**, to design a reinforced concrete Grecian temple with a storage basement and classical columns inside and outside the front door. When **Homer Delawie** redesigned and expanded the building in 1974, he incorporated the original building within the new, adding two inner courtyards and a community meeting room. Take note of the engraved names of famed thinkers—Byron, Dante, and Chaucer—near the ceiling. Two 60-foot-high star pines and two rose gardens frame the library's entrance. A $9 million renovation and expansion project in 2004-2005 added 17,000 square feet of additional space, including a much-needed computer lab. The video selection is huge and a good resource for families on extended stays in town. Nonresidents can get a $5 library card good for one year—a handy resource for library addicts. ♦ Daily. 640 Orange Ave (between Seventh and Sixth Sts). 522.7390

10 TIDELANDS PARK

This wildly popular 22-acre park under the northwest side of the bridge has four athletic fields, a children's play area, a skateboard park, a beach on San Diego Bay, a wide-angle view of downtown, clusters of picnic tables, and rest rooms. Originally the old ferry landing area, it was turned into a park in the early 1980s as part of the development of this waterfront land. ♦ Glorietta Blvd (at Fourth St). 522.7342

11 ORANGE AVENUE

Coronado's main boulevard is named for the orange trees that originally lined its wide median strip. Jackrabbits devoured the orange trees in no time, but the name stuck. In the late 1940s and early 1950s, perfectly formed cedar trees were planted along the median, each with a plaque commemorating the donor's loved ones. Flower gardens line the median beneath the trees and are lovingly tended by volunteers. This strip of trees is lit with Christmas lights for much of December and leads to the city's main Christmas tree in a small green called **Rotary Park** at the intersection of Park Place and Orange Avenue. The median becomes a casual reviewing stand during the annual Fourth of July parade, when families with generations of local history in their genes stake out their traditional patch of grass for the day. ♦ From Tenth to First Sts

12 SPRECKELS PARK

J.D. Spreckels donated this 8-acre piece of land to Coronado in 1909. Originally known as **East–West Plaza**, the park was renamed in honor of Spreckels in 1927, a year after his death. The result was a town square complete with a bandstand that remains the island's and city's social center. The park is a popular spot most weekends, with kites flying over family picnics. Art shows are held here the first and third Sunday of the month, featuring fine art by San Diegans. Summer band concerts are a hometown tradition and occasionally feature local musicians who've made it to the big time. ♦ Bounded by C and Orange Aves and by Seventh and Sixth Sts

13 SACRED HEART CATHOLIC CHURCH

One of Coronado's most visible examples of **Irving Gill**'s work is this simple and graceful church, designed in 1920. An enhanced version of a Mission-style tower is topped with a blue mosaic tile dome and a gilded cross. Thin panels of stained-glass windows recessed in arches depict the Last Supper, the disciples, and the Virgin Mary. The walls are lined with ceramic dioramas of the birth of Christ and other events. ♦ 672 B Ave (between Seventh and Sixth Sts). 435.3167

14 NIGHT & DAY CAFE

★$ Frank Sinatra croons "My Way" on the jukebox (when it's working) as the short-order cook slides plates piled with hash browns and eggs along the counter. Easily the least expensive and most casual of Coronado's eateries, this is the place to come for inexpensive burgers, meat-loaf sandwiches, and homemade chili. ♦ American ♦ Daily, 24 hours. 847 Orange Ave (between Ninth and Eighth Sts). 435.9776

15 STEPHENS-TERRY HOUSE

The epitome of Tudor splendor, this manse has a massive chimney, a spotted roof of red and green tiles, and several A-frame dormer windows, topped by what looks like a gun tower or turret. The house was originally designed by **Hebbard & Gill** in 1898 and was remodeled between 1926 and 1930. It's a private residence. ♦ 711 A Ave (at Seventh St)

16 PRIMAVERA RISTORANTE

★★$$$ Superb Northern Italian cuisine is served inside this elegant, split-level dining room. Although all of the dishes are excellent, you won't go wrong with the scampi primavera (shrimp sauteed with wild mushrooms and champagne), braised veal shanks, or risotto with lobster. For dessert, the tiramisù stands out among the very best. ♦ Northern Italian ♦ Daily, dinner. Reservations recommended. 932 Orange Ave (between Tenth and Ninth Sts). 435.0454. www.primavera1st.com

17 CHRIST EPISCOPAL CHURCH

Hand-hewn granite gives a mountain-lodge feel to this Gothic A-frame church designed by **James Reid** in 1894. The blue and purple floral-patterned Tiffany windows took 4 years to complete. ♦ 1028 Ninth St (between C and Orange Aves). 435.4561

18 STRETCH'S CAFE

★$ This long, narrow eatery seems bright and fresh thanks to mirrored walls, several healthy trailing plants, a white trellis used as wainscoting, and grass-green tablecloths. There's no meat on the menu, just plenty of fresh, healthful selections, including spinach and sprout salads, melted cheese on seven-grain bread, and baked potatoes stuffed with everything from butter and sour cream to broccoli. ♦ Vegetarian ♦ Daily, breakfast, lunch, and dinner. 943 Orange Ave (between Tenth and Ninth Sts). 435.8886

19 GRAHAM MEMORIAL PRESBYTERIAN CHURCH

Elisha Babcock gave architect **James Reid** little time to recover from the construction of the **Hotel Del** and commissioned him to design several other buildings, including this

---

Restaurants/Clubs: **Red** | Hotels: **Purple** | Shops: **Orange** | Outdoors/Parks: **Green** | Sights/Culture: **Blue**

Victorian-Gothic church. Opened in 1890, the structure was named in honor of the parents of his wife, Isabella. Green shingles cover the pointed steeple in picturesque contrast to the white and yellow fish-scale shingles on the façade. The massive gray Victorian house next door, used as the church's offices, was built in 1887 for C.T. Hinde of the Spreckels Company; in 1894, Hinde had the **Christ Episcopal Church** across the street constructed in memory of his daughter. ◆ 975 C Ave (between Tenth and Ninth Sts). 435.6860

20 REW-SHARP ESTATE

A chest-high concrete wall surrounds an entire block, marking the original boundaries of the 1919 estate built for George Rew, president of Calumet Baking Powder Company. The identity of the original architect is unknown, but there are elements of the Spanish-Moorish designs being used at that time in **Balboa Park**. The front door of the house is framed by ornate molded pilasters; the original façade was covered in concrete mixed with pebbles, giving a rough texture to the walls. The mansion was purchased in 1926 by the wealthy T.E. Sharp; **Sharp Hospital** in San Diego is named for his son. The estate was subdivided over the years (the wall has been cut in sections to make way for driveways), but the main house is still quite impressive. It is a private residence. ◆ 1124 F Ave (between Ocean Blvd and Tolita Ave)

21 BABY DEL

This miniature version of the **Hotel Del** was built in 1887 in southeast San Diego and rescued in 1983 by historic preservationist Chris Mortenson (who was responsible for much of the **Gaslamp Quarter**'s redevelopment in downtown). Mortenson had the home moved to Coronado by barge and restored the pale gray Queen Anne house to its former beauty. It's not open to the public. ◆ 1410 Isabella Ave (at Ocean Blvd)

When the city began reconstructing the sidewalks along Orange Avenue in 2001, workers discovered 100-year-old stamps left in the concrete by the original contractor. The current workers cut out the old stamps and embedded them in the new sidewalks.

There are 19 public tennis courts on Coronado, including eight courts at 150-1 Glorietta Boulevard, six by the Coronado Library, and five at Coronado Cays. Courts are open between sunrise and 6PM. For information, call 435.1616.

22 MOOTIME CREAMERY

★$ A life-size Elvis and a full-grown cow guard the door to this funky ice-cream parlor. If you miss the statues, look for the bold blue-neon sign atop the building or the long line at the front door. Inside is some of the best ice cream you'll ever taste. Waffle irons give off the heady, sugary scent of cones in the making, and rows of glass jars display potential mixings. Pick your flavor (the dark chocolate-orange is divine) and a few tasty tidbits—nuts, crushed cookies, even gummy worms. The counter attendants will scoop your ice cream onto a marble slab, mix your blend, and fill a cone before your lusting eyes. Don't miss it. ◆ Ice-cream parlor ◆ Su-Th, 10AM-11PM; F, Sa, 11AM-11PM. 1025 Orange Ave (at Tenth St). 435.2422. ఉ www.mootime.com

23 BAY BOOKS

Plan to spend some time at this excellent shop, browsing the shelves and perusing international newspapers and magazines. The clerks post written reviews beside their favorite books, the better to help you choose even more purchases. ◆ M-Sa, 9AM-9PM; Su, 9AM-6PM. 1029 Orange Ave (between C Ave and Tenth St). 435.0070

24 CORONADO VILLAGE INN

$ This three-story European-style inn from the 1930s stands on the site of the **Blue Lantern Cafe**, the **Hotel Del**'s biggest restaurant competition in the 1920s. The original café building was moved from the site in 1926, and the square brick and stucco **Blue Lantern Inn** was built in its place. The building is dark and plain, but the proprietors have created a cozy feel within, stocking the lobby and lounge with magazines, flyers, and books. Although the 15 guest rooms have been renovated and modernized, an Old World feel remains, with antique dressers and armoires, incredibly tiny bathrooms, and canopy beds. Some have small balconies with chairs. Guests have use of the kitchen, where a continental breakfast is served free daily. ◆ 1017 Park Pl (between Flora and Isabella Aves). 435.9318. www.coronadovillageinn.com

25 McP's Irish Pub

★$ The Guinness flows like water at this lively neighborhood pub owned by Greg McPartland, a former Navy SEAL who heartily welcomes men and women in uniform. Patrons are a fun and festive lot who enjoy good ale and hearty grub. It's the only place in town serving mulligan stew and corned beef and cabbage. ♦ Irish pub ♦ Daily, 11AM-2AM; dinner served until 9PM and a modified menu until closing. 1107 Orange Ave (between B and C Aves). 435.5280. www.mcpspub.com

26 Star Park

One of the prettiest lawns in all of Coronado is this half-acre in the center of Star Park Circle, where several small residential streets converge. Another J.D. Spreckels donation, the circle is framed by enchanting bungalows with gorgeous flowerbeds. Years ago, the ocean was visible from the little park, but the view disappeared as mansions rose on Ocean Boulevard and the surrounding streets. The park is particularly enjoyable when the magnolias blossom in late spring. ♦ At Loma Ave, Flora Ave, and Park Pl

27 Claus Spreckels House

J.D. Spreckels's first Coronado home was this 1908 beach cottage designed by **Harrison Albright**. Spreckels subsequently gave the house to his son Claus as a wedding gift. The cottage is nearly hidden by tall eugenia bushes, but you can get a glimpse of it from across the street. It is a private residence. ♦ 1043 Ocean Blvd (at Loma Ave)

27 Crown Manor

This English-Tudor estate is a modest home with *only* 17 bedrooms and 13 baths semihidden behind a wall. The home was originally designed in 1901 by **Hebbard & Gill** for Bartlett Richards, a Nebraska cattleman and banker. In 1913 Richards's widow sold the home to Walter and Florence Dupee of Chicago, who commissioned **Frederick Roehrig** to add two wings to the house in 1914, increasing its size to 20,000 square feet. Walter Dupee was instrumental in creating both the **Coronado Country Club** and the **Coronado Beach Polo Club**, which became world renowned. The house gained national notoriety when President Bill Clinton and his family vacationed here in the middle of Republican territory. It is a private residence. ♦ 1015 Ocean Blvd (between Loma La and Loma Ave)

28 Lemeche-Meade House

The pale yellow bungalow with blue shutters and window boxes to the right facing **Star Park** was a favorite retreat for L. Frank Baum, author of *The Wizard of Oz*. The house was built in 1896, and Baum wintered there for several years, completing several books in what must have been a serene and inspirational hideaway. The house is a private residence. ♦ 1101 Star Park Cir (between Loma and Flora Aves)

29 Chez Loma

★★★$$$$ A more romantic dining spot than this converted 1890 Victorian house can't be found in Coronado. The inside dining room is filled with antiques and subdued candlelight; the enclosed sidewalk terrace gives the feeling of a private garden, with a few tables set amid vines and potted plants. From the fine selection of cuisine, savor the filet mignon with black truffle jus (an outstanding dish), the salmon with roasted horseradish crust, or the house specialty—roasted duckling with cherry, burnt orange, and green-peppercorn sauce. Save room for the heavenly gingerbread cake with vanilla-bean ice cream. Take your time. Dinner here is a sublime experience. Prix-fix menus and early-bird specials make the restaurant a possible splurge for those on a budget. ♦ Continental ♦ Tu-Su, dinner. Reservations recommended. 1132 Loma Ave (at Orange Ave). 435.0661. www.chezloma.com

29 Museum of History and Art

Volunteers worked for many years to create this fascinating museum run by the Coronado Historical Association. The neoclassical **Bank of Commerce** building, which sits on a V-shaped corner by Rotary Park, was the island's first bank when it opened in 1910. It now holds four exhibit spaces with permanent exhibits on the history of the island and the navy's presence there. The photos of **Tent City** are especially fascinating, and temporary exhibits have included shows on the history of surfing and poster images from World War II. The museum has a gift shop and the **Tent City Café**, a good spot for coffee or a light lunch. ♦ Donation suggested. M-F, 9AM-5PM; Sa, Su, 10AM-5PM. 1100 Orange Ave (at Loma Ave). 437.8788. www.coronadohistory.org

Within the museum:

CORONADO VISITOR CENTER

Helpful clerks at the desk beside the front door assist tourists with maps, directions, brochures, and tips on what to do while on the island. ♦ M-F, 9AM-5PM; Sa, Su, 10AM-5PM. 437.8788

29 EMERALD CITY SURF 'N SPORT

The hottest brands and styles of beach gear are arrayed under neon-bright surfing posters, surfboards, and skateboards. Wet suits, bathing suits, and T-shirts in the hippest styles and colors tempt even youngsters to cash out their allowance savings. ♦ Daily. 1118 Orange Ave (at B Ave). 435.6677

29 SPRECKELS BUILDING

In 1916 John D. Spreckels declared that Coronado needed only two more institutions to make it a complete city—a bank and a theater. He commissioned **Harrison Albright** to design a block-long structure to house both, as well as several shops and residences. The resulting neoclassical edifice was one of Coronado's finest until it gradually fell into disrepair over the decades. Entrepreneur Paul Swerdlove bought the building in 1992 and restored the original façade. The following year, the **Lamb's Players** signed a lease on the old theater and remodeled it to the tune of $2.5 million. Trendy cafés and boutiques along the block have established it once again as a centerpiece of life in "The Village." ♦ Orange Ave (between B and C Aves)

Within the Spreckels Building:

CAFE 1134

★$ This sleek coffeehouse-café-gallery serves salads, sandwiches, and coffee drinks in a stark setting. Grab a seat at the sidewalk tables for a great street scene. Dogs lap cool water and munch on biscuits by the seats on the back patio. Either place is perfect for a bracing espresso and peanut butter cookies. ♦ Café ♦ Daily. 1134 Orange Ave (between B and C Aves). 437.1134. ♿

LAMB'S PLAYERS THEATRE

J.D. Spreckels's original **Silver Strand Theatre** opened in 1917 with a performance by Madame Ernestine Schumann-Heink, the most famous contralto of her day. In the 1930s it became a movie house, called the **Coronado Theatre**, which lasted until 1952 when more modern theaters with "refrigerated air" were in vogue. The lobby became a retail space and the theater remained dark until restoration began in 1993. Architect **Douglas Whitmore** found that most of the

original details had been removed, including the seven Tiffany glass skylights. He managed to replicate the ornate columns and capitals from the original design and created an intimate 340-seat auditorium for the **Lamb's Players**, a nonprofit theater ensemble. The theater reopened in 1994, and plays are scheduled throughout the year. ♦ Admission. 1142 Orange Ave (between B and C Aves). 437.0600. ♿ www.lambsplayers.org

IN GOOD TASTE

Looking for the perfect hostess gift? Or maybe a special treat to snack on in your room? This is your place. The shelves are stocked with gourmet cookies, crackers, teas, and coffees; the display case presents a tempting array of cheese tortes; and the chocolates are to die for. ♦ Daily. 1146 Orange Ave (between B and C Aves). 435.8356

PLUMS

Picture frames, cookbooks, stuffed animals, jewelry—there are enough trinkets and treasures in this little shop to satisfy the pickiest shopper. ♦ Daily. 1158 Orange Ave (between B and C Aves). 435.5542

RHINOCEROS CAFE & GRILLE

RHINOCEROS CAFE & GRILLE

★★$$ Floor-to-ceiling windows make this white-on-white café a bright and cheery place to dine on huge salads, cioppino, shrimp with trout cream, and Southwest

Coronado's strange configuration is due in part to Palm and Olive Avenues, two 100-foot-wide boulevards (planted, of course, with palm and olive trees) running diagonally from the peninsula's northwest and southwest corners to a central point in Spreckels Park.

meat loaf with a mild Ortega chile on grilled focaccia. Grab a table by the windows and watch the street scene. ♦ Daily, lunch and dinner. 1166 Orange Ave. 435.2121. www.rhinocafe.com

30 LA AVENIDA INN

$$ A gray-and-purple awning marks the entryway to this 29-room, motel-like establishment on the former site of **La Avenida Cafe**, once one of Coronado's most beloved landmarks. All the guest rooms have king- or queen-size beds, and all rooms are nonsmoking. There's no restaurant, but complimentary coffee and breakfast pastries are served in the lobby in the morning. A small swimming pool provides refreshment on hot days. ♦ 1315 Orange Ave (at B Ave). 435.3191, 800/437.0162; fax 435.5024. & www.laavenidainn.com

31 ROBERT HOUSE

This simple off-white adobe home designed by **William Templeton Johnson** in 1916 looks like it belongs in Santa Fe rather than facing San Diego Bay. It is tucked behind ancient succulents (including a rare dragon tree) planted by **Balboa Park** landscape designer Kate Sessions. It is a private residence. ♦ 1000 Glorietta Blvd (at San Luis Rey Ave)

32 CORONADO GOLF COURSE

Like many of San Diego's waterfront attractions, this golf course actually stands where the waters of the San Diego Bay once bordered Glorietta Boulevard. The course was created from tons of dirt dredged from the bay, plus topsoil from along the strand, all molded into a 200-acre strip of emerald lawns stretching from the old navy housing lots on the north side of the bridge to the yacht club on Glorietta Bay. Now golfers can look toward the office towers of downtown as they enjoy their weekday games on the 18-hole course designed by Jack Daray in 1955. The clubhouse restaurant has an awesome view of the water and downtown and serves inexpensive sandwiches and salads. It's open to the public and is an undiscovered gem for casual dining. The adjacent **Coronado Tennis Center** has courts open to the public. ♦ Greens fee. Daily, 6AM-6PM. 2000 Visalia Rd (at Glorietta Blvd). 435.3121. www.golfcoronado.com

33 OCEAN BOULEVARD AND SEAWALL

From the beginning, Ocean Boulevard was the most desirable address in Coronado, and

lavish mansions were the preferred type of residence. When a severe storm threatened the homes in 1905, boulevard residents voted in a $145,000 bond issue to finance building a seawall. Spreckels, the railroad magnate, built a rock foundation in front of the **Hotel Del** to extend the **Belt Line Railroad**'s tracks toward the boulevard, then hauled some 67 tons of rock from the Sweetwater Valley to construct the wall. The rocks did minimize storm damage for a while, but eventually the rocks themselves were used by the forces of nature as weapons when fierce tides and winds tossed the boulders onto the boulevard. The seawall was reinforced in 1912, and again several times since. A long and deep beach was eventually created between the seawall and the sea, which kept the waves from beating directly on the wall and boulevard. Today, sand dunes topped with succulents help hold the water at bay, making the beach one of the most scenic in the county, and several fire rings line the beach's north end. The city installed a 145-foot-long pathway made of recycled rubber for wheelchair access to the beach.

Across the street is **Sunset Park**, a popular spot for volleyball games. There is a second entrance to North Island here; just inside the gate (where a sign says "patrolled by military working dog teams") is the **North Island Naval Air Station**'s golf course. ♦ Ocean Blvd (between Flora Sue and Ocean Dr) &

34 BRIGANTINE

★★$$$ Locals swear by the juicy, thick burgers, crisp fish and chips, and gigantic Cobb salads at "the Brig," where cozy booths line the walls. Salty types flock to the dark, nautical bar for spirits and boat talk. The grilled fish is always good, and the swordfish marinated in soy, Dijon mustard, and garlic is superb. The Sunday-to-Thursday early-bird dinners are a great deal. ♦ Steak/seafood ♦ M-F, lunch and dinner; Sa, Su, dinner. 1333 Orange Ave (between Adella and B Aves). 435.4166. & www.brigantine.com

34 EL CORDOVA HOTEL

$$ Character and charm make this rambling old hacienda a great choice for those who want casual comfort and a homelike setting. The original building was Elisha Babcock's home, built in 1902; the other Spanish-style buildings were added in the 1930s. Wide stairways are lined with Mexican tiles; wrought-iron balconies face a quiet stretch of Orange Avenue, and the pool and gardens

are tucked beneath ancient bird of paradise plants. The peach stucco and green trim on the hotel's exterior are showing their age, and the furnishings in the 40 rooms (some without a/c) are well worn, but some accommodations have kitchenettes and living rooms where you can set up housekeeping by the day, week, or month. Underground parking is available for a fee. ◆ 1351 Orange Ave (at Adella Ave). 435.4131, 800/229.2032; fax 435.0632. www.elcordovahotel.com

Within El Cordova Hotel:

MIGUEL'S COCINA

★$ One of the most popular restaurants in Coronado is this courtyard patio covered with latticework and *palapas* (thatch-roof huts). The waitresses wear colorful costumes, Mexican ballads play in the background, and a festive attitude prevails among the clientele. Like most old-line Mexican restaurants, this place has its own secret preparations for all the standard fare. The quality of the food has gone way downhill, and the staff has a *mañana* attitude toward service. But the place is still packed, and you can count on waiting for a table on weekend nights. Stick with the least expensive tacos and burritos. ◆ Mexican ◆ Daily, lunch and dinner. 1339 Orange Ave (at Adella Ave). 437.4237

34 ADELLA PLAZA

A tiled fountain splashes in the middle of this small plaza lined with benches and palms. Look for the plaque on the wall commemorating one of Coronado's proudest achievements. In 2000, the city was given a Great American Main Street Award by the National Trust for Historic Preservation. The award is prestigious and much coveted. Orange Avenue, with its gardens and carefully restored historic buildings, was deemed worthy by a panel of noted architects and city planners. ◆ Adella Ave (at Orange Ave)

35 GLORIETTA BAY INN

$$$ When sugar baron J.D. Spreckels moved to Coronado, he commandeered an entire block above Glorietta Bay (where his yacht

could be safely berthed) and commissioned **Harrison Albright** in 1908 to build a mansion that suited his position within the community. A marble-and-brass staircase with leather handrails leads from the hotel's lobby to the 11 guest rooms furnished with antiques. Be sure to take a look at the music room, added to the mansion in 1912 to house Spreckels's Aeolian organ and its 2,000 pipes. Brass and copper doors were installed in the long horseshoe-shaped room, along with indirect lighting behind handmade curved plaster moldings next to the ceiling. Newspaper magnate Ira Copley bought the house in 1926; when he died in 1949, his family sold the entire block for $90,000. Several two-story buildings were built on the grounds in later years and now are tucked amid mature tree ferns and palms. The variety of rooms, from low-priced but comfortable standards to delightful mansion suites, makes this a good choice for all types of visitors. Some units have kitchenettes and separate bedrooms; all have refrigerators and free high-speed Internet. There's no restaurant, but guests are served a complimentary continental breakfast in the Music Room, along with warm drinks, lemonade, and gingersnaps in the afternoon. The hotel has a warm, friendly feeling; it has received many awards for its service. Perhaps that's why many guests return annually. Room rates rise significantly during the summer and on holidays. ◆ 1630 Glorietta Blvd (between Orange Ave and Ynez Pl). 435.3101, 800/283.9383; fax 435.6182. ◆ www.gloriettabayinn.com

36 HOTEL DEL CORONADO

$$$$ The oldest (completed in 1888) Pacific Coast resort from Alaska to Acapulco, this renowned, celebrated, and venerated hotel is the place to live out aristocratic fantasies. Start in the regal lobby, a handsome room of polished dark Illinois oak and Honduran mahogany that feels like the inside of an English millionaire's country estate. The lobby was originally used primarily by men registering their families at the front desk and dragging in their catches from hunting and fishing trips around the barren island. The women used a separate entrance and lobby, freshening up before riding one of three birdcage electric elevators to their rooms.

Elisha Babcock and H.L. Story were nothing short of visionaries when they conceived of building an oceanfront resort so spectacular that even jaded Easterners would be drawn west by its grandeur and style. Architects

James and **Merritt Reid** designed this Queen Anne castle, working with a general vision, conceptual drawings, and a generous amount of flexibility, rather than specific plans. Chinese laborers and skilled craftsmen of varied nationalities were brought in from San Francisco, and hundreds of thousands of feet of redwood, fir, cedar, hemlock, pine, and oak trees were shipped in to build the largest all-wood structure in the country. Advanced sprinkler systems were installed throughout the hotel, but to this day there hasn't been a fire. A 200-foot-long tunnel was dug to install water, steam, gas, and electrical power lines that led to a separate powerhouse and laundry. An estimated two million red shingles cover the peaked roofs, dormers, and towers. Perhaps the building's most spectacular feature at the time was its use of electricity. A cable was run underneath the bay from San Diego during construction, furnishing the current for the lights that illuminated the site for the night crews. When the hotel opened, each bedroom had an electric light, a novelty at the time.

A formal opening was held in February 1888, a mere 11 months after construction began. The entire project cost $1 million, and J.D. Spreckels repeatedly rescued Babcock and Story from financial ruin in the hotel's early years; by the time he moved from San Francisco to San Diego in 1906, he had taken over, with Babcock working as an employee. The hotel flourished through the early Spreckels years, much aided by the owner's investments in **Tent City** and the railroad lines that brought a steady flow of guests. Although the Great Depression, World War II, and the next few owners all left their mark, the hotel remained a star (though sometimes a tarnished one)—attracting luminaries and celebrities who recorded the hotel's charms in letters, books, and films. *Some Like It Hot*, starring Marilyn Monroe, Jack Lemmon, and Tony Curtis and directed by Billy Wilder, was filmed here in 1958.

In 1963, the Hotel Del Corporation purchased the property and spent the next 20 years and $80 million restoring the main building's structural and mechanical supports. The addition of a seven-floor tower created a disgruntled stir among longtime Coronado residents. But many of the hotel's original features, including the gazebo in the garden (which still contains palms planted by landscaper Kate Sessions in 1888) and the porte cochere at the entrance were restored. Another $55 million major restoration was completed in 2001, and yet another major renovation reached completion in 2007. The Spa at the Del was enlarged to include 21 treatment rooms, an expanded fitness center, and a private pool.

The hotel initially had 399 guest rooms and 75 bathrooms (the largest number of indoor toilets anywhere in the country at that time). Today, each of the 381 rooms in the original building has a private bath, and the configurations formed by these additions make for some strangely shaped rooms. Another quirk: Rubbernecking is a must in some ocean-view rooms. Staying in the original building is a treat, though you may feel like you're on display while on your balcony—when the hotel's busy it feels more like a tourist attraction than a serene getaway. Still, few places feel more romantic. There are also 293 rooms in the more modern tower with great ocean and bay views. Other assets include two swimming pools above a pristine beach, six tennis courts, several galleries and boutiques, four restaurants, and two bars. ♦ 1500 Orange Ave (between Ave del Sol and Ocean Blvd). Reservations, 435.6611, 800/468.3533; fax 522.8262. ♿ www.hoteldel.com

Within the Hotel del Coronado:

CROWN ROOM

★★$$ Sunday brunch in this majestic dining room with the second-largest unsupported domed ceiling in the US (the first is the Mormon Tabernacle in Salt Lake City) is a treat worth experiencing at least once. Just make sure you don't try it on Easter Sunday or Mother's Day, when reservations are a must and buffet lines are extreme. L. Frank Baum, author of *The Wizard of Oz*, designed the room's original crown chandeliers, which have since been replaced. On Sunday mornings, hundreds of diners line up at long tables filled with salads, entrées, and sinful desserts, lingering for hours, listening to harp music over the din of happy chatter. Some find the brunch to be overpriced and overcrowded, but it still holds a special charm for first-timers. ♦ American ♦ Su, brunch. Reservations recommended. 522.8490

1500 OCEAN

★★$$$ The Del's weary Prince of Wales Grill has been replaced with this casually elegant dining room with sea-blue accents and glass walls. Oversized booths with sheer draperies provide a sense of dining in private with a few friends (the booths hold four), while the terrace tables overlooking the Windsor lawn feel more casual. Ingredients from California and Baja are highlighted in the menu. Don't miss the divine cheeses, especially the buffalo mozzarella featured in several appetizers. A new chef had arrived at press time, but the menu will likely continue

to feature local seafood and angus beef.
♦ Californian ♦ Daily, dinner. 522.8490. ₺

Beach Village

$$$$ The newest development at the Del is this "resort within a resort" complex of 35 luxurious oceanfront cottages and villas available as whole-ownership, limited-use condominiums. The buildings contain 78 guest rooms and suites that can be reserved like hotel rooms in a separate enclave with its own front desk, concierge services, and private pools and hot tubs. The ultra-luxe suites with one to three bedrooms have ocean views, fireplaces, kitchens, and dining and living spaces along with high-end amenities including Bose sound systems, flat-panel TVs, and large soaking tubs in the bathrooms. Guests have full use of the entire resort's amenities and priority for dining reservations, but the Village section is restricted to those guests staying there.
♦ Reservations, 435.6611, 800/468.3533; fax 522.8262. ₺ www.hoteldel.com

37 Glorietta Bay Civic Center and Promenade

Coronado's **City Hall and Community Center,** designed by the architectural firm **Robbins Jorgenson Christopher,** opened in spring 2005. A series of landscaped parks, pedestrian-friendly courtyards, and interactive plazas encourage public use of the $33 million public improvement project, which includes a community center with a gymnasium, banquet facility, community playhouse, fitness facility, pool, and climbing wall. A wave-and-shell sculpture and fountain designed by San Diego artist James Hubbell sits at the formal entrance to the promenade. ♦ Strand Way (along Glorietta Bay). 522.7300

38 Coronado Boathouse 1887

★$$$ The **Hotel Del**'s original boathouse was designed by **James** and **Merritt Reid** and built in 1887 by Chinese laborers practicing the skills they later used so impressively in constructing the hotel. The building, on the edge of Glorietta Bay, is a fantastic miniature of the hotel, with red-shingle turrets and gables and peaks poking out from the white wooden façade. A bathhouse was once connected to the boathouse, providing heated dressing rooms and bathing suits rented for 35 cents. In the summers of 1903 and 1904, biologist William E. Ritter from the laboratory of the University of California at Berkeley studied the marine life of Glorietta Bay here. Ritter attracted the attention of wealthy San Diegans like J.D. Spreckels, William Marston (the force behind much of **Balboa Park**), and the Scripps family, who later provided

him with the beginnings of La Jolla's famed **Scripps Institution of Oceanography**. The boathouse also served as the headquarters for three different yacht clubs and has housed several restaurants. A Coronado native owns the restaurant and knows his customers' preferences. The bartender mixes a mean margarita, the perfect accompaniment when watching the glow of the setting sun on Glorietta Bay. Macadamia-crusted halibut is the most popular dish—or maybe it's the chocolate lava cake with caramel sauce and crunched up Heath Bars. ♦ American ♦ Daily, dinner. Reservations recommended. 1701 Strand Way (at Ave del Sol). 435.0155. www.coronado-boathouse.com

39 The Shores

As if the bridge weren't enough of a shock to Coronado's tranquility, these glaring 15-story concrete and steel condo towers, designed by **Krisle & Shapiro,** began poking up from the sands south of the **Hotel Del** in 1971. Now there are 10 buildings on 35 acres bordered by a 2,100-foot-long seawall. The community reacted by creating a 40-foot, three-story limit on all future buildings. Units in the 10 towers are available for rent on a monthly basis. These are private residences. ♦ Ave de las Arenas (at Orange Ave). 435.6238

40 Coronado Boat Rentals

Sailboats, motorboats, Windsurfers, and canoes are all available at this spot by **Glorietta Bay Park**, where boaters line up early on weekend mornings to launch their vessels from the public ramp. ♦ Daily. 1715 Strand Way (between Aves Lunar and del Sol). 437.1514

41 Naval Amphibious Base

Swarms of Navy SEALs practice their maneuvers at this amphib base, established during World War II, storming the beaches at the north end of the Silver Strand. ♦ North end of Silver Strand

42 Silver Strand State Beach

This spectacularly wild and windswept beach became a state park in 1932 and is still one of the best beaches in the county for surf fishing and clam digging. A campground for recreational vehicles is available on a first-come, first-served basis (no reservations), and there are four parking lots, public rest rooms, showers, and fire rings. ♦ Camping fee. Daily, 8AM-7PM. Silver Strand Blvd (at Coronado Bay Rd). 435.5184

43 Loews Coronado Bay Resort

$$$$ It's hard to imagine that into the 1990s there was still a 15-acre undeveloped

peninsula on the **Silver Strand**. Then Loews Corporation hired architect **C.W. Kim** to design a 440-room resort and 80-slip marina. It sits on Crown Isle just north of the **Coronado Cays** and is surrounded on three sides by water with views of the bridge, downtown, and the marina. All spacious, soothing rooms and suites feature waterfront views and private balconies. The bayside villas are especially enchanting, with their private decks right over the water. A dreamy spa, salon, and fitness center called **Sea Spa** opened in 2004, making the resort a complete escape. In addition to the typical treatments, the spa has a watsu pool for awesome underwater massage. A spa menu was added to the restaurants and room service and features an unusual dietary system based on food colors. The Commodore Kids Club has supervised activities for kids ages 3 to 12 and is open year-round and on Friday and Saturday evenings in summer—a major plus for parents who want a romantic interlude at one of the hotel's fabulous restaurants or a sunset cruise in a gondola. Other pluses include three tennis courts, three swimming pools, and a fascinating herb garden. Locals pack the **Market Café** during Sunday brunch—a culinary festival of fresh seafood, carved meats, unusual salads, and to-die-for desserts. Shops include **R.R.R.'s Market**, with its irresistible selection of gourmet foods, beachwear, straw hats, and kids' toys. The Loews is a bit removed from downtown Coronado, which makes it an idyllic hideaway. There's a shuttle to downtown San Diego if you must leave the property. ◆ 4000 Coronado Bay Rd (at Silver Strand Blvd). 424.4000, 800/235.6397; fax 424.4400. & www.loewshotels.com

Within the Loews Coronado Bay Resort:

MISTRAL

★★$$$$ A wide, sweeping staircase leads to this second-story dining room with windows looking out to the bay and central Coronado. Formerly an elegant space called Azzura Point, the restaurant was updated and renamed in 2007. The refreshed decor is unpretentious and less elegant than in the past, and all tables have a view of the floor-to-ceiling windows framing the sunset. Chef de cuisine Martin Batis designed his new menu to emphasize fresh local produce and seafood with unpretentious preparations and presentation. The new menu features steamed mussels, heirloom tomato and mango salad, white sea bass, and a hefty 16-ounce T-bone with truffle pommes frites. Sommelier Kurt Kirschenman has reworked the wine list to add more Mediterranean vintages. ◆ Mediterranean ◆ Tu-Su, dinner. Reservations recommended. 424.4000, ext. 6300

44 CORONADO CAYS

One of the most exclusive residential communities in Coronado is built on the site of the **Hog Ranch**, one of the most heavily disputed plots of land on **Silver Strand**. The ranch was in its prime during the days of **Tent City**, when the garbage from that resort served as bountiful fodder for the livestock on this ranch 4 miles south of the resort. The Riis family operated the farm, and when it was washed out by a high tide in 1916, they moved their operation to the mainland. Coronadans continued to dump their junk on the property, and the *Coronado Journal* reported at one point that "the Navy never disposed of anything smaller than a used battleship there." In 1954, the city council designated the area off-limits for dumping, the navy announced the land would not be needed for military purposes, and the controversy began over **Rancho Carrillo** (as the Hog Ranch became known). Fourteen years later the Atlantic Richfield Company purchased the land for $4 million and built **Coronado Cays**, a 1,500-unit residential community. The development is home to Hollywood stars, retired navy officers, and others seeking a private hideaway. These are private residences. ◆ Silver Strand Blvd (at Coronado Cays Blvd)

UPTOWN

A cluster of centuries-old suburbs and villages, each with its own character, uptown includes the communities of **Mission Hills, Hillcrest, Bankers Hill,** and **University Heights**. It borders **Balboa Park**, the city's urban treasure, and **Mission Valley**, where cattle ranges have given way to shopping malls. A wide variety of people populate the area: middle-class families, upper-class dynasties, ethnic minorities, gays and lesbians, and up-and-coming singles.

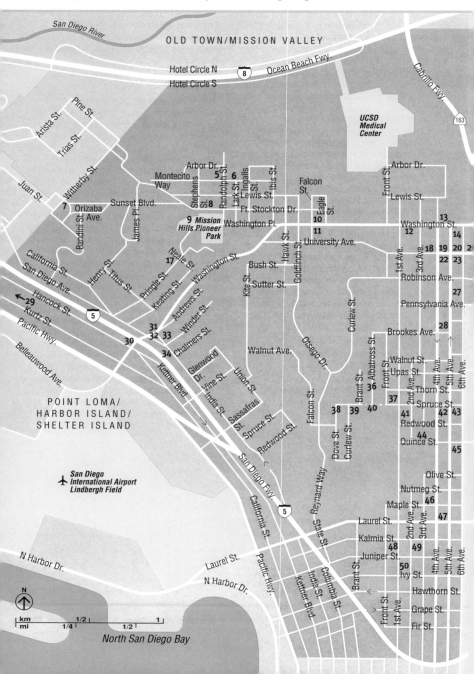

High-society settlers in the late 1800s headed straight to Mission Hills after hearing steamship captain Henry James Johnson vividly describe the hillside's beauty and his 65 acres of land overlooking **San Diego Bay**. Quite the salesman, the captain was successful in quickly selling parcels to these pioneers. As the city grew, the canyons and parklands of Mission Hills remained relatively natural and wild, with coyotes, owls, and deer browsing behind palatial estates housing wealthy families whose surnames were synonymous with San Diego history. It's a place where all of San Diego's leading architects have built residences: This is **Irving Gill**

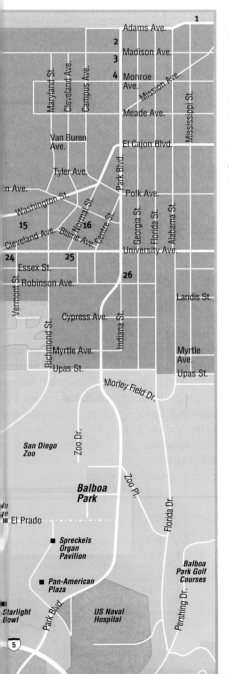

country, with plenty of examples of works by **William Templeton Johnson, Richard Requa, Sam Hamill, the Quayle Brothers, John Lloyd Wright**, and **Homer Delawie** as well. Architectural styles range from Italian Renaissance to Mission Revival, Spanish Colonial, Moorish, Craftsman, and Victorian. The neighborhood still holds the prestige of old, with streets named after local judges and financiers, and homes in the grandest Spanish hacienda style bordering the rolling lawns of the original presidio and Old Town. In the spring, when the jacarandas bloom, entire neighborhoods are shrouded in a purple haze. It's no wonder Kate Sessions, **Balboa Park**'s first gardener, chose to live here. During the 1980s, gentrification of Mission Hills and a growing appreciation for Craftsman homes took hold and the neighborhood became one of the city's most sought-after addresses.

Hillcrest was also a desirable address when downtown was in its nascent prime and bankers and bureaucrats erected their mansions looking down upon the center city. Only those with horse-drawn carriages could afford to live atop the steep incline of **Fifth Avenue**. Exclusivity was established as early as 1907, when developer William Wesley Whitson purchased 40 acres for $115,000 and began selling lots. *For profit or for comfort buy in a restricted tract*, read his ads. *If you buy now your investment may double before your second payment is due.*

In the 1920s, Hillcrest was the city's first suburb, complete with trolley stop, movie theaters, restaurants, and parks. In

1940, local merchants were so proud of their thriving commercial district that the mounted a giant sign boldly emblazoned with the name *Hillcrest* atop two tall woode posts and stretched it across Fifth Avenue at **University Avenue**. Eventually the post were replaced with cement pillars, but in the 1960s, when residents began to move t more peaceful suburbs, business declined. The sign fell into disrepair and was removed

In the 1980s, a new wave of yuppified gays, lesbians, and straights took interes in the cottages built during Whitson's time, and Hillcrest's charms were restored The subsequent gentrification has driven away many of Hillcrest's landmark old time businesses as a result of spiraling rents and the proliferation of minimalls. Ye excellent restaurants and cafés abound, and despite all its modern urban trapping Hillcrest has retained its neighborly feeling. The 1940s bold red sign spelling ou "Hillcrest" was refurbished in 1983. On 16 August 1984, the mayor and other loca VIPs lit the new sign, sparking a nightlong celebration that became the genesis fo CityFest, one of the city's largest street fairs.

Hillcrest is most broadly bounded by **Washington Street** and **Walnut Avenue**, an by **Park Boulevard** and **First Avenue.** It borders **Balboa Park** and is home to many o the city's grandest churches, synagogues, homes, and hospitals. Many of the area's ol Victorian homes are headquarters for medical clinics and social services agencies. Th avenues on the south side of Hillcrest are a veritable museum of San Diego's architec tural styles, with homes designed by many of the same architects as in Mission Hills West of Balboa Park, the hill sloping toward downtown and I-5 is called **Bankers Hil** (and sometimes **Pill Hill** in reference to the many doctors in residence). Outstandingl renovated Victorian homes, many from the late 1800s, now house small inns, attor neys' and doctors' offices, and the offspring of some of San Diego's founding families

Until the building of the **Uptown District**—a 14-acre complex of condos, cafés, an shops—was completed in 1989, Hillcrest's eastern edge was an area sprinkled wit discount warehouses and transvestite bars. A smaller complex, Village Hillcrest, revive the block of **Fifth Avenue** between University Avenue and Washington Street and th multiplex theater, showing American independent and foreign films, is the bigges draw. These two additions prodded a 1990s upswing, and a development craze tha continues in fits and starts, with the current Uptown push focused on Universit Avenue, around Richmond (Uptown District, again). Past Uptown is the Universit Heights neighborhood, clustered around Park Boulevard, north of University Avenue The modern, street-spanning neon sign announcing this neighborhood is topped by red trolley car—a tip of the hat to the trolley barn that signaled the end of the line from downtown in the 1890s (a park now occupies the site on Adams Avenue). There are few businesses along Park Boulevard, but for the most part this is a charming middle class quarter marked by more Craftsman and Spanish stucco bungalows, bordered o its north and west by the finger canyons that define much of the Uptown area.

1 ADAMS AVENUE GRILL

★$$ A fun restaurant with locally made art on the walls, this is a place you can take your parents, your boss, a date, or your friends. Interesting soups (try the fabulous carrot-ginger) and weekly specials (such as eggplant Parmesan or stuffed red peppers) keep the faithful regulars from getting bored There's a wide variety of tastes, from spicy Asian dishes to American comfort foods like the ever-popular Yankee pot roast.
◆ American/eclectic ◆ Sa, Su, breakfast; daily, lunch and dinner. Dinner reservations recommended. 2201 Adams Ave (at Mississippi St). 298.8440. ఉ

2 El Zarape

★★$ Locals depend on this neighborhood fast-food restaurant for delicious Mexican food at good prices and in large portions. The menu offers lots of seafood—try the fabulous shrimp burritos. Vegetarians can ask for many of the same dishes to be made without meat. ♦ Daily, breakfast, lunch, and dinner. 4642 Park Blvd (between Madison and Adams Aves). 692.1652

2 Bourbon Street

The crowd at this New Orleans–style bar is diverse, attracting young and old, straights, gays, and lesbians. Several contiguous homes have been opened up and revamped to make this super-fun bar feel like home. Smokers congregate around the fountain on the open back patio. The bar itself is dark and seductive; one corner has a piano where Barbra Streisand wannabes sing heartfelt songs in competition most nights for prizes and the acclaim of their peers. ♦ M-Sa, 4PM-2AM; Su, 1PM-2AM. 4612 Park Blvd (between Madison and Adams Aves). 291.4043. & www.bourbonstreetsd.com

3 Twiggs Coffee Shop

★★$ The owners of this popular coffee spot live in the neighborhood and are a real part of the community. Adjoining the comfortable neighborhood café is the **Green Room**, a performance space used for live Celtic music (Sundays, 4-6PM), poetry readings (second and fourth Mondays at 8PM), and AA meetings. Clients line up prior to these events to order excellent coffee, homemade pastries, cookies, and pies (made in **Twiggs**'s own bakery across the street). You can order salads and sandwiches as well, and sit on the living room furniture, at tables and chairs, or outside along one of the more attractive stretches of Park Boulevard. ♦ M-Th, 6:30AM-11PM; F, 6:30AM-midnight; Sa, 7AM-midnight; Su, 7AM-11PM. 4590 Park Blvd (at Madison Ave). 296.0616. www.twiggs.org

4 Buddha's Light

Located in the revitalized area of Park Boulevard near the beginning of Adams Avenue, this very Zen book shop sells books on religion and spirituality. Likewise, you'll find yoga magazines and some gift items, mainly statues of Buddha. ♦ Daily, 10AM-6PM. 4538 Park Blvd (at Monroe Ave). 298.2800

5 Francis Parker School

Architect **William Templeton Johnson**, who shaped much of the physical appearance of San Diego in the early 1900s, also contributed to its spirit by founding and designing this independent private school that remains prestigious today. The school is named for Colonel Parker, a prescient educator who espoused independent thinking and individual instruction. As was his forte, Johnson designed the school in 1913 in the Spanish-Colonial style with classrooms opening onto canyons, courtyards, and porches. It's not open to the public. ♦ 4201 Randolph St (between Montecito Way and Arbor Dr)

6 Kate O. Sessions House

William Templeton Johnson is said to have designed this home in 1912 on land owned by Kate Sessions, which the horticulturist used for growing plants for her nursery. An anomaly for Mission Hills, this neoclassical stucco-and-brick rectangle at the edge of a canyon was rescued after some years of neglect, and rebuilt entirely from the ground up due to its questionable earthquake viability. But the exterior of the building is identical to its original design, right down to the wood-framed arch windows and perforated brick parapets, all fronted by a garden of roses. Interestingly, the home facing the Sessions residence (on the other side of the circular driveway) was also designed by Johnson, in a style much more typical of the houses that were springing up in Mission Hills circa 1912. ♦ 4159 Lark St (at Montecito Way)

7 Edward Tindall Guymon Residence

This Italianate mansion designed by **Robert S. Raymond** in 1921 is a great example of the grandeur and elegance of early Mission Hills. Though the gray-blue trim against beige walls seems too modern for the imposing façade, the wide, sweeping lawns are a reminder of the vast spaces available for private homes back when few streets etched through the hills. This is a private residence. ♦ 2055 Sunset Blvd (between Couts and Witherby Sts)

8 Mission Hills Nursery

California and Iceland poppies bob above midnight blue lobelia and snow white alyssum in the flower bed bordering the nursery yards where **Kate Sessions** sold the palms and junipers that now tower above

Mission Hills estates. Sessions opened this nursery in 1910 when she was forced to leave her planting grounds at **Balboa Park** to make way for the 1915 exposition. She was San Diego's leading horticulturist between the 1870s and the 1930s, greatly influencing and creating the landscape of today's San Diego. When she moved to Mission Hills in 1903, the canyons and hayfields were undisturbed, with a view west to the bay and east over Mission Valley. During her stay, she persuaded builders to follow the land's natural curves instead of subdividing the hills into square lots. Within 10 years, she felt the neighborhood had become too crowded for her acres of seedlings, and she began amassing land in Pacific Beach. Gradually, her assistant, Giuseppe Antonicelli, took over the nursery, then turned it over to his son Frank, who sold it in 1989. As in Sessions's day, the nursery is a botanical garden filled with the ordinary and odd plants that flourish in San Diego. One yard is filled with healthy perennials, another with trees and vines. There's a room with gardening books and another moist and shady with ferns. Get your housewarming gifts here. ◆ Daily. 1525 Fort Stockton Dr (between Randolph and Palmetto Sts). 295.2808

9 MISSION HILLS PIONEER PARK

Children playing at this neighborhood park might become wide-eyed if they heard of its origins. The park was once the **Calvary Cemetery**, founded in 1874 with 5 acres of burial grounds for Catholics and 5 for Protestants. About 2,000 San Diegans were interred here, including many of the city's original pioneers; the last burial took place in 1960. In the early 1970s, Mission Hills residents closed the cemetery and turned the land into a park, which opened on 11 December 1977. About 40 tombstones large and small are clustered together at one corner of the park, and there is a rusty plaque listing the names of all those known to be buried beneath the immaculate lawns where the living play Frisbee and touch football. Facilities include playground equipment, rest rooms, and tennis courts. ◆ Washington Pl (at Randolph St)

10 VENISSIMO CHEESE

Artisanal cheeses from around the world are the stars of this shop that's a must for anyone who likes cheese—and who doesn't? The rotating selection generally exceeds 100, and is hardly limited to favorites like Spanish Manchego or fine Stilton (staples you can easily pick up at gourmet markets). No, a visit to Venissimo might feature Delice Pommard, a triple cream from Burgundy rolled in mustard husks; Gjetost, a caramelized whey from Norway; or Hook's

Cheddar, a delicious 10-year-aged variety from Wisconsin. These specialty products don't come cheap, with some picks topping $30 a pound. But samples are freely offered and after a couple of tastes you'll be hooked on a new favorite. With a selection of bread (from Bread & Cie), fruit, and treats, you can assemble a great impromptu picnic. ◆ M-Sa, 10AM-6PM. 754 W Washington St (between Eagle and Falcon Sts). 491.0708. www.venissimo.com

parallel 33

11 PARALLEL 33

★★$$$$ It's hard to categorize this eclectic gourmet fusion food restaurant, where decorations of woven baskets and tall reeds are enhanced by subdued lighting. The concept is food from regions and countries that border parallel 33, including California, Morocco, Lebanon, and the world's earliest breadbasket—the Tigris–Euphrates river valley. Enticing appetizers and salads lead to sharing of plates; the main dishes are less alluring, somehow, although the udon noodles with spinach, eggplant, Kalamáta olives, dried tomatoes, and feta is a definite go. For dessert there's a wonderful date cake. ◆ Fusion ◆ M-Sa, dinner. 741 W Washington St (at Falcon St). 260.0033. &

12 BRONX PIZZA

★$ Choices are refreshingly limited at this bustling New York–style pizza parlor decorated with decades of prizefight photos and the standard red-and-white-checked tablecloths. Order an 18-inch pie or a slice with spinach and ricotta cheese, eggplant and roasted red peppers, or more traditional sausage and pepperoni. Homemade calzone is available; no salad or beer, but you can bring the latter to drink on the premises. ◆ Italian ◆ Daily. No credit cards accepted. 111 Washington Street (between Third and First Aves). 291.3341. &

13 SOMMERSET SUITES HOTEL

$$ All 80 units at this hotel have full kitchens with microwave, dishwasher, and toaster and comfortable living rooms and bedrooms. This building has the ambience of

an apartment complex for instant transplants, with all the necessities (alarm clocks, coffeemakers, etc.). There's no restaurant, but a complimentary continental breakfast is served in a pleasant dining room, and dozens of restaurants are within a short walk. The second-floor pool is surrounded by tropical plants. Ask for a room away from the traffic on Washington Street. ♦ 606 Washington St (between Fifth and Fourth Aves). 692.5200, 800/962.9665; fax 692.5299. &. www.sommersetsuites.com

14 VILLAGE HILLCREST

Hillcrest took on an upscale look when this mixed-use development opened in 1991. The buildings—with walls painted in various hues of wheat, gold ochre, rust, greens, and pinks—comprise an entire city block and house retail shops, restaurants, offices, and a theater complex. The underground parking lot is a major plus in this congested area. ♦ Bounded by Sixth and Fifth Aves and by University Ave and Washington St. 296.4051. &.

Within Village Hillcrest:

PIZZA NOVA

PIZZA NOVA

★★$$ Hungry for something quintessentially California? Try the Thai shrimp pesto pizza or tequila-chicken atop spinach fettuccine with jalapeño cream sauce at this trendy, casual bistro. The salads are outstanding and can be a full meal unto themselves. If you're dining with a partner, order a salad and a pizza and you'll have leftovers to take home. There's a nice variety of outdoor and indoor seating areas, with very comfortable booths in the main restaurant. ♦ Italian ♦ Daily, lunch and dinner. 3955 Fifth Ave (between University Ave and Washington St). 296.6682. &. www.pizzanova.net

14 LANDMARK'S HILLCREST CINEMAS

The latest art and foreign films are featured at this five-plex movie house. Though this theater may lack the charm of its older Uptown siblings, the now-defunct **Guild** and

The median family income in San Diego is a little over $60,000.

Park, it's infinitely more comfortable and plush. The seats have holders for drinks and popcorn, on which real butter, not "golden flavoring," is drizzled. ♦ Admission. Daily. 3965 Fifth Ave (between University Ave and Washington St). 819.0236. &. www.landmarktheatres.com

14 KAZUMI SUSHI

★★★$$ Owner and head chef Kazumi supervises the bustling crew of his tiny, unpretentious, and totally dependable neighborhood sushi bar. In addition to well-rendered classics like tempura and sashimi are such inspired creations as a puff pastry of scallops and fish topped with a creamy ponzu sauce. ♦ Tu-F, lunch; Tu-Su, dinner. 3975 Fifth Ave (between University Ave and Washington St). 682.4054

15 UPTOWN DISTRICT

Lorimer-Case designed the eastern section of this massive development to house 320 apartments, town houses, and condos; and the **SGPA** group drew up plans in a variety of styles for the commercial buildings that fill the western section. Some of the shops in the commercial area look like mining-town banks; others have Mission-style arches and Spanish wrought-iron gates. In the residential part, balconies face inner courtyards, and pathways lead from the parking lots past fountains and flower gardens. When it opened in 1990, the development seemed like an overwhelming intrusion into the neighborhood; now it's become an integral part of Hillcrest and a model for integrated housing and business development. ♦ Bounded by University Ave and Washington St and by Richmond St and Tenth Ave

16 FARMERS MARKET

Held every Sunday at the impersonal venue of the Department of Motor Vehicles building off Washington Street, the **Farmers Market** is a fun place to shop for fresh flowers, baked goods, and Kalamáta olives as well as pesticide-free fruits and vegetables. ♦ Su, 9AM-1PM. 3960 Normal St (between Blaine and Lincoln Aves).

17 NEALE STREET

The canyons north of Washington Street are a backdrop for a mélange of architectural styles. One such example is the house at **1820** built in 1949 by **John Lloyd Wright**, the son of famed architect **Frank Lloyd Wright**. A low, wide wood-shingle roof shades and shelters the house like a Japanese pagoda, and a window corner looks into and across the canyon. At **1833**, architect **Homer Delawie** perched his narrow, rectangular wood home on the side of a canyon in 1963, blending the structure in naturally with the brown dirt, rocks, and eucalyptus trees. Delawie even created a living-room garden space, integrating an old California pepper tree that had been growing on the lot. These are both private residences. ♦ At Pringle St

18 BREAD & CIE

Hungry customers can't resist the aroma of this cavernous bakery's extraordinary breads that are made in the open kitchen throughout the day. Try the anise-and-fig loaf or the black-olive loaf. Unusual sandwiches abound: There's tuna with capers, walnuts, and basil piled on a crusty baguette; turkey breast with hot-pepper cheese on rosemary bread; and imported mozzarella layered with roasted peppers and red onions and served on focaccia. If you can't wait until you get home to devour these delicacies, sit indoors under the original art lining the walls or outside on the shaded open patio. ♦ Daily. 350 University Ave (between Fourth and Third Aves). 683.9322. ₺

19 THE CORVETTE DINER, BAR & GRILL

★$$ Noise, fun, and general pandemonium reign amid 1950s décor at this eatery—a neon Statue of Liberty, a genuine yellow Corvette, and a soda fountain with soda jerks. Kids love it and birthday parties are an hourly event. Ponytailed waitresses sling meat loaf and gravy, chicken-fried steak, and good-natured barbs at the temporarily infantile crowd. If you're not driving, try the Jell-O shooters flavored with peach schnapps and mai tai mix—they pack a powerful wallop. This may be the only burger

Kate Sessions's advertising slogan for her nursery in Mission Hills was "Never plant a $5 tree in a 50¢ hole."

Newspaper baron E.W. Scripps called San Diego "a busted, broken-down boom town" when he arrived in 1890. Then again, he called his autobiography *Damned Old Crank*.

joint in town with valet parking and a live DJ. ♦ American ♦ Daily, lunch and dinner. 3946 Fifth Ave (between University Ave and Washington St). 542.1476. ₺ www.cohnrestaurants.com

19 KEMO SABE

★★$$$ Small, modern, and noisy, Kemo Sabe is distinguished by the luscious and sometimes outrageous look of dishes prepared by chef Deborah Scott. Portions are large, but because of the stylish presentation, the Asian-fusion dishes beg to be eaten in rather than taken home. It's best, therefore, not to order too many appetizers or side dishes. The bar bustles with those cruising for a night out, quaffing the wide variety of martinis. Like much of the food, the jalapeño martini is fiery hot. ♦ Fusion ♦ Daily, dinner. Reservations recommended. 3958 Fifth Ave (between University Ave and Washington St). 220.6802. ₺ www.cohnrestaurants.com

20 502 UNIVERSITY AVENUE

Security Commercial and Savings Bank built this ornate antebellum-style neoclassical box of a building with third-floor balconies and hand-painted ceiling murals in 1927. Between stints as a branch for various banks, the edifice was a mental health facility and senior center. In 1960, a modern false façade completely covered the curlicues and sculpted moldings, supposedly giving the bank's customers a sense of future prosperity. FarWest Savings bought the building and land in 1976 and hired architects **M. Wayne Donaldson** and **Mark Lyon** to oversee its restoration in 1987. The bank closed a few years later, and the building has several tenants, with a Prudential Realty office occupying the central corner space. ♦ 502 University Ave (at Fifth Ave)

21 TASTE OF SZECHUAN

★$ Good food preempts mediocre mauve décor at this laid-back Hillcrest eatery in a university-street strip mall. If the color scheme is mismatched, at least the leatherette booths are comfortable. Maybe this is why the restaurant seems even more popular for take-out than for sit-down dining. The food, however, is quite tasty. The salt-and-pepper chicken is predictably salty, bone dry, and light as popcorn; it is served with white rice only. Go at lunch for the inexpensive combos, which include a reasonably priced entrée plus soup, egg roll or fried chicken wing, rice, and tea. ♦ Chinese ♦ Daily, lunch and dinner. 670 University Ave (between Seventh and Sixth Aves). 298.1638

22 BABETTE SCHWARTZ, THE STORE

Named for and owned by a celebrated local drag queen, this emporium of pop-culture kitsch purveys everything from "Nunzillas" (wind-up nuns shooting sparks from the mouth) to "trailer trash Barbies" to Day of the Dead miniatures and an assortment of Virgin of Guadalupe candles. Don't miss the wacky selection of greeting cards. ♦ M-Sa, 11AM-9PM; Su, 11AM-5PM. 421 University Ave (between Fifth and Fourth Aves). 220.7048. www.babette.com

COLUMN ONE

22 COLUMN ONE

This fabulous shop has everything one needs for a beautiful garden—except the plants. There are sculpted stone statues, cement benches, and cherubs and saints in a variety of materials. Wandering among the fountains and waterfalls and smattering of ethnic, outdoor-oriented bric-a-brac serves both to relieve the stress of shopping elsewhere and to give you terrific ideas for improving your patio or backyard. Delivery is available at extra cost. ♦ Daily. 401 University Ave (between Fifth and Fourth Aves). 299.9074

23 KAHN BUILDING

One of the oldest commercial buildings in Hillcrest (constructed in 1928), this structure is highlighted by an elaborate sculpted mural of giant fruits along the building's upper edges. The mural and other decorations were covered with stucco for many years, but when plans to demolish it were made public, Hillcrest residents resorted to furtive guerrilla tactics and began chipping the stucco off the ornamental panels. The building was saved and remodeled and became the **City Deli**, a mediocre restaurant and bakery that's an okay place to come as a last resort after midnight, Friday and Saturday. The building's most remarkable aspect, its bas-relief fruit mural in reds, yellows, and greens, could benefit from a touch-up. ♦ 535 University Ave (between Sixth and Fifth Aves) &

23 WEAR IT AGAIN SAM

Looking for just the right gown for that black-tie affair? Try this vintage-clothing shop's collection of capes and beaded and bangled evening dresses. The farther back in the shop you go, the farther back in time, starting with the 1960s and finally just touching the 19th century. There's a good selection of men's clothing at the front of the store; for women, you'll find shoes, hats, handbags, jewelry, and even old-fashioned bathing suits and halter tops in season. ♦ Daily. 3823 Fifth Ave (between Robinson and University Aves). 299.0185. www.wearitagainsamvintage.com

24 POMEGRANATE

An interesting and reasonably priced mix of practical yet fashionable furnishings sheds light on the Hillcrest lifestyle. In living, dining, and sleeping sections are sofas, tables, and beds along with lamps, vases, frames, and other pleasing accessories that are modern but somehow classic as well. In the bedroom area are books on how to teach yourself to dream; in the living room is a stack of books titled *The 100 Simple Secrets of Happy People*. ♦ 1037 University Ave (between Vermont St and Tenth Ave). 220.0225

24 RALPH'S

Park in the underground lot, grab a shopping cart, and ride the rubberized ramp up to this store, then try to resist the dazzling display of state-of-the-art grocery merchandising (and the social "meet" market). ♦ Daily, 24 hours. 1030 University Ave (between Vermont St and Tenth Ave). 298.2931. &

24 ACE HARDWARE

Here you'll find every kind of household item: from turkey basters to tea lights, potting soil and plant food to rat poison, and more. It's a fun, modern, well-organized hardware store in the heart of the Uptown shopping district. ♦ 1007 University Ave (between Vermont St and Tenth Ave). 291.5988. www.hillcresthardware.com

25 ICHIBAN

★$ This Japanese eatery, with tiny tables packed together on the sidewalk and in the minuscule dining room, is eternally crowded. But the food is good, cheap, and abundant, with no frills. The sushi and sashimi are as fresh as they can possibly be; also available are bountiful portions of sesame or teriyaki chicken. Although the sidewalk patio has been expanded to accommodate the constant flow of foot traffic, it's still crowded.

Restaurants/Clubs: **Red** | Hotels: **Purple** | Shops: **Orange** | Outdoors/Parks: **Green** | Sights/Culture: **Blue**

If seating is a problem, get your sushi to go and sit on a bench at the **Uptown District** across the street. ♦ Japanese ♦ Daily, lunch and dinner. 1449 University Ave (at Normal St). 299.7203

26 MY BEAUTIFUL DOG-O-MAT

Three large washtubs for bathing dogs and a boutique of all things canine are available at this do-it-yourself dog wash. Even if you don't have a pet, it's worth checking out. Cats are also welcome. ♦ Daily. 3789 Park Blvd (between Robinson and University Aves). 295.6140.
www.mybeautifuldogomat.com

27 BUSALACCHI'S

★★★$$$ Diners feel at home here: It's a restored two-story Victorian house with a lively bar. Even dieters can't resist the pastas; the chef will also prepare a low-fat sauce with fresh tomatoes, basil, and garlic. Other Sicilian comfort foods include calamari Parmigiana, calamari steaks breaded, baked, and topped with mozzarella cheese and marinara sauce; and Pollo Piccata a boneless chicken breast sautéed with mushrooms, lemon, capers, and white wine. The large, enclosed sidewalk patio is ideal for a leisurely lunch. ♦ Italian ♦ Daily, lunch and dinner. Reservations recommended. 3683 Fifth Ave (between Pennsylvania and Robinson Aves). 298.0119. ♿ www.busalacchis.com

28 HASH HOUSE A GO GO

★★★$$ Award-winning breakfasts are the main draw, but late breakfasts also lure, with scrambled eggs garnished with roasted rosemary and garlic. For lunch, try the sloppy joe, roasted chicken, or a meat-loaf sandwich with a side of cucumber salad or french fries. For dinner, there's rib eye, salmon with goat cheese, or rack of lamb, each with baked potato and appropriate side dishes. If you haven't guessed it already, this is quintessential American cuisine. ♦ Tu-Su, 7:30AM-2PM and 5:30PM-9PM. 3628 Fifth Ave (between Brookes and Pennsylvania Aves). 298.4646.
www.hashhouseagogo.com

29 BUFFALO BREATH

Ali Baba? Check. Sexy Mrs. Santa? Check. Admiral Nelson? You bet. The San Diego location of the national chain is *the* place to indulge your clothing-related fantasies. The store boasts 25,000 costumes, most for sale or rent, in sizes small through extra large. It's helpful that many outfits are accessorized: the caveman and -woman come with large plastic clubs; the Marie Antoinette, with a wig and necklace in addition to an impressive dress made of

miles of material. The least expensive rental is $49 per day; "Scrappy," the 8-foot rubberized robot costume, isn't for sale, but you can rent it for $500 per day. ♦ M-Sa, 2050 Hancock St (between Washington St and Witherby Ave). 297.1175.
www.buffalobreath.com

30 MISSION BREWERY PLAZA

Early San Diego's German community included brewmasters from across the Atlantic who quickly responded to the immigrants' thirst for home-style beers. In 1912, August Lang, president of Bay City Brewing Company, hired the premier brewery architect of the time, **Richard Griesser**, to build a Mission Revival–style brewery by San Diego Bay. Mission Brewing Company opened in 1913, producing Old Mission and Wurzberger beers using imported Bavarian hops and San Diego water (considered superior at the time). The burgeoning Temperance Union and wartime animosity toward Germans began to affect business; a new nonalcoholic beer, Hopski, did little to attract more customers, and the brewery closed in 1918—2 years before Prohibition.

The brewery served as a seaweed-processing plant for American Agar from 1923 until the company relocated to Spain in 1987. Later that decade, developer Mike Foote took interest in the site at the foot of Mission Hills, overlooking the airport and bay. He originally planned to raze the brick building but gradually became entranced by the idea of restoring and reopening the brewery. A successful ballot initiative exempted the building from coastal height limitations, and the original 80-foot brick chimney, tile roof, and cupola were restored in 1989 by architect **Jim Galvin** and the roof topped by a 140-pound welded copper weather vane made by sculptor Robert Feeley. The brewery was added to the National Register of Historic Places in 1989. Today, in addition to the brewery, low-rise office suites and commercial spaces—following the original brick and wood design—make up this plaza. Don't come expecting a cold one, however; there's no pub on the premises. ♦ 1751 Hancock St (between Washington and Keating Sts)

31 YOSHINO

★★★$ Only the freshest translucent yellowfin tuna slices are used for sashimi in this outstanding dining spot, where the sesame chicken also gets a high score. In a bow to current tastes, the owners finally added sushi to the menu. But they've done little else to update the place. The ambience is coffee-shop plain, with slick, Formica-topped tables that are slightly askew, sometimes causing teacups to slide around. The beyond-efficient waitresses keep the lunchtime crowd of attorneys, accountants, and carpenters moving at a brisk pace. Dinner is a bit less popular, so the lines for a table are somewhat shorter. ◆ Japanese ◆ Tu-F, lunch; Tu-Su, dinner. 1790 W Washington St (at India St). 295.2232. ♿

32 MIDDLETOWN

When hunger strikes, head for the intersection of India and Washington Streets, where a lineup of inexpensive restaurants and take-out stands survives changing taste trends. When **Raoul Marquis** bought the southeast corner of India Street at Washington in the 1970s, he put out a sign calling the cluster of houses and shops the **India Street Art Colony**. Marquis was a lawyer, architect, sculptor, and Renaissance man and wanted to surround himself with like-minded talents. The now-defunct **India Street Poets Theater** was formed and the annual jazz festival was a riot of eclectic creativity. Rickety wooden stairs led up a small hill to small shops, where newly immigrated Hmong artisans from Cambodia found a lucrative outlet for their needlework. Gradually, the shops became burger stops, and the poets, playwrights, and painters moved on. Still, the corner never gave way to tacky take-out places and strip malls. Instead, one-of-a-kind restaurants opened, trying to capture the India Street character. Some failed miserably; others have survived and thrived. At times, it seems like the artists' colony could be revived, with the help of an appropriate gathering spot. The neighborhood's quiet back streets and canyons still attract writers, architects, and transients; if you're a patient driver, or a curious walker, wander the hillside's network of one-way alleys and streets between India and Goldfinch Streets on the south side of Washington Street and note how the homes become more extravagant as the harbor view becomes more distinct. ◆ India St at Washington St

33 SHAKESPEARE PUB & GRILLE

★★$$ Order a pint of Abbott Ale and a plate of fish and chips (or bangers and mash) and grab a table on the sun-dappled patio of this airy, authentic English pub. The gregarious owners, known simply as Paul and Frasier, formerly tended the taps at **Princess of Wales** (now

the **Princess Pub and Grille**) down the street (see page 51). ◆ Pub ◆ Daily, lunch and dinner; Sa, Su, breakfast, lunch, and dinner. 3701 India St (between Winder and Andrews Sts). 299.0230. www.shakespearepub.com

33 SAFFRON NOODLES AND SATÉ

★★★★$ Owner Su-Mei Yu grew up in Bangkok and missed the grilled chicken she used to buy at ramshackle huts by the Thai city's boxing arena. Now Su and a slew of cooks serve up fragrant marinated chicken with peanut sauce and jasmine rice from a tidy storefront. She's added a noodle and saté shop next door and expanded the menu so even regulars can find new favorites. Yu has become a celebrity, with two Thai cookbooks and many TV appearances, but she still spends most of her time at her tiny cafés. ◆ Thai ◆ Daily, lunch and dinner. 3731 India St (between Winder and Andrews Sts), 574.0177; Saffron Noodles and Saté, 3737 India St (between Winder and Andrews Sts), 574.7737. www.sumeiyu.com

33 GELATO VERO CAFFE

★★$ There is a steady lineup of Vespas next to the sidewalk tables at this popular café, where flaky *palmiers* (puff pastry cookies), giant blueberry scones, espresso drinks, and sublime gelati are the main draws. ◆ Coffeehouse ◆ Su-Th, 7AM-midnight; F, Sa, 7AM-1AM. 3753 India St (at Washington St). 295.9269. www.gelatovero.net

El Indio

34 EL INDIO

★★$ Ralph Pesqueria Jr. followed his father's example and kept this over-50-year-old Mexican take-out stand simple and straightforward, though he did add an indoor dining area with booths and Southwestern décor. On sunny days, snag a picnic table on the patch of pavement across the street. Best bets include giant quesadillas stuffed with cheese and guacamole, *taquitos* (deep-fried

Restaurants/Clubs: **Red** | Hotels: **Purple** | Shops: **Orange** | Outdoors/Parks: **Green** | Sights/Culture: **Blue**

85

rolled tacos) with shredded beef, homemade tamales, and *carnitas* (marinated pork served with tortillas, rice, and beans). This place's legendary chips and salsa are often flown to homesick pols in Sacramento and Washington, DC, and can be found at even the swankiest La Jolla parties. ♦ Mexican ♦ Daily, breakfast, lunch, and dinner. 3695 India St (between Chalmers and Winder Sts). 299.0333. &

35 3500 BLOCK OF SEVENTH AVENUE

Bordered on three sides by **Balboa Park**, this block was one of San Diego's most exclusive neighborhoods in the early 1900s when **Irving Gill** and **W. S. Hebbard** designed homes for a number of San Diego's prestigious residents. Alice Lee and Katherine Teats, two avid supporters of Gill's work, commissioned three cottages clustered around a common garden designed by **Kate Sessions** in 1906. The two women lived in neighboring houses and shared their gardens with the neighbors; today the cottages are nearly overgrown with ivy, and the Kate Sessions garden is off-limits to the public. Across the street at **3565** and **3575** are two brick houses from Gill's New England stage that have been significantly altered. The Gill house at **3526** demonstrates yet another style, with its break from the boxes and cubes of the other houses to a multiwing, multifloor style. The **Marston House** at **3525** has been restored by the San Diego Historical Society as a part of **Balboa Park** (see page 14). Together, this collection of houses represents a mini-museum of Gill's early work. These are all private residences. ♦ From Upas St to Pennsylvania Ave

36 ALBATROSS CANYON COTTAGES

The master plan for development along the edge of Albatross Canyon included eight homes to be designed by **Irving Gill**. Four cottages, at **3407**, **3415**, **3367**, and **3353 Albatross Street**, were completed between 1912 and 1913 and still stand today; the others were never put up. The wood-frame stuccoed cottages were built as rental units for Alice Lee and Katherine Teats and have similar arched entrances and windows, simple lines, and abundant landscaping. They have all been restored with the traditional Gill colors of beige stucco with green, gray, and brown trim.

According to the US Census Bureau, California has the highest percentage of foreign language–speaking residents in the US. Overall, San Diego ranks 14th in percentage of residents who speak a foreign language at home, at 33%.

Large hedges screen the last home on the block, 3353, from view. Across the street are lovely vintage homes with leaded glass windows; this is a great neighborhood for a walk. These are private residences. ♦ At Upas St

37 SELF-REALIZATION FELLOWSHIP

Irving Gill designed this white Mission-style building in 1908 for the **Bishop's Day School**. It was converted to apartments, and in the early 1940s was home to noted San Diego artists Dan Dickey and Belle Baranceanu. Today it houses the Self-Realization Fellowship, whose members often gather on the wide green lawns in front of the building's arched windows, or within the simple meditation garden overlooking San Diego Bay. ♦ 3072 First Ave (between Spruce and Thorn Sts). 295.0170

38 435 WEST SPRUCE STREET

Three massive retaining walls shelter the elaborate gardens—and the view—of this 1913 Mediterranean villa, which has been called the finest local example of **Richard Requa**'s work. Construction lasted for more than a year—understandable, given the many stacked levels of gardens and living space. The house is a private residence. ♦ At Curlew St

39 407 WEST SPRUCE STREET

William Templeton Johnson designed this sandstone-colored Mediterranean house in 1928. In 1991, **Mark Tarasuck** oversaw the house's remodeling and expansion, with a fanciful eye toward the original design. The addition includes molded concrete windows in the Moorish design favored by Johnson. It is a private residence. ♦ At Brant St

40 SPRUCE STREET FOOTBRIDGE

Children love running across this 375-foot-long suspension bridge over a deep, forested canyon. The bridge was originally built in 1912 by **Edwin M. Capps** to give residents on the east side of the canyon access to the trolley running to Hillcrest from downtown. ♦ Between Front and Brant Sts

41 3162 SECOND AVENUE

Carleton Winslow designed this Mediterranean mansion in 1915 for Hortense Couter, a singer and cultural maven who was a member of the Wednesday Club and sponsored appearances by symphonies and opera companies in San Diego. This off-white building with gray trim around the arched

TREKS AND TOURS

Coronado's beauty inspires residents to support all sorts of options designed to ensure that visitors thoroughly appreciate their city. Choose one or all of the following touring possibilities to get a bird's-eye view of the peninsula.

The **Coronado Shuttle** (233.3004), actually the No. 904 bus, is a shuttle bus that runs from the **Ferry Landing** through downtown, along **Orange Avenue**—passing the **Hotel Del**—and down the **Silver Strand**. It operates daily every hour on the half hour between 10:30AM and 6:30PM.

Coronado Touring (435.5993) features local Nancy Cobb, who leads a 1.5-hour walking tour of Coronado's historic sites. The excursion stops at the **Glorietta Bay Inn**, Hotel Del, and **Star Park**, and along **Ocean Boulevard** and Orange Avenue, and is filled with juicy

tidbits of gossip and local lore. Tours (admission charged) depart Tuesdays, Thursdays, and Saturdays at 11AM from the Glorietta Bay Inn.

The **Museum of History and Art** (435.7242, 437.8788 for tour info) offers a Promenade Through the Past walking tour that meanders past many of the finest Craftsman, Victorian, and Spanish Colonial homes in town—a must for architecture buffs. Tours (admission charged) depart from the museum at 2PM on Wednesdays and 10:30AM on Fridays. The **Gondola Company** (429.6317) offers gondola rides through the Coronado Cays from the Loews Coronado Bay Resort. Totally romantic on a starry night (bring your own champagne), the tours (admission) include hors d'oeuvre or dessert, a warm blanket, a wine bucket and glasses, and discreet gondoliers.

windows has an imposing appearance and provides a sense of gentility. The ancient pines in the front yard are loaded with pinecones in the spring. The house is a private residence. ♦ Between Redwood and Spruce Sts

Jimmy Carter's Cafe

42 JIMMY CARTER'S CAFE

★$ You can get hearty portions of standard American bacon and eggs here, or something a bit more exotic from the Mexican and Indian menus. This eclectic, unpretentious café is a neighborhood favorite, especially for breakfast. Count on standing in line on weekend mornings. ♦ American ♦ Daily, breakfast, lunch, and dinner. 3172 Fifth Ave (at Spruce St). 295.2070

43 PARK MANOR SUITES

$$ Actors appearing at the Old Globe frequent this seven-story brick hotel across the street from **Balboa Park**. Constructed around 1926, the hotel was designed by **Frank P. Allen Jr.**, chief architect for the 1915 Panama-California Exposition. The ambience is similar to what you'd find in an old European hostelry, which means it's low on California glitz but high on coziness and charm. Accommodations include studios and one- and two-bedroom suites with

kitchenettes, some with views of the park. Rates include a complimentary continental breakfast and free Wi-Fi. The **Top of the Park**, with some of the best views of downtown and the bay, is most definitely the spot for gay men to wind down Friday evenings (5PM-10PM). The **Inn at the Park** restaurant serves continental cuisine. ♦ 525 Spruce St (between Sixth and Fifth Aves). 291.0999, 800/874.2649; fax 291.8844. www.parkmanorsuites.com

44 QUINCE STREET BRIDGE

When the city planned to close this 236-foot-long wood-trestle bridge in the late 1980s, neighbors were aghast. **George A. d'Hemecourt** designed the bridge in 1905 so residents could cross a deep canyon filled with palms and eucalyptus to reach a trolley stop. More recently, walkers, joggers, and nature lovers had found the bridge a quick and scenic shortcut across the canyon. Their protests convinced the city to refurbish and reopen the bridge, where neighbors once again can run. ♦ Quince St (between Fourth and Third Aves)

45 EXTRAORDINARY DESSERTS

★★★$ One of the top pastry chefs in town, Karen Krasne, graduated from Le Cordon Bleu in Paris and opened this wonderful bakeshop. Supremely exquisite desserts—white chocolate linzertorte, *truffe framboise* (raspberry truffle), toasted macadamia caramel cheesecake—are displayed on a

Restaurants/Clubs: Red | Hotels: Purple | Shops: Orange | Outdoors/Parks: Green | Sights/Culture: Blue

SEALIFE CALENDAR

San Diego residents are fascinated with the underwater seasons. Many depend on the sea for their livelihoods; many more, for their fun. Anglers, divers, and seafood lovers divide the year by their prey:

* **January through March:** rock cod
* **March through September:** bonita and barracuda

* **Late spring:** yellowtail, bass, and bonita
* **4 July through October:** marlin, albacore, bluefin tuna, and shark

Divers follow these seasons:

* **May through June:** mussels, clams, and other bivalves found along coast are poisonous now

* **October through March:** lobsters are in season

* **December:** squid spawn off **La Jolla** shores

sleek granite counter. Browsers are encouraged to relax with a cup of Kona coffee (ground fresh for each customer) at the counter or one of the coveted tables. Krasne approaches her work with an artistic eye, shaping macaroons into pyramids, weaving ribbons and flowers around her cakes. It's the perfect place to buy a cake to go with a fabulous feast or indulge a craving for sweets on the spot. Krasne opened a stunning bakery/café downtown in 2004. It was an instant hit with office workers and downtown residents. ◆ Bakery ◆ M-Th, 8:30AM-11PM; F, 8:30AM-midnight; Sa,

10AM-midnight; Su, 10AM-11PM. 2929 Fift Ave (between Palm and Quince Sts). 294.2132. Also downtown at 1430 Union S (between Ash and Beech Sts), with similar hours. 294.7001.
www.extraordinarydesserts.com

46 BRITT SCRIPPS INN

$$$ Conveniently situated between Bankers Hill, Balboa Park, and downtown, this 1887-era Queen Anne Victorian mansion got a face-lift in 2005 when it was transformed into this lavish B&B. Entrepreneur Gordon Hattersley III lavished

$6 million on the project, polishing the original two-story stained-glass window and flying staircase of white oak and adding a wealth of antiques. The nine rooms are individually decorated, and most have 12-foot ceilings and the kind of amenities today's bankers might demand, starting with 1,000-thread-count linens and posh plumbing. ♦ 406 Maple St (at Fourth Ave). 230.1991, 888/881.1991. www.brittscrippsinn.com

47 BERTRAND AT MISTER A'S

★★$$$ High atop the **Fifth Avenue Financial Center**, this is the best place for a heart-stopping view of downtown San Diego and jets passing by the 12th-story windows as they approach **Lindbergh Field**. San Diego's old guard lost its longtime gathering place for martinis and Manhattans when the legendary **Mr. A's** closed in 2000. Tournedos of beef, chateaubriand, and cherries jubilee were replaced with contemporary American cuisine with Mediterranean inspiration when it reopened in 2001. However, the restaurant maintains its traditionally lavish display of Christmas lights wrapping the building between Thanksgiving and New Year's—a good time to stop by for cocktails or to drink in the view from the balcony. ♦ Eclectic ♦ M-F, lunch and dinner; Sa, Su, dinner. Reservations recommended. 2550 Fifth Ave (between Laurel and Maple Sts). 239.1377. www.bertrandatmisteras.com

48 LONG-WATERMAN HOUSE

This astounding example of Queen Anne–Victorian eccentricity features bay and dormer windows, gables, and towers protruding from all sides and an intricate original latticework porch railing that curves around the side of the house. The house was originally designed by **D.P. Benson** in 1889 for John Long, a lumberman in Colorado who supplied much of the veneers used throughout the interior. California Governor Robert Waterman purchased it in 1893, and the house was the

center of social and cultural life at the turn of the 19th century. The building has been faithfully preserved and houses private offices. ♦ 2408 First Ave (at Kalmia St)

49 KEATING HOUSE

$$ Nestled on a quiet residential street, this gay-owned bed-and-breakfast in a historic 1888 Victorian home offers nine comfortable rooms; all have a private bath, but only some have a bathtub. If you're at all tall or of ample girth, ask for the room with the largest bed—most seem tiny by today's standards. The **Cottage**, built in 1905, consists of the Garden Suite on the first floor and the Butler's Room on the second floor. The Craftsman-style suite includes a sitting room, bedroom, kitchenette, and bathroom with shower and tub. The Butler's Room overlooks the gardens and has a queen and twin bed. A full breakfast is served each morning, and there's always a bottle of tawny port on the sidebar for a pre- or postprandial drink. Smoking is not allowed inside the house. Don't confuse this comfy adobe with the very high-end and ultra-modern Keating Hotel downtown. ♦ 2331 Second Ave (between Juniper and W Kalmia Sts). 239.8585, 800/995.8644; fax 239.5774. www.keatinghouse.com

50 HOB NOB HILL

★$ One of the most popular hangouts in town since 1944 when it opened as a 14-stool lunch counter named **Juniper Cafe**, this place still offers a down-home menu and ambience. It's frequented by some of San Diego's most prominent politicians, doctors, attorneys, and accountants, who conduct their power-breakfast deals over beef hash and eggs, oatmeal with pecans, or sunny-side-up eggs with thick slices of hickory-smoked bacon. Breakfast (served all day) is the best meal here, but such rib-sticking repasts as fried chicken; roast leg of lamb or pork with vegetables, potatoes, gravy, and bread; and hot turkey sandwiches drenched in gravy are also quite pleasing. Multiple-generation families assemble here for a traditional Sunday dinner, and the waitresses (some of whom have been here for decades) know them all by name. ♦ American ♦ Daily, breakfast, lunch, and dinner. 2271 First Ave (at Juniper St). 239.8176. www.hobnobhill.com

Hillcrest by the numbers: median age, 39; approximately 37% have college degrees; almost 10 times as many residents rent as own homes. What the census figures don't indicate is that of the estimated 36,000 folks who reside here, about half are gay.

Restaurants/Clubs: Red | **Hotels: Purple** | Shops: Orange | **Outdoors/Parks: Green** | Sights/Culture: Blue

OLD TOWN AND MISSION VALLEY

Old Town San Diego State Historic Park is the best place to learn about San Diego's history. The first Spanish mission in Alta California (as opposed to Baja California, which is in Mexico and was the site of California's first missions) overlooked the tidy patch of streets and parks laid out in the mid-1800s. Within the park's boundaries are several original adobe structures and an original schoolhouse, stable, and San Diego's first newspaper office.

For many years the park's historic buildings were overshadowed by the **Bazaar del Mundo**, San Diego's most popular attraction. Savvy entrepreneur Diane Powers realized the park's potential in the 1970s and leased a large section of the historic park from the state. The site included an 1824 wood and adobe home with eight entrances facing a central courtyard. It was the center of society in the burgeoning community of early San Diego, and when Powers took over the property, she made it the focal point of her Bazaar del Mundo. The Bazaar's colorful Mexican-flavored shops were among the best in the city for textiles, furnishings, books, and folk art,

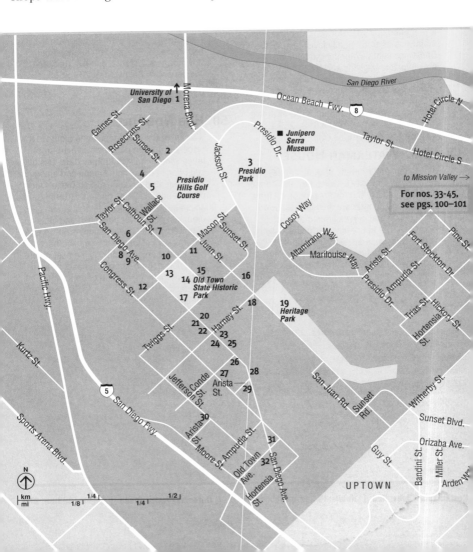

and the restaurants' festive décor, immense margaritas, and decent Mexican cuisine drew crowds year round. Powers lost her lease for the Bazaar in 2005, after years of rumors and wrangling, and the festive ambience drifted away. The lease was awarded to the Delaware North Corporation of New York, which replaced the Bazaar with the **Plaza del Pasado**, a more historically accurate re-creation of the businesses that would have existed in the mid-1800s.

Parking is free and abundant except in the busiest of seasons; tour and city buses make regular stops here, as does the **San Diego Trolley.** It's easy to ditch your vehicle and make foot power your mode of transportation here. But you'll need to get back into your car to make it up **Presidio Hill,** the site of San Diego's first fort in the 1700s. The view west, beyond civilization to the ocean and bays, and east over Mission Valley to the **Cuyamaca Mountains,** is outstanding, especially on a clear day.

Mission Valley, ranging east along the **San Diego River,** is a tribute to the automobile and to a more modern style of prosperity. Its main street, aptly named **Hotel Circle,** is lined with convenient places to stay. Every major freeway in town hits the valley at some point—see those terrifying overpasses swooping through the sky? The frontage roads on this stretch of the freeway are packed with shopping centers, restaurants, and chain hotels. The **Blue Line** of the San Diego Trolley goes east from Old Town through the valley to **Qualcomm Stadium** and **San Diego State University.** Condo and townhouse complexes, modern shopping plazas, and trendy restaurants are cropping up along both sides of the river, once the most fertile cattle-raising area in the county. The valley has become a major residential area in the past decade, and now has more than 20,000 residents.

OLD TOWN

1 UNIVERSITY OF SAN DIEGO

The white Spanish tower and sky-blue tile dome on the hills above I-5 crown the **Immaculata Church** at the **University of San Diego** (USD), one of the most beautiful campuses in the county. The independent Catholic university began as the **San Diego College for Women** in 1949 and was modeled after the University of Alcalá de Henares near Madrid in the Spanish Renaissance style. The first building for the **Women's College** included a chapel (now called **Founders' Chapel**), lavishly decorated with a white Botticino marble altar from Italy, gold leaf gilding on the interior architectural details, 14 stained-glass windows, and a rose marble floor. Weddings are booked back-to-back here on most weekends, as well as at the Immaculata Church, which stands like a grand cathedral at the heart of the campus. *Our Lady of Grace*, a statue by artist Chris Mueller, stands atop the dome—no small feat, because the cast-stone prayerful Virgin weighs about 4.5 tons and stands 11 feet high. All the buildings added to the campus (called **Alcalá Park**) have complemented the original style, creating a picturesque setting. USD's students, some of whom live above their classrooms in historical landmark buildings, are attracted by the school's reputation of excellence in law, nursing, and business administration, as well as its natural setting. ♦ 5998 Alcalá Park (at Linda Vista Rd). 260.4600

2 PADRE TRAIL INN

$$ This basic motel has the cheapest rooms within walking distance from Old Town's shops and restaurants. The motel has 100 rooms, a pool, and a restaurant open only for breakfast. It's a viable option for those wishing to spend the big bucks on other things. ♦ 4200 Taylor St (between Sunset St and Morena Blvd). 297.3291. & www.padretrailinn.com

Restaurants/Clubs: Red | Hotels: Purple | Shops: Orange | Outdoors/Parks: Green | Sights/Culture: Blue

3 PRESIDIO PARK

There's no better vantage point from which to see the contrast between old and new San Diego than atop **Presidio Hill**. The view encompasses much of the county, and you can easily imagine how spectacular it was before smog and commerce took over. To the west lie Mission and San Diego Bays and the Pacific Ocean. To the east, freeways carve into the canyons of Mission Valley, sending a ribbon of traffic toward the Cuyamaca Mountains. Within the park, the frenzy of civilization seems remote. It's easy to see why early settlers chose to live here.

Padre Junípero Serra founded the first Franciscan mission in Alta California (as opposed to Baja California, which is in Mexico) on 16 July 1769, beside the first Spanish fort on Presidio Hill. The soldiers, who thoroughly abused the local Kumeyaay tribe, made poor neighbors, and the mission was moved farther east (in what's today Mission Valley) in 1774. (In 1775, the Kumeyaay destroyed the new mission, but it was rebuilt at the same site.) The Mexican flag appeared above the hill in 1824; the US flag replaced it in 1847.

At the turn of the 20th century, merchant and philanthropist George White Marston purchased the land for **Presidio Park** piece by piece, spending more than $392,000 over a span of 22 years. In 1929 he presented the park and its historical landmarks to the city as a gift. Architect **William Templeton Johnson** set to work on the **Junípero Serra Museum**; landscape architect John Nolen plotted long swaths of green grass down the hillsides and planted several secluded groves of eucalyptus and pine trees. Sculptor Arthur Putnam cast the *Indian* and the *Padre* in bronze; a bronze cannon, *El Jupiter*, marks the spot where the US flag first flew. Presidio Park is one of San Diego's overlooked treasures. It is an outpost of natural gentility, a lovely setting for an afternoon garden wedding. The palatial homes of Mission Hills overlook its sloping lawns and miniforests of pines and oaks.
♦ Bounded by Harney and Taylor, Juan, and Mason Sts.

Within Presidio Park:

JUNÍPERO SERRA MUSEUM

Architect **William Templeton Johnson** paid full tribute to San Diego's heritage in this reinforced concrete Spanish-Colonial mission with its red-tile roofs, white stucco arches, colonial windows, and narrow, shaded passageways. The museum contains Father Serra's records and vestments; a cross outside the building was made from adobe bricks from the remains of the original mission. ♦ Admission. F-Su, 1PM-4:30PM. 2727 Presidio Dr (at Taylor St). 297.3258

FORT STOCKTON MEMORIAL

When Mexico lost the battle for **Presidio Hi** in 1846, US soldiers renamed the hill **Fort Stockton** for Robert Stockton, commander of the American Pacific Squadron. Later tha year, Stockton and his men built walls from sand and dirt, mounted 12 guns, and dug a moat. The fort no longer exists, but a flagpole, bronze statues, and several monuments mark the site. ♦ Jackson St (o south side of park)

4 BAZAAR DEL MUNDO

The Bazaar's colorful enclave of blooming hibiscus, mariachis, and margaritas was synonymous with Old Town for nearly 30 years, and locals and frequent visitors were sadly disappointed when the complex close in 2005. Interior designer Diane Powers created the Bazaar in buildings leased from the state's historic park in 1971. At its height, the Bazaar had 16 specialty shops displaying folk art, jewelry, furnishings, textiles, books, and all sorts of irresistible treasures. Powers has relocated some of th stock to a much smaller venue just north of Old Town, and done all she can to make it a festive and colorful locale.

Within the shopping area are several small shops (all using the same phone number ar address). The **Design Center** displays napkins and table runners in vivid Guatemalan fabrics, glassware, and dishes from Italy and Mexico, and all sorts of clever kitchen gadgets. **Artes de Mexico** offers fine Majolica tableware, place settings from Guadalajara, and an assortment of fun, less expensive Mexican handicrafts. The **Guatemala Shop** is packed with dresses, vests, and jackets made from gorgeous textiles, as well as woven purses and shawls and a good selection of fabrics. **Libros Bookstore** contains a small, fascinating selection of nonfiction books on Latin America and contemporary fiction. **The Gallery** features colorful women's clothing, and jewelry by Native American Indian and Latin American artisans. Also here are mugs jewelry, and clothing by Laurel Burch and a fine collection of John Swanson serigraphs with colorful, highly detailed religious themes done in a primitive style. ♦ All shops open Tu-Sa, 10AM-9PM; Su, M, 10AM-5:30PM. 4133 Taylor Street St (at Juan St). 296.3161. ♿ www.bazaardelmundo.com

4 CASA GUADALAJARA

★★$$ A festive atmosphere prevails at this typically colorful Mexican restaurant, especially when strolling mariachis entertain (W-Su, 6-9:30PM) or when San Diegans show up after work for the happy-hour drink specials. You'll find all the typical Mexican plates of tostadas, burritos, and tacos, as well as many seafood specialties. Indoors, cutout flags (called *papel picado*) decorate the festive, multilevel dining room. Outside on the charming patio—scented in summer with blooming jasmine—diners are soothed by the rumbling water sounds of a lovely fountain and shaded by café-table umbrellas and an enormous pepper tree. ♦ Mexican ♦ Daily, lunch and dinner; Sa, Su, breakfast, lunch, and dinner. 4105 Taylor St (at Juan St). 295.5111. ♿ www.casaguadalajara.com

5 LA PIÑATA

★$ You'll find more locals than tourists at this colorful veteran dining spot which has offered decades of service to families who enjoy the peaceful patio, peach margaritas, Mexican pizza, sizzling fajitas, and guacamole tostadas. Dine inside, where small piñatas hang from the low ceiling, or outside on the small shaded patio. There's a large lot for free parking. ♦ Mexican ♦ Daily, lunch and dinner. 2836 Juan St (between Wallace and Taylor Sts). 297.1631. www.lapinataoldtown.com

6 ROBINSON-ROSE HOUSE AND VISITORS' CENTER

The park offices and visitors' center are located in a reconstruction of an 1853 house that served as law offices, railroad headquarters, and a newspaper office. Park rangers cheerfully dispense up-to-the-minute information, and a few books on Old Town are for sale. Public rest rooms, pay phones, and parking are all available here. Take time to visit the rooms that have been outfitted with period furnishings. The **Silvas-McCoy House**, adjacent to the visitors' center, was built in 1869 by James McCoy, a wealthy Irish immigrant who served as San Diego's sheriff and state senator. ♦ Free. Guided, one-hour tours of the park and some of the museums offered daily at 11AM and 2PM. 4002 Wallace St (between San Diego Ave and Calhoun St). 220.5422

7 PLAZA DEL PASADO

When Bazaar del Mundo lost the concession for shops and restaurants here in 2005, it was awarded instead to the Delaware North Corporation of New York, whose successful bid entailed a venue less colorful but more historically accurate. The Mexican and Latin American boutiques that previously enlivened the area have been replaced by shops that are both less lively and less successful. The restaurants have changed as well, and have yet to achieve the quality and popularity of their predecessors. Dining options in Plaza del Pasado now include **Casa de Reyes** (Juan and Calhoun Sts at the old Casa de Pico; Mexican; 220.5040) and **The Cosmopolitan** restaurants (at old Casa de Bandini, Mason and Calhoun Sts; American/Mexican; 209.3525). Both are open daily for early lunch through dinner. ♦ 2754 Calhoun St (at Wallace St). 297.3100. ♿ www.plazadelpasado.com

Within Plaza del Pasado:

CASA DE SERRANO

Browse here for Talavera and Majolica pottery and place settings from Mexico (Guanajuato, Guadalajara, and the major tile- and ceramic-making centers) and Spain, as well as charming art naïf clay renditions of churches and Indian musicians from Peru, and smaller gift items. ♦ 293.7520

ROPERÍA

This boutique offers extravagant hats from England, lovely Bolivian shawls, open-weave tops from Brazil, and Spanish fans, among other finery. All of the merchandise is unusual, feminine, and fun. ♦ 220.5048

8 LA CASA DE MACHADO Y STEWART

The Silvas and Machado families lived in this house for over 100 years. The kitchen and dining room have been converted to a minimuseum, set up as they would have been had the family been about to dine, with authentic tableware and foods in the kitchen. A walk through the kitchen takes you to the herb garden. There are periodic demonstrations of the art of making tortillas. ♦ Free. Daily. San Diego Ave (between Mason and Wallace Sts). No phone

9 RACINE & LARAMIE

The aroma of pipe tobacco pervades the air in this reconstruction of San Diego's first tobacco shop, an 1830s store-turned-saloon, which burned down in 1872. The wooden boxes of custom cigars are a good gift for a discerning smoker; antiques lovers should check out the items in the glass-and-wood display cabinets. ◆ Daily. 2737 San Diego Ave (between Mason and Wallace Sts). 291.7833

10 OLD TOWN PLAZA

Also called **California Plaza** and **Plaza de las Armas**, the town green is marked by a flagpole at the site where the American flag was first raised here in 1846. Art shows are sometimes held here. ◆ Bounded by Mason and Wallace Sts and by San Diego Ave and Calhoun St

11 BLACK HAWK LIVERY & BLACKSMITH

J.B. Hinton began blacksmithing here in the 1860s. Today the smithy has been restored and vintage blacksmithing techniques are demonstrated. ◆ Free. W, 10AM-4PM (Memorial Day through Labor Day also open F-Su). Mason St (between Calhoun and Juan Sts). No phone

12 MASON STREET SCHOOL

This classic one-room schoolhouse displays artifacts such as students' and teachers' desks and textbooks. Read the comments of its teachers, including those of Mary Chase Walker, who arrived from Massachusetts in 1865 and said of her new hometown: "Of all the dilapidated, miserable-looking places, this is the worst." She later married the president of the school board. ◆ Free. Daily. Mason St (between Congress St and San Diego Ave). 297.1183

13 LA CASA DE ESTUDILLO

This beautifully restored adobe was once the home of *Capitán* José María Estudillo, a retired fort commander, during California's Mexican period. The house was first restored under the direction of architect **Hazel Waterman** in 1910; the state restored the home again in 1969 for San Diego's bicentennial. The house is furnished with items representative of the 16th through 20th centuries with assistance from the National Society of Colonial Dames of America. ◆ Free. Daily. Mason St (between San Diego Ave and Calhoun St). 220.5426

14 OLD TOWN STATE HISTORIC PARK

A cluster of buildings and 13 acres of land that formed the center of early San Diego became a state historic park in 1968. Architects **Delawie, Macy & Henderson** were consulted to help create a master plan for the complete restoration of Old Town. Archeologist Ray Brandes excavated sections of the park to determine the exact location and dimensions of former buildings. Restored structures, most from the mid-1800s, include several adobe and wood houses and stores. Cars are banned from the park, allowing pedestrians to wander and congregate on park benches beside the central lawn, where art shows are often held. Take a self-guided walking tour of the park's historic buildings; they're all set around the park lawn. ◆ Bounded by Twiggs and Mason Sts and by San Diego Ave and Juan St. 220.5422. ⸜ www.parks.ca.gov

15 SEELEY STABLES

The original terminal of the **Seeley and Wright Stage Line**, which was conveniently located next door to old San Diego's largest hotel, now houses the **Roscoe Hazard Museum**, a collection of stagecoaches and other horse-drawn vehicles, saddles, and Western artifacts. A 20-minute film on early San Diego history is shown throughout the day. ◆ Free. Daily. Calhoun St (between Twiggs and Mason Sts). 220.5427

16 MORMON BATTALION MEMORIAL VISITORS CENTER

The center is staffed by Mormon volunteers from various countries who devote their time to educating their guests about how Mormons contributed to the settling of Old Town. ◆ Daily. 2510 Juan St (between Harney and Twiggs Sts). 298.3317

17 SAN DIEGO UNION NEWSPAPER HISTORICAL BUILDING

This restored wood-frame structure was built in Maine in 1851, then shipped around Cape Horn. The first edition of the *San Diego Union* (still San Diego's daily newspaper) came off the presses here in 1868. Visitors can see the original printing presses. ◆ Free. Daily. San Diego Ave (between Twiggs and Mason Sts)

18 BEST WESTERN HACIENDA SUITES-OLD TOWN

$$ The original tenant of this hilltop compound was a highly unsuccessful shopping center, and it seemed the hacienda-style buildings and terraced patios would be destroyed. But crafty developers envisioned hotel rooms where knickknack shops once stood, and spent a year renovating and expanding the complex into a very successful, charming, all-suites

hotel overlooking Old Town. The 220 large, high-ceilinged rooms are-spread over several levels, with fountains bubbling on brick patios, wooden balconies looking out to the street, and rustic wood furnishings imported from Mexico. The rooms have kitchenettes with microwaves, coffeemakers, and refrigerators. There's plenty of room for children to roam, but anyone who has trouble climbing stairs and hills might be unhappy here. ♦ 4041 Harney St (between San Diego Ave and Juan St). 298.4707, 800/888.1991; fax 298.4771. www.bestwestern.com

19 HERITAGE PARK VICTORIAN VILLAGE

Some of San Diego's most precious historic Victorian houses line the cobblestone walks of this 7.8-acre park, operated by San Diego County. The concept of creating a park where historic houses slated for destruction could be preserved was born at meetings of a group of nostalgia buffs, led by San Diego artist Robert Miles Parker, who began the Save Our Heritage Organization (SOHO). Saved from demolition in other parts of the city, several grand Victorian homes and a temple have been moved to the park and restored and now contain offices, shops, and a bed-and-breakfast. ♦ Bounded by Sunset Rd and Harney and Juan Sts. For information, call the San Diego Parks and Recreation Department, 858/565.1699. www.sandiegohistory.org

Within Heritage Park:

SHERMAN-GILBERT HOUSE

This 20-room house was designed by **Comstock & Trotsche** in 1887 in the Stick-Eastlake style named after Charles Eastlake, English author and furniture designer. The style's distinctive applied stick-, lattice-, and scrollwork are evident in the bright white trim and the peaked widow's walk. The Gilbert family purchased the house in 1897, and sisters Bess and Gertrude, active in the arts, hosted many soirées for famous guests, including the Von Trapp Family Singers and Yehudi Menuhin, until Bess died in 1965. The house originally was on the edge of downtown; in 1940, the widow's walk was removed because it obstructed the flight path to Lindbergh Field. The house was moved to Heritage Park in 1971 and lovingly restored, with the widow's walk intact once again. ♦ Free. Daily. Heritage Park Row (between Sunset Rd and Harney St)

HERITAGE PARK BED & BREAKFAST INN

$$ The Queen Anne–style Christian House, built in 1889 by merchant Harfield Timberlane Christian, now houses this peaceful, picturesque inn, easily the most charming hostelry in Old Town. The 12 bedchambers (all with private baths) are appointed with period antiques, finished wood floors, and Oriental rugs. Modern amenities include meeting facilities with fax, computer, and audiovisual equipment; Old World touches include fireplaces and afternoon tea. Breakfast is included, of course. ♦ 2470 Heritage Park Row (between Sunset Rd and Harney St). 299.6832, 800/995.2470; fax 299.9465. & www.heritageparkinn.com

BUSHYHEAD HOUSE

Edward Wilkerson Bushyhead was an early San Diego sheriff and a founder of the *San Diego Union*. He built this Italianate-style Victorian in 1887 in the same fashionable downtown neighborhood as the Sherman-Gilbert house; in the 1920s, it became a rental unit, then deteriorated over the next 50 years. In 1976, SOHO moved the house to the park and restored it. Today it is part

of the Heritage Park Bed & Breakfast Inn, with three rooms available to guests.
♦ 2460 Heritage Park Row (between Sunset Rd and Harney St). 299.6832, 800/995.2470. ♿

TEMPLE BETH ISRAEL

This odd, Victorian-eclectic-style building was the first synagogue in Southern California and was used for the first time on Rosh Hashanah eve, 25 September 1889. The interior has been restored as a community hall available for rent to the public. ♦ Open during events only. 2455 Heritage Park Row (between Sunset Rd and Harney St)

20 IMMACULATE CONCEPTION CHURCH

Just as construction of this Catholic church was under way, Alonzo Horton began building his New Town, and Old Town's good fortunes ceased. The cornerstone of the church was laid in 1868, but it wasn't dedicated until 1919 and was finally completed in 1937.
♦ 2540 San Diego Ave (between Harney and Twiggs Sts). 295.4148

21 GALLERY OLD TOWN

Some of our favorites and some rare and previously unreleased images from *Life*'s top photojournalists are for sale in this small gallery. Hand-signed photographs by Margaret Bourke-White, Alfred Eisenstaedt, and Joe Rosenthal are framed and ready to be hung on your wall. ♦ 2513 San Diego Ave (between Harney and Twiggs Sts). 296.7877

22 CHUCK JONES STUDIO GALLERY

Showcasing the animation art of one of Warner Bros.' former (and most famous) artists, this large gallery is home to the likenesses of Bugs Bunny, Daffy Duck, and Wile E. Coyote, as well as fine art drawings by the artist. ♦ Su-Th, 11AM-7PM; F, Sa, 11AM-8PM. 2501 San Diego Ave (between Harney and Twiggs Sts). 294.9880

23 WHALEY HOUSE

Thomas Whaley, entrepreneur, merchant, and pillar of the community, came from a family with ancestors at the Battle of Hastings and the Boston Tea Party. His 1856 Old Town home was a solid two-story brick mansion, now completely restored and authentically furnished. The house served for a time as a theater and in 1869 became the **County Courthouse**. The last Whaley to live in the house was Corinne Lillian, youngest of the Whaleys' six children, who died in 1959 at the age of 89. The house's four resident spirits—Mr. and Mrs. Whaley, a young girl, and Jim Robinson (who was hanged near the house)— have been featured in television shows and books and are said to favor dreary cold days near Christmas. The ghosts are a hit with schoolkids—over 10,000 visit the house each year. ♦ Admission. Closed W (open daily June-August). 2482 San Diego Ave (between Conde and Harney Sts). 297.7511. www.whaleyhouse.org

24 OLD TOWN MEXICAN CAFE AND CANTINA

★★★$ One of Old Town's most enduringly popular Mexican restaurants, this eatery is famous for the *carnitas* (marinated pork) served with tortillas fresh from the grill, beans and rice, and a tray of condiments including cilantro, onions, and guacamole. Breakfast hangover cures (served all day) include an egg-and-*chorizo* taco and saucy *chilaquiles* (fried tortilla strips in red sauce) with fried eggs. The restaurant keeps expanding to outdoor patios and more dining rooms, but that never seems to shorten the lines of patrons waiting for tables.
♦ Mexican ♦ Daily, breakfast, lunch, and dinner. 2489 San Diego Ave (between Conde and Harney Sts). 297.4330. www.oldtownmexcafe.com

25 NEW ORLEANS CREOLE CAFE

★★$$ If you've had enough tacos and tostadas, how about some red beans and rice, jambalaya, or mac and cheese? New Orleans transplant Mark Bihm and business partner Humberto Villegas have teamed up to offer a petite restaurant overlooking the gardens of the Whaley House, in the heart of Old Town. From Mark's grandma's and other Big Easy recipes, choose a po' boy sandwich or the house coup de grâce, a creamy crawfish etouffeé. For dessert, order coffee to cut the sweetness of an enormous portion of Red Velvet cake, an oh-so-yummy red-dyed chocolate cake draped in cream cheese frosting. Eat outside on the open patio or, for a romantic evening tête-à-tête, inside the tiny vintage wooden building, moved from downtown San Diego at the same time other rescued buildings were moved to create Heritage Park. ♦ Creole
♦ Daily, lunch and dinner May-Oct; closed W, Nov-April. 2476 San Diego Av (between Harney and Conde Sts, behind the Whaley House). 542.1698. www.neworleanscreolecafe.com

26 APACHE INDIAN ARTS GALLERY

Navajo, Zuni, Hopi, and Santo Domingo Indian art, kachina dolls, rugs, and the requisite moccasins are all for sale here. ◆ Daily, 10:30AM-7:30PM. 2425 San Diego Ave (between Arista and Conde Sts). 296.9226

27 OLD ADOBE CHAPEL

Dedicated as a chapel in 1858, this small adobe house served as the **Immaculate Conception Church** in Old Town for far longer than expected, because it took over 60 years to build the current church. It is now listed as a California state historical landmark. ◆ Conde St (between Congress St and San Diego Ave)

28 ZOCALO GRILL

★$$$ Named for the main plaza in Mexico City, Zocalo replaced the popular Brigantine that stood on this corner for years. The same owners redid the interior with a Southwest décor and updated the menu. Steaks, seafood, and chicken are spiced up with various chiles and salsas; prices are high at dinner. Better deals are the shrimp torta and steak sandwich at lunch. ◆ American/Mexican ◆ M-Sa, lunch and dinner; Su, brunch and dinner. 2444 San Diego Ave (at Conde St). 298.9840. & www.zocalogrill.com

28 CAFE PACIFICA

★★★★$$$$ The sleek white dining rooms have twinkling white lights, murals on the walls, and plenty of mirrors for studying the who's-who crowd. The café was the first venture for the now-revered dining duo of Kipp Downing and Deacon Brown. Offerings include excellent fresh seafood, including Hawaiian ahi with shiitake mushrooms and ginger butter, and mustard catfish. The new lunch menu features salads and small plates. Long-time general manager Frank Busic bought Cafe Pacifica in 2001 and has since introduced live abalone, farm-grown in Ensenada, Mexico, to the menu. There are two presentations, abalone piccata, served with lemon, butter, and white wine, or herb–crusted abalone with panko bread crumbs. Be sure to call ahead for availability. The crème brûlée is a must, especially when topped with fresh raspberries. ◆ Seafood ◆ W-Sa, lunch; daily, dinner. Reservations recommended. 2414 San Diego Ave (between Arista and Conde Sts). 291.6666. www.cafepacifica.com

28 EL CAMPO SANTO

🅿 The Sacred Field was Old Town's original cemetery: Many of San Diego's original settlers are buried here behind an adobe wall. ◆ San Diego Ave (between Arista and Conde Sts)

29 JACK AND GIULIO'S ITALIAN RESTAURANT

★★$$$ This father-and-son team brings decades of restaurant experience to Old Town (Giulio's **Pacific Beach** restaurant was an institution until it closed a few years ago). The atmosphere is open and light, with bright red leatherette booths along one wall and an umbrella-shaded patio out front. Most often requested are scampi Giulio, butterfly shrimp sautéed with mushrooms and garlic, and the filet mignon au cognac with fresh rosemary. There is a full bar with both California and Italian wines available. ◆ Italian ◆ Daily, lunch and dinner. 2391 San Diego Ave (at Arista St). 294.2074. & www.jackandgiulios.com

30 COURTYARD SAN DIEGO OLD TOWN

$$$ The first hotel on this site was far more elegant, and less convenient, than the current one. The **Gila House Hotel**, built by Juan Bandini in 1850, was the center of old San Diego's social life and looked out to the bay where steamships brought new pioneers to town. Today's incarnation overlooks I-5—which makes it easily accessible. Ask for a room away from the freeway, facing into the courtyard. The sights of Old Town are within reasonable walking distance, and the hotel is popular for medium-size group meetings. The 176 rooms and suites are pleasantly comfortable; suites have microwaves, hair dryers, and refrigerators. The shaded pool is heated, the beds and bedding are new and improved, and there's free wireless in the lobby and free high-speed Internet in guest rooms. ◆ 2435 Jefferson St (at Arista St). 260.8500, 800/255.3544; fax 298.2427. & www.marriott.com

31 EL AGAVE RESTAURANT AND TEQUILERIA

★★★$$$$ Often touted as serving the most authentic regional Mexican food in San Diego, El Agave has a varied menu and an even more extensive tequila listing. With over 1,800 different types of tequila ranging in price from a few dollars to over $100 for a single shot, the proprietors here will tell you that they offer more selections than any other restaurant in the country. Seafood, beef, and chicken dishes are prepared as they are in Mexico. If you have never tried *mole* (pronounced "MO-lay"), this may be the place to take the plunge. A spicy, unique sauce prepared with everything from chilies to chocolate, El Agave features six different kinds, usually served over chicken or pork. The cozy dining room is located upstairs. ♦ Mexican ♦ Daily, lunch and dinner. 2304 San Diego Ave (at Old Town Ave). 220.0692. www.elagave.com

32 HOLIDAY INN EXPRESS

$$ The peaceful peach-and-pink rooms are clustered around a winding walkway and courtyard, with bubbling fountains and tall palms. Pseudo-antique armoires and floral quilted spreads give an old-fashioned feel to the 125 rooms and suites, whereas high-speed Internet access, refrigerators, and coffeemakers offer modern convenience. The long, three-story buildings and gated pool area create a motel-like appearance; underground parking is a somewhat steep $12 per day. Old Town's shops and restaurants are just west of the hotel, the entrance to I-5 is a block west, and the trolley is about five blocks (a 10-minute walk) along pleasant Old Town streets. ♦ 3900 Old Town Ave (between Jefferson St and San Diego Ave). 299.7400, 800/972.2802; fax 299.1619. &. iwww.ichotelsgroup.com

33 CROWNE PLAZA SAN DIEGO

$$$ Of the dozens of hotels lining I-8 in Mission Valley, this one stands out as a curiosity and a reliable hostelry. Formerly the Hanalei (and then The Red Lion) hotel, it retains a Polynesian tropics theme. The palms and flowering shrubs have matured since planted in the 1960s, giving the courtyard pool area a soothing Hawaiian ambience. The 416 rooms have recently been upgraded with dreamy "seven-layer" bedding, lavender pillow spray, and a relaxation CD to promote a good night's sleep. The location is great for hopping on a freeway to anywhere in the county. Facilities include several restaurants and lounges, a business center, and a fitness center revamped in 2007. ♦ 2270 Hotel Cir N (between Fashion Valley Rd and Taylor St). 297.1101, 800/2-CROWNE; fax 297.6049. www.ichotelgroup.com

34 FASHION VALLEY CENTER

Opened in 1969, when malls were just hitting their forward stride, this compound offered direct competition for **Mission Valley Center** and formed a shopping combo that would make Mission Valley the retail—as well as the geographic—heart of the county. It boasts **Neiman Marcus**, **Nordstrom**, and **Macy's**; all

sorts of specialty shops, and several restaurants and theaters. The addition of a **Bloomingdale's** (the first in San Diego) in 2007 further upped the mall's cachet, and it's now the venue of choice for fashionistas seeking the latest Burberry or Betsey Johnson design. ♦ Daily. Fashion Valley Rd (between Hotel Circle N and Friars Rd). 297.3381

35 HANDLERY HOTEL & RESORT

$$ Built in 1956 by the Handlerys, this 222-room hotel was called the **Stardust** at one point but has reverted once again to the family name. With its close proximity to the **San Diego Zoo** and **Sea World**, as well as baby-sitting services and complimentary shuttle service to area attractions, it's a popular choice with families. The pool and hot-tub area are spacious enough to be attractive to folks of all ages. The **Riverwalk Golf Course**, a 27-hole championship course is adjacent to the hotel. ♦ 950 Hotel Cir N (between Hwy 163 and I-5). 298.0511, 800/676.6567; fax 298.9793. www.handlery.com

36 TOWN AND COUNTRY HOTEL

$$ Restaurateur Charles H. Brown built this hotel in the 1950s amid dairy farms in the bucolic river valley. Brown's vision of Mission Valley as a center of commerce became realit in the next two decades, and in 1970 the **Town and Country Convention Center** opened beside the hotel. Today the 40-acre resort includes 1,000 rooms and suites in high-rise towers and ranch-style bungalows, four restaurants and bars, four pools, a full-service spa and beauty salon, and all the services necessary to keep travelers and conventioneers satisfied, if not excited. The compound seems outdated, especially when compared to San Diego's new downtown **Convention Center** and hotels, but it attract a considerable number of midsize conventions on everything from aerobics to Zen. Business travelers appreciate the phones and desks by the beds, the proximity to all major freeways, and the variety of restaurants on the grounds. Check out the archway of 20-foot-high palms at the entranceway. ♦ 500 Hotel Cir N (between Camino de la Reina and Fashion Valley Rd). 291.7131, 800/854.2608; fax 291.3584. &. www.towncountry.com

37 ADAM'S STEAK 'N' EGGS AND ALBIE'S BEEF INN

★★★$$ These tandem restaurants in front of the **Travel Lodge Mission Valley** are traditional local favorites for hearty no-nonsense food. **Adam's** has a mountain lodge décor and is open only for breakfast—superb steak and eggs, corn fritters with honey butter, *carne asada* (grilled beef) with eggs, beans and tortillas, grits and home fries, and outrageous waffle concoctions. **Albie's** is a classic steak house—dark and woodsy, with red leather booths. Try the top sirloin, New York steak, or the chicken-fried steak with mashed potatoes and gravy. ◆ American ◆ Adam's: daily, breakfast. Albie's: M-F, lunch and dinner; Sa, dinner. 1201 Hotel Cir S (between Hwy 163 and I-5). 291.1103. & www.adamsandalbies.com

38 MISSION VALLEY RESORT

$$ This two-story Southwestern-style property spreads across a valuable 20-acre lot at the edge of I-8. Formerly a Quality Inn, the hotel offers a lot for your buck. Many of the 202 rooms have two beds and foldout couches for families, and guests have access to the adjacent health club. Facilities include tennis courts, several swimming and wading pools, a restaurant, a market, and a sports bar, and there's free parking and shuttle service to **Fashion Valley Center** and Old Town. ◆ 875 Hotel Cir S. 298.8281, 800/362.7871; fax 295.9610. www.missionvalleyresort.com

39 HAZARD CENTER

As Mission Valley has expanded into a major residential community, several shopping and entertainment minimalls have opened to serve the rapidly expanding community. This complex includes a high-rise hotel, office tower, shopping/dining area, movie theaters, and a park along the northern banks of the San Diego River. A paved sidewalk runs along the riverbank, a perfect place to unwind and stretch your legs. ◆ Hazard Center Dr (between Camino de la Reina and Friars Rd). www.hazardcenter.com

Within Hazard Center:

TROPHY'S SPORTS GRILL

★★$ The name says it all. Sports fans are happy here watching games on wide-screen TVs while devouring stone-fired pizzas, mesquite-grilled burgers, and bountiful salads and sandwiches. The food is good, the crowd friendly and lively, and the setting family-oriented, with a separate menu for children. ◆ American ◆ Daily, lunch and dinner; Su, brunch and dinner. 7510 Hazard Center Dr (between Camino de la Reina and Friars Rd). 296.9600. & www.trophys.tv

PREGO RISTORANTE

★★$$$ This Italian restaurant is an offshoot of a San Francisco–based chain. The style is trendy and chic, with a bustling Italian market atmosphere and an exhibition kitchen that turns out nice gourmet pizzas—the one with smoked mozzarella, goat cheese, portobello mushrooms, basil, and tomato is especially good. Also on our list are the meat lasagna and risotto of the day. ◆ Italian ◆ M-F, lunch and dinner; Sa, Su, dinner. Reservations suggested. 1370 Frazee Rd (between Hazard Center Dr and Friars Rd). 294.4700. & www.pregoristorante.com

DOUBLETREE HOTEL

$$$ This 300-room hotel is favored by business travelers who appreciate ample work space and both Wi-Fi and high-speed Internet access in their rooms, a spacious dining room for doing lunch, and easy freeway access. Other amenities include a health club with fitness center, two lighted tennis courts, an indoor lap pool, and an outdoor pool and hot tub. Another plus is the hotel's proximity to the **Hazard Center's** shops, movie theaters, and restaurants. ◆ 7450 Hazard Center Dr (between Camino de la Reina and Friars Rd). 297.5466, 800/222.8733; fax 297.5499. & www.doubletree.com

40 WESTFIELD SHOPPINGTOWN MISSION VALLEY CENTER

Mission Valley seemed the likely location for San Diego's first modern mall, which became the cornerstone of the valley's transformation from farming to commerce in 1961. The center has a 20-theater movie complex, a **24-Hour Fitness** gym, **Nordstrom's Rack**, and about 100 specialty stores. The anchor stores include **Macy's**, **Target**, and **Bed, Bath & Beyond**. ◆ Daily. Mission Center Rd (between Camino del Rio N and Friars Rd). 296.6375. www.westfield.com/missionvalley

---

Restaurants/Clubs: Red | Hotels: Purple | Shops: Orange | Outdoors/Parks: Green | Sights/Culture: Blue

Within Mission Valley Center:

SEAU'S THE RESTAURANT

★★$$$ Owned by the former San Diego Chargers' hometown hero, linebacker Junior Seau (now with the New England Patriots), this huge restaurant boasts 57 television monitors, with the daddy of them all, an 11×14–foot projection screen suspended from the 30-foot-high ceiling. The menu encompasses classic American grill fare (pizzas, pasta, steaks, and burgers) with a few of "Mama Seau's" Samoan-style recipes thrown in as well. This isn't the place to come for a quiet lunch, but it is a fun place to enjoy good food and maybe catch a glimpse of your favorite sports star. The Raw Mana Sushi Lounge serves nigiri, sashimi, udon noodle bowls, and other Japanese fare. ♦ Eclectic ♦ Daily. 1640 Camino del Rio N (at Mission Center Rd). 291.7328. &. www.seau.com

41 BULLY'S

★★★$$$ Hungry for real beef? Then this is your place: It's legendary for its thick prime rib served with baked potato, crisp iceberg-lettuce salad with chunky blue cheese dressing, and plenty of spicy horseradish. The steaks are good, as are the chicken and seafood dishes, but it's the prime rib that keeps the place filled. The red leather booths are the best seats, but the place gets so busy

on weekend nights you'll be happy with a table in the center of the dimly-lit dining room. Early-bird dinners, served nightly (4:30PM–5:30PM), are a great bargain. For companionship, single diners gravitate toward the large, horseshoe-shaped table at the end of the bar. ♦ American ♦ Daily. 2401 Camino del Rio S (at Texas St). 291.2665. &.

42 SAN DIEGO MARRIOTT MISSION VALLEY

$$$ This elegant hotel, with an abundance of marble and granite, claims to be the accommodation closest to **Qualcomm Stadium** (see opposite), making it an obvious choice for pro-team players appearing for games. The Modernist pool area with sleek waterfalls and plenty of lounging space is the gathering spot for visiting celebs. The 350 rooms were remodeled in 2004. ♦ 8757 Rio San Diego Dr (between I-8 and Stadium Way). 692.3800, 800/842.5329; fax 692.0769. www.marriott.com

Established 1982

43 DAVE & BUSTER'S

★★$$ For all you kids masquerading in grown-up bodies, **Dave & Buster's** is the playground for you. This place is gigantic, with 48,000 square feet devoted to an astonishing array of state-of-the-art video games and simulators. The pool tables are top-notch and custom-made, as are the shuffleboard tables. The front of the building houses the restaurant, with a turn-of-the-19th-century feel with lots of stained glass and dark wood. Seafood, chicken, and salads are tastefully

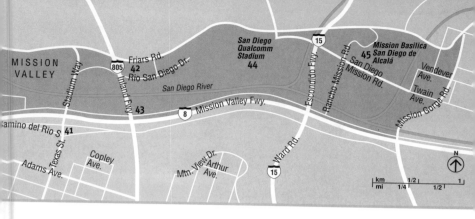

prepared, with an enticing dessert selection offering key lime pie and triple chocolate cake. The bar has two banks of elevated televisions with continuous sports coverage, though you may be too busy playing games yourself to watch. ♦ American ♦ 2931 Camino del Rio N (at the I-805–I-8 interchange). 280.7115. &

MISSION VALLEY

44 QUALCOMM STADIUM

Upgraded in 1997 to the tune of $78 million, the 71,500-seat stadium is home to the San Diego Chargers. Since the San Diego Padres got a brand-new downtown baseball stadium, however, the Chargers

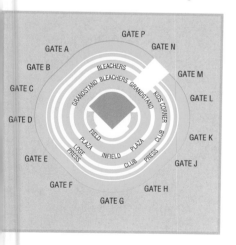

have been considering moving, and are negotiating for a new stadium with other cities, some within San Diego County. The stadium, built in 1967, has in recent years made itself useful as a venue for the multi-day Street Scene music festival, flower shows, and various community events. With its vast parking lot and trolley stop, it's easily accessible. ♦ 9449 Friars Rd (between Hwy 15 and Stadium Way). 641.3100

45 MISSION BASILICA SAN DIEGO DE ALCALÁ

The first Franciscan mission in California was the **Mission San Diego de Alcalá**, established by Padre Junípero Serra in 1769 on **Presidio Hill** overlooking Mission Valley and Old Town. The mission was moved six miles upriver to this location in 1773, then nearly destroyed in an Indian uprising in 1775. But by the early 1830s the mission was firmly established and the Native Americans were either converted or displaced. The mission was restored in 1931. The church is a simple, small wooden chapel with little adornment. The **Father Luis Jayme Museum** at the mission is a permanent interfaith ecclesiastical art museum and includes original mission records, liturgical robes, books, and relics. The museum was named after Father Jayme, a Franciscan missionary who was martyred by the Kumeyaay during the 1775 uprising. Mass is held morning and afternoon most days, with multiple services on Sunday. ♦ Admission to tour buildings and grounds. Daily. San Diego Mission Rd (between Mission Gorge and Rancho Mission Rds). 281.8449. www.missionsandiego.com

POINT LOMA/ HARBOR ISLAND/ SHELTER ISLAND

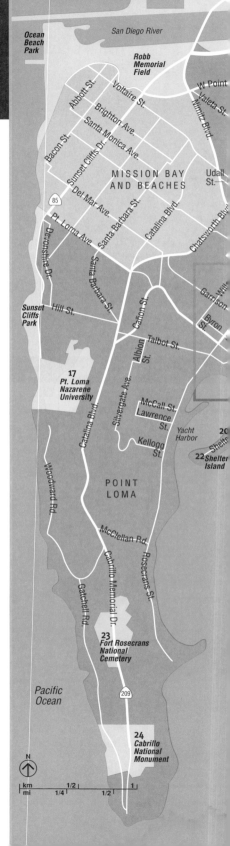

Point Loma may be the most beautiful spot in San Diego (with the possible exception of the more refined La Jolla). Pines and junipers twist and bend in the stiff winds atop the point's treacherous cliffs, jutting 500 feet above sea level. Handsome homes and gardens rise proudly behind protective hedges on twisting streets named for authors from Byron to Zola. **Fort Rosecrans**, a 71-acre garden with bright white tombstones, guards the point's southern end like a silent sentinel protecting the sloping hillsides from encroachment. At the tip, **Cabrillo National Monument**, where Juan Rodríguez Cabrillo landed in 1542, perches above the waves, offering rugged nature, nautical vessels, gray whales, and spectacular views. As befits Point Loma's seafaring history, the US Navy and the Marine Corps have commandeered much of the land with large compounds that include the **Marine Recruit Depot**, the **Fleet Anti-Sub Warfare School**, and the **Space and Naval Warfare Systems Center**.

Various settlers were determined to bring Point Loma fame and financial gain. Nineteenth-century residents lived in shacks made of cowhides while they operated lucrative tanneries and tallow-rendering businesses. Chinese immigrants anchored their junks along the point's shores, beginning the fishing industry that would be passed on to the Italians and then the Portuguese, whose descendants still dock their boats in Point Loma's marinas.

Point Loma was also the home of the colorful Madame Katherine Tingley, a dedicated theosophist. Madame Tingley created a commune named **Lomaland**,

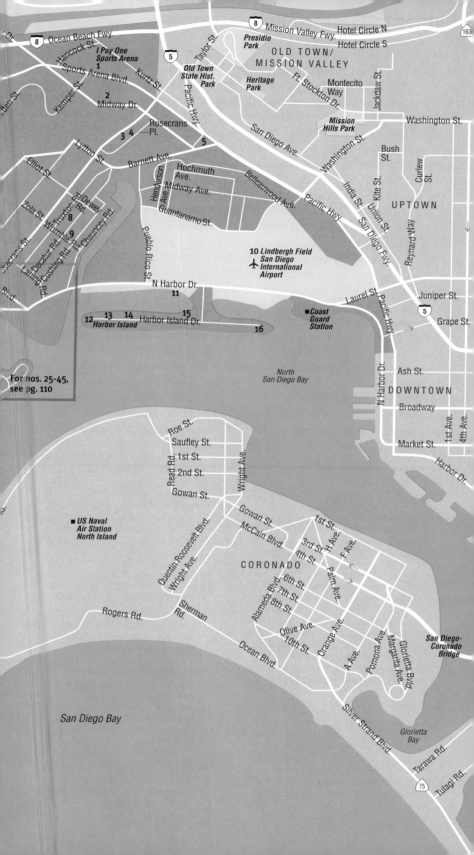

which caused quite a stir from 1897 to 1942. Residents sought divine wisdom through the study of comparative religion, philosophy, literature, theater, and art. By the 1930s, however, spiritualism was on a steady decline and the community began to fall apart. Treasured buildings were destroyed, and the lands passed through a series of owners until taken over by **Point Loma Nazarene College,** which has its administration offices in one of the remaining houses from Madame Tingley's utopia. Point Loma gained notoriety once again in 2004 when a former restaurant on the waterfront was converted into a customized 5,000-square-foot house for MTV's 2004 *The Real World: San Diego* show.

The point's neighbors are not as naturally and historically endowed. Two of the most popular spots—Harbor Island and Shelter Island—were both created from landfill. Both have become picturesque tourist enclaves, where hotels, restaurants, and parks flourish amid lush lawns and majestic palms, and marinas fill the bay with private boats. Nearby is **Lindbergh Field,** San Diego's international airport.

Harbor Island was built from 3.5 million tons of silt and sludge dredged from the **San Diego Bay** to make way for the navy's aircraft carriers. Hotels soon lined the fake island and were eventually joined by a lineup of restaurants, including one in a paddle wheeler (now closed).

Shelter Island is a former submerged shoal that rose above the water line as another dumping ground for dredged dirt. Ever since the city built a causeway on top of the landfill in 1950, hotels, boatyards, and restaurants have steadily filled every inch on the shores, facing east to the lights of downtown and west to the palatial estates and steep cliffs of Point Loma. On weekend mornings, hundreds of boats launch for scuba diving and fishing trips along the point or out in the open sea. The island's nautical bent is firmly anchored by the **San Diego Yacht Club** and by San Diego's most venerable boat brokerages and builders.

1 iPayOne Center

This outdated eyesore, formerly the **San Diego Sports Arena,** holds too few people (14,200) for a major-league hockey or basketball franchise, and is a dismal place for concerts. Still, it's the biggest indoor venue in town, so music lovers have to put up with the nosebleed seats and lousy acoustics for now. The arena is best used for ice shows, volleyball tournaments, and exhibition games. The parking lot is used for a giant swap meet on Saturday and Sunday during daylight hours. ◆ Box office: daily. 3500 Sports Arena Blvd (between Rosecrans and Hancock Sts). Office, 224.4171. www.sandiegoarena.com

2 Fairouz

★★$ Owner Al-Nashashibi, a native of Jerusalem, was an attorney in Kuwait before coming to San Diego and opening this restaurant; he has since brought in many family members to help run it. The food is consistently good and inexpensive, especially the excellent hummus, falafel, and stuffed grape leaves. The combination plates—big enough to split—offer generous samplings of many dishes. There's a bountiful, inexpensive vegetarian lunch buffet, and the dinner menu has been expanded to include chicken, beef, and lamb dishes. ◆ Middle Eastern ◆ Daily, lunch and dinner. 3166 Midway Dr (near Rosecrans St). 225.0308

3 Newbreak Coffee Co.

★$ There's a good array of pricey cakes, muffins, desserts, breakfast burritos, and omelettes to accompany the standard espresso coffee drinks. Patrons scrunch into movie-house seats rescued from the **Loma Theater** and dangle their feet from high bar stools. There's a small shop with an excellent selection of coffees, teas, and accoutrements. ◆ Coffeehouse ◆ M-Sa, 6:30AM-7PM; Su, 8AM-5PM. 3145 Rosecrans St (between Lytton St and Midway Dr). 224.2891. &

4 Bookstar

Movie lovers moaned in unison at the passing of the 1945 **Loma Theater,** one of the last big screens in town. Just when it

BIRD'S-EYE VIEWS

The **San Diego Bay** area is known for its sweeping vistas. Here are several of the very best:

* **Coronado Bridge**
* The top of the 70-foot dip on the **Giant Dipper** roller coaster in **Belmont Park**
* Landing at **Lindbergh Field**
* Hot-air balloons over **Del Mar**
* **Sea World Tower**
* The **Skyfari** ride at the **San Diego Zoo**

* **Cabrillo Monument**
* **Bertrand at Mr. A's** restaurant
* **Fort Rosecrans Cemetery**
* **Salk Institute**
* **Mount Soledad**
* **Palomar Observatory**
* **Mount Helix**

seemed the theater would certainly be torn down to make space for a new strip mall, the **Bookstar** chain bought the building and commissioned **Alamo Architects** to refurbish it. The restored tail-fin marquee touts the latest best-sellers, whereas the old silver screen is the backdrop for an impressive newsstand. You can use your Barnes & Noble membership cards here. M-Th, 10AM-9PM; F, Sa, 10AM-10PM. 3150 Rosecrans Pl (between Lytton St and Midway Dr). 225.0465. ⅃

5 US MARINE CORPS RECRUIT DEPOT

During the military's boom years, thousands of recruits passed through here so quickly that graduations were held every Friday morning. The compound, originally designed in 1920 by **Balboa Park**'s master architect **Bertram Goodhue**, contains several Spanish-style buildings with red-tile roofs and classic archways. Stuccoed in a soft gold color, these buildings seem almost to glow in the sunlight. Pacific Hwy (between Barnett Ave and Rosecrans St). Information, 524.4426

6 POINT LOMA ELLIOT HOSTEL

$ Affiliated with Hostelling International, this well-tended, colorfully decorated hostel with a very welcoming vibe is inexpensive and well situated in a residential neighborhood on a main bus route. A grocery store, library (with free Internet access), and Laundromat are located nearby. Ocean Beach is a 30-minute walk or 10-minute bus ride west. There are 52 beds in private and shared rooms. All rooms have shared baths. Kitchen facilities are available. ♦ No credit cards accepted. 3790 Udall St (at Worden St). 223.4778; fax 223.1883. www.hihostels.com

7 THE VENETIAN

★★$$ Owner Vince Giacalone, who opened this pizza parlor in 1965, now counts on his sons Frank and Joey to help run the business. Many Point Lomans grew up on the Venetian's pizza, which is among the best in town. The secret is a crisp crust—not too thin, not too thick—topped with an unusually spicy sauce. It's great with masses of paper-thin onion slices and fresh tomatoes on top. Takeout is available. ♦ Italian ♦ M-F, lunch and dinner; Sa, Su, dinner. 3663 Voltaire St (between Chatsworth Blvd and Worden St). 223.8197

8 WINE STEALS

This informal wine bar draws all comers but has a knack for attracting friends who come for reasonably priced wine sold by the glass or bottle (slightly above liquor store prices, plus reasonable corkage). The 200-plus selection features some offbeat choices from California, Argentina, France, and Australia, and a short menu of comestibles includes pizzas, panini, and artisan cheese boards. ♦ Su and Tu-W, 11AM-11PM; M, 4PM-11PM; Th-Sa, 11AM-midnight. 2970 Truxtun Rd (between Womble and Dewey Rds). 221.1959; also at 1243 University Ave (between Richmond and Vermont Sts). 295.1188. ⅃ www.winestealssd.com

Restaurants/Clubs: Red | Hotels: Purple | Shops: Orange | Outdoors/Parks: Green | Sights/Culture: Blue

9 LIBERTY STATION

Between 1923 and 1999, the navy used this prime waterfront property adjacent to the airport for the **US Naval Training Center**. When the base was closed, proposals for the property included a waterfront park and a man-made river connecting downtown and Mission Bay. Few were shocked when all those lofty ideas were scuttled in favor of a $500 million, 361-acre mixed-use commercial development. The residential development has 349 homes; the 125 acres designated for parks and open space include a boat channel and existing 9-hole golf course. The development is gradually becoming a city within the city, with an elementary school, a high-tech high school, and **The Rock Church and Academy**, a Christian mega-church with about 7,000 worshippers. Families have moved into rows and rows of attached housing. Business districts with markets, restaurants, and services are gradually opening and becoming established. The chains have moved in (Trader Joe's, Panera) and are providing stiff competition for small businesses in Point Loma. A farmers' market, concerts, and other events draw outsiders. Marriott is planning to open a Nickelodeon Hotel (the first of its kind) in 2010, though not all permits were issued by press time. If built, it could have a large water-park feature and all sorts of company-themed activities and treats. A **Marriott Courtyard** is under construction and slated to open in 2008. ♦ 2750 Womble Rd (between Cushing and Decatur Rds). 794.1428. www.libertystation.com

10 LINDBERGH FIELD SAN DIEGO INTERNATIONAL AIRPORT

When Charles Lindbergh was practicing his moves in the *Spirit of St. Louis* back in 1927, the tidelands along the bay seemed a perfect launching pad. Today they seem an odd use of space for an international airport, with jets roaring over crowded neighborhoods less than 3 miles from downtown. For detailed information and a map, see the Orientation chapter. ♦ 3707 N Harbor Dr (between Laurel and Pueblo Rico Sts). 686.8095

11 SPANISH LANDING

Take the afternoon off to enjoy a picnic on this beautiful strip of grassy, tree-shaded land overlooking the harbor. The view of sailboats adrift in the bay makes this the perfect spot for harborside walks, though the traffic from North Harbor Drive is distracting. Barbecues, picnic tables, and rest rooms are available. The **Cancer Survivors Park** at the south end of the landing is one of a series in the country donated by Richard Bloch, a two-time cancer survivor. The park, designed to provide encouragement and comfort for those with cancer, includes a waterfall, bronze figurines, and plaques with inspirational messages, all topped by white sails that glow at night. ♦ N Harbor Dr (between Harbor Island Dr and Nimitz Blvd

12 TOM HAM'S LIGHTHOUSE

$$$ This restaurant's working Coast Guard beacon flashes every 5 seconds from a 55-foot cupola, which is an exact replica of the **Old Point Loma Lighthouse** tower. Because the building juts out into the water, the view, if not the food, is terrific, and the interior boasts an extensive collection of California seafaring memorabilia. It's worth a visit, but stick with lower-priced entrées. The champagne brunch is a big hit, especially on Easter, Mother's Day, and graduation weekends. ♦ Steak/seafood ♦ M-F, lunch and dinner; Sa, dinner; Su, brunch and dinner. 2150 Harbor Island Dr. 291.9110. &

13 THE BOAT HOUSE

★$$$ One of the first businesses on the island, this restaurant has been through several remodelings and still has one of the best views of the bay. The menu features well-prepared seafood and steak; try the halibut with lemon–macadamia nut butter or the chicken teriyaki. The island is full of mediocre restaurants; this is one of the better options. ♦ Seafood ♦ Daily, lunch and dinner; Su, brunch. Reservations recommended for dinner and brunch. 2040 Harbor Island Dr. 291.8011. &

13 HARBOR SAILBOATS

This is the place to charter a sailboat (with or without captain) or to sign up for sailing lessons. ♦ Daily. 2040 Harbor Island Dr. 291.9568. www.harborsailboats.com

14 HILTON SAN DIEGO AIRPORT HARBOR ISLAND

$$ One of the oldest hotels on the island, this isn't flashy and luxurious, but it's a good bargain for lodgings on the water and often has special rate discounts. The lobby and 207 rooms are acceptable but hardly exciting, with a staid hunter-green-and-burgundy color scheme, but the rooms have all the right amenities for business travelers, from coffeemakers to irons to dataports. The restaurant is only fair, but the health club

and pool are fine. ♦ 1960 Harbor Island Dr. 291.6700, 800/445.8667; fax 293.0694. ♿ www.sandiegoairport.hilton.com

15 SHERATON SAN DIEGO HOTEL AND MARINA

$$$ Two hotels in one, the **Sheraton** has 1,044 rooms in its two towers. In the original 698-room **East Tower**, the lobby's ceiling frescoes are lit by a computerized system designed to replicate sky patterns at different times of the day. The rooms here are smaller than in the **West Tower**, but proximity to the recreation facilities is a plus. The West Tower's 345 rooms have separate seating areas, work spaces (if you must), and amenities like terry-cloth robes. All rooms have coffeemakers and hair dryers and the dreamy Sheraton Sweet Sleeper™ bed with plush-top mattress and a choice of pillows. The two towers share lavish facilities, including three pools, three tennis courts, a health club and spa, jogging trails, three restaurants, and a marina. Though the airport is actually within walking distance (if you're not hauling luggage), the noise from the jets is not bad. ♦ 1380 Harbor Island Dr. 291.2900, 800/325.3535; fax 692.2363. ♿ www.sheraton.com/sandiegomarina

16 REUBEN E. LEE

This Mississippi-style paddle wheeler was built specifically as a restaurant. It operated as a restaurant geared toward groups of tourists (lousy food, great view) for many years but eventually closed down. It's still there, but is used only for private functions. 880 E Harbor Dr.

16 ISLAND PRIME & C LEVEL

★$$$ The Cohn family operates many of Downtown's most popular eateries, and took over the view off Harbor Island when the Reuben E. Lee closed. They opened a side-by-side restaurant and lounge with extraordinary views of San Diego Bay and Downtown. Chef Deborah Scott, who's gained a local following at Little Italy's Indigo Grill, created a steak and seafood menu that suits tourists' expectations for Island Prime. The steaks outshine the overcooked seafood, and the views from the window-side table far outshine those from other seats. The room is cacophonous, but not nearly as loud as in **Level C**, the site's very happening lounge. Waiters rush about the waterside tables crammed close together, and steamer clams and oysters, beer-battered fish and chips, and other bar fare in the lounge are

better bets for hungry diners on a budget. ♦ Steak/seafood ♦ Daily, lunch and dinner. 880 E Island Harbor Dr. 298.6802

17 POINT LOMA NAZARENE UNIVERSITY

You couldn't dream of a better setting for an institute of higher learning than here along Point Loma's ridge, on rugged cliffs above the Pacific. This priceless property, originally built in 1895, housed Madame Katherine Tingley's **Theosophical Institute**; her ghost reportedly haunts the campus. Tingley and her followers opposed the materialism of science and all dogmatic theology. She was also opposed to war, capital punishment, and electric power poles. One of the institute's original buildings, **Mieras Hall**, stands in the middle of the campus, its purple domes (which bear a startling resemblance to red onions) acting as a landmark. It's hard to imagine any studying getting done here, with dorms looking out to sea and tennis courts above the ocean. The view from the campus is breathtaking. ♦ 3900 Lomaland Dr (off Catalina Blvd). 849.2200. www.pointloma.edu

18 BAY CLUB HOTEL AND MARINA

$$ This low-rise, wood-shingled resort hotel offers a welcome escape from the predominant tropical theme of other Shelter Island resorts. The rooms at the back of the hotel have balconies looking out to the boats moored at marinas and at gorgeous homes and Point Loma; the rooms at the front look across the way to downtown; and second-floor rooms have views both ways. The 105 rooms and suites have refrigerators and desks, and there's a small pool, spa, and weight room. There's no restaurant, but a full complimentary breakfast buffet is available. Relax on one of the comfortable bamboo couches near the fireplace in the lounge, which overlooks the marina. Complimentary airport and Amtrak station shuttles are available. ♦ 2131 Shelter Island Dr. 224.8888, 800/672.0800; fax 225.1604. www.bayclubhotel.com

19 BEST WESTERN ISLAND PALMS HOTEL

$$ Cozy first-floor marina-view suites and rooms have terraces, but the rooms without views tend to be small. The best of the 93 rooms are the 29 suites with kitchenettes, and slips are available in the marina. The sundeck features a whale-shaped pool and whirlpool overlooking the marina. The **Blue Wave Bar & Grill** serves all meals. The rates

---

Restaurants/Clubs: Red | Hotels: Purple | Shops: Orange | Outdoors/Parks: Green | Sights/Culture: Blue

are among the lowest on the island. This is a good choice for conventioneers willing to drive 10 minutes to downtown. ◆ 2051 Shelter Island Dr. 222.0561, 800/922.2336; fax 222.9760. www.islandpalms.com

20 Kona Kai Resort

$$ Built in 1952 as the Kona Kai, this resort was a Polynesian-style post–World War II honeymooners' dream. It's been revived with more modern Mediterranean architecture and décor and has changed names over the years. It's back to Kona Kai now, though some sundries still carry the former Shelter Pointe name. The 237 guest rooms and suites are decorated with bleached wood armoires and desks, king or double beds, and blue floral drapes and spreads. Most have a view of the 516-slip marina or the gardens. The townhouse suites have separate bedrooms and kitchens. Amenities include two swimming pools, two tennis courts, a health spa, and a waterfront restaurant. ◆ 1551 Shelter Island Dr. 221.8000, 800/566.2524; fax 221.5953. www.shelterpointe.com

21 Tunaman's Memorial

This bronze sculpture by F. Vianello of three larger-than-life fishermen casting their lines for yellowfin tuna was erected in 1986. The inscription reads: "Honoring those that built an industry and remembering those that departed this harbor in the sun and did not return." ◆ East side of Shelter Island (south of the fishing pier)

22 Yokohama Friendship Bell

Dedicated to San Diego from her sister city in Japan, this 2.5-ton bronze bell was installed at the end of Shelter Island Drive in

Eight weeks after Easter, Point Loma's Portuguese community celebrates the Festa do Espirito Santo, a feast of thanksgiving, which climaxes with a festive parade.

The first lighthouse in the harbor was installed in 1769 and consisted of a pole formed from the tallest tree on the point equipped with a rope to haul a lantern to the top at sunset each day. Tallow candles provided the light.

There once was a canyon on the south side of Point Loma dubbed Hermit's Canyon. A hermit made the canyon his home, planting fig, lemon, and orange trees; carving chairs from sandstone; and making a tub for collecting rainwater.

In the Ice Age, Point Loma was an island.

1960 as a symbol of eternal friendship. **James Hubbel** added a sculpture near the park in 2004. Titled *Pacific Spirit,* the bronze piece depicts a graceful female form rising from the water. ◆ Southern tip of Shelter Island Dr

22 Pacific Rim Park

◐ Designed by architect **James Hubbell** with architecture students from San Diego's sister cities in China, Mexico, and Russia, this small park is a peaceful setting for surveying the harbor. The park's tiled mosaics flow around a spurting fountain and under an ironwork archway and are meant to represent peace and unity among nations. ◆ Southern tip of Shelter Island Dr

23 Fort Rosecrans National Cemetery

◐ Seventy-one acres of white headstones flank both sides of Cabrillo Memorial Drive. One of California's five national cemeteries, it has been the burial site for San Diego's military personnel since 1899. A 75-foot obelisk honors 60 men who were killed in the USS *Bennington* boiler explosion of 1905. A stroll along the grounds affords a spectacular and moving view of the San Diego Harbor and beyond. ◆ Daily. Cabrillo Memorial Dr. 553.2084

24 Cabrillo National Monument

◐ The most awesome panoramic view in San Diego can be had from a rocky promontory 400 feet above sea level at the tip of Point Loma. From its heights, one can see the Pacific, San Diego Harbor, Coronado, and south to Mexico. The point is a seafarer's delight, a navigational pointer marking the entrance to San Diego Bay and the continental US. In 1542, a Portuguese explorer named Juan Rodríguez Cabrillo sailed into this "closed and very good harbor," anchored inside what is now Ballast Point (formerly known as Fort Guijarros, which translates to "Fort Cobblestones"), and named the bay San Miguel. Spanish explorers and pirates charted the point and the bay; three centuries later, the US Navy claimed the point, which now is closed to the public and used as a submarine base.

When President Woodrow Wilson established Cabrillo National Monument in 1913, it was half an acre in size, the smallest national monument in the US. President Dwight Eisenhower transferred 80.6 acres from the navy to the National Park system in 1959; ever since, the military and the park have kept the point a relatively undisturbed natural habitat. For a good overview of the continued military presence in San Diego,

MUSICAL NIGHTS

Between May and October, the lawn between **Humphrey's** restaurant and the marina fills with folding chairs for intimate nighttime concerts under the stars. Lazy San Diego nights are stirred by such blues players as B.B. King, Buddy Guy, and Robert Cray; such jazz musicians as Al Jarreau, Huey Lewis & the News, Dave Brubeck, and George Benson; and such comedians as Dana Carvey, David Spade, and Jay Leno. Freeloaders catch the show from dinghies and kayaks bobbing in the water by the stage or listen to the amplified music on the lawns outside Humphrey's. Dinner packages include a pre-show meal and guaranteed seating for the concert in rows 2–7. Tickets can be purchased at Humphrey's box office (recorded information, 523.1010; restaurant, 224.3577). Tickets can also be obtained by phone through Ticketmaster (220.8497).

check out the observation deck behind the gift shop and the charts of military ships and aircraft based along the point and across the bay at the **North Island Naval Air Station**. You too will be able to tell the difference between a carrier and a sub. A small exhibit hall includes a scale model of Cabrillo's sailing ship, the *San Salvador*. Slide shows about the whales and tide pools are presented throughout the day in the auditorium. The park's bookstore and gift shop are worth a visit, especially if you're into local history or nautical stuff. Save your souvenir shopping for here. ◆ Admission; parking fee. Daily. Take Rosecrans St to Cañon St to Catalina Blvd. Proceed on Catalina Blvd, which changes to Cabrillo Memorial Dr, to end of the point. 557.5450. www.nps.gov/cabr

Within Cabrillo National Monument:

CABRILLO STATUE

A statue of Juan Rodríguez Cabrillo was sculpted by Portuguese artist Alvario de Bree in 1904. Through a series of mishaps, it sat in storage until 1942, when California State Senator Ed Fletcher somehow "kidnapped" the statue and had it installed near the harbor. In 1949, the statue was moved to the grounds of Cabrillo National Monument, where it weathered the winds until 1988, when a visiting Portuguese admiral commented on its sad condition. A sandstone statue took its place in 1989. ◆ East of the Visitors' Center

WHALE OVERLOOK

Ⓟ Between December and February, you may see the annual migration of the gray whales as they pass Point Loma on their way from the Bering Sea to the lagoons of Baja, California. The lookout perched above the point's tip has a good vantage point, but the whales are becoming less visible each year as they swim farther from shore to avoid the hordes of whale-watching boats. ◆ West side of the point

OLD POINT LOMA LIGHTHOUSE

Beaming its beacon a whopping 462 feet above sea level, the original lighthouse served as the southernmost Pacific Coast beacon in the US from 1855 to 1891. Called Star of the Silver Gate, it was designed in Cape Cod style by **Francis Kelly** and **Francis Gibbons**. The lighthouse deteriorated miserably until 1933, when the National Park Service took responsibility for its restoration. You can't actually climb the tower or visit the rooms, but you can peek in. The building is distinctive and beautiful. ◆ Center of the park

BAYSIDE TRAIL

Ⓟ This winding dirt trail curves down the rocky slopes of the point, passing the former hunting and gathering grounds of the Kumeyaay people, who inhabited the shores long before Cabrillo anchored. Take note of the panting hikers headed back uphill and gauge your distance accordingly. A map of the hike with good sketches and descriptions of native plants is available at the ranger-station counter in the gift shop. Wear sturdy shoes when you hike around the cliffs and stay away from the edges, which can crumble with the slightest provocation. ◆ South of the *Cabrillo* statue

TIDE POOLS

Ⓟ The rocky coast of the point's western side harbors a flourishing colony of tide pools. The best time to see the 100 or so different species of marine flora and fauna is during the low tides of fall, winter, and spring. Check the tides in the newspaper or local TV news. Wooden fences and dirt trails lead to

Restaurants/Clubs: Red | Hotels: Purple | Shops: Orange | Outdoors/Parks: Green | Sights/Culture: Blue

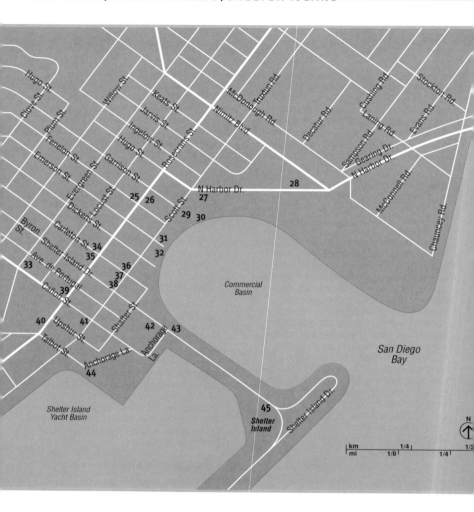

several good pools. Watch your footing—those rocks get slippery. ♦ Cabrillo Rd (at Cabrillo Memorial Dr)

HOTEL

25 THE PEARL HOTEL

$$ One doesn't expect to find a Palm Springs mid-century hotel amid taco stands and KFC on busy Rosecrans Street. But entrepreneurs betting on a renaissance have taken a rundown motel and turned it into a little gem with 23 high-style rooms, heavy on tech toys (Wi-Fi, LCD, Internet radio), that have a vintage-modern flair. Everything was still coming together at press time, but the property is slated to have a restaurant,

lounge/bar, saltwater pool with a projection screen, and all sorts of fun amenities. A special after-midnight "Play & Stay" rate is available if you lack a designated driver. ♦ 1410 Rosecrans St (between Fenelon and Garrison Sts). 877/PEARL-SD; fax 226.6161 www.thepearlsd.com

26 RAMADA LIMITED SAN DIEGO AIRPORT

$ Popular with fishermen and boaters, this streetside chain property has only 80 rooms which means you can usually get a lounge chair by the heated pool. The harbor views are excellent from the top-floor rooms; many have balconies. Microwaves, refrigerators, and coffeemakers in the rooms make the hotel a good choice for those on a budget. The **Captain's Quarters** bar and restaurant hosts a popular Monday-night steak dinner.

♦ 1403 Rosecrans St (between Fenelon and Garrison Sts). 225.9461; fax 225.1163. www.ramadasandiegoairport.com

27 PIZZA NOVA

★★$ This two-story building with great water views from the upstairs deck is one of a wildly successful chain of gourmet pizza-pasta cafés. Best bets include the tequila chicken fettuccine, roasted garlic shrimp pizza, Oriental chicken salad, and chopped salad with turkey, ham, and cheese. Check local papers for the frequent coupons, and get by inexpensively with the pizza or pasta and salad lunch specials. Delivery is available. ♦ Californian ♦ Daily, lunch and dinner. 5120 N Harbor Dr (off Scott St). 226.0268. www.pizzanova.net

28 HOLIDAY INN SAN DIEGO BAYSIDE

$$ This four-story brown-and-white hotel offers marina luxury at inland prices. The basic rooms were remodeled in 2006-2007 and have fresh carpeting and linens; reserve a room on the top floor on the south side for a good view of the boats in the bay. The proximity to the airport and marinas makes up for the lack of luxury. The 237 rooms have refrigerators and coffeemakers, and the hotel has a coffee shop, fitness center, and small beach on the bay. Kids' rooms have bunk beds and Playstations. Children under 12 eat free when dining with a parent at the inn's Point Loma Cafe. ♦ 4875 N Harbor Dr (off Nimitz Blvd). 224.3621, 800/345.9995; fax 224.3629. & www.holinnbayside.com

29 FISHERMAN'S LANDING

A fleet of short- and long-range boats are available for charter or party-boat fishing trips; whale-watching and long-range trips are also available. ♦ 2838 Garrison St (at Scott St). 221.8500; recorded information on boats and fish count, 224.1421. www.fishermanslanding.com

30 MUNICIPAL SPORTFISHING PIER

Although the majority of San Diego's tourists hop from the **Convention Center** to **Old Town** to the **Zoo**, a special breed heads here. They usually carry coolers and tackle boxes and crash at various budget hotels no more than a block from their boats. They're up at 5AM, stalking tuna, yellowtail, and dorado; stop by in the afternoon for a survey of the day's catch. Several commercial sportfishing boats depart from this pier; most companies also offer whale-watching tours. Parking is at a premium. ♦ Scott St (at the foot of Garrison St). No phone

31 H&M LANDING

This is one of the largest sportfishing operations in San Diego, with private charters and party boats to the Point Loma kelp beds, the Coronado islands, and San Diego Bay. Also available are long-range trips to Baja, and in the winter, whale-watching trips. ♦ 2803 Emerson St (at Scott St). 222.1144; daily fish count, 224.2800

31 LEE PALM SPORTFISHERS

This outfit's *Red Rooster III*, a 105-foot boat specially outfitted for sportfishing, is one of the most popular among serious anglers. The fishing trips last anywhere from 3 to 21 days. Anglers rave about the crew and revere the cooks. ♦ 2801 Emerson St (at Scott St). 224.3857. www.redrooster3.com

32 POINT LOMA SEAFOODS

★★★$ A terrific seafood experience can be had at this take-out seafood café and retail fish market, which is always noisy and jammed. Take a number for your order—a squid or crab-salad sandwich on soft sourdough; ceviche still tasting of the sea; fresh albacore with mayonnaise, celery, and red onions; heaping plates of fried shrimp, scallops, fish, and squid with fries and slaw; fresh lemonade; chocolate-chip cookies. Take your food to the enclosed patio or the outdoor tables by the waterfront for a postcard view of the marina. The fish market is the best in town, with the pinkest, freshest selection of local catches and a lavish display of smoked fish and sushi. Offer to bring dinner, then stop here for swordfish or wild salmon (worth their weight in dollars), red snapper, yellowfin tuna, or halibut. Add a loaf or two of savory sourdough, a bottle of wine, and some brownies—and a lemon, of course. Don't miss this place! ♦ Seafood ♦ Daily. 2805 Emerson St (at Scott St). 223.1109. www.plsf.com

33 ST. AGNES ROMAN CATHOLIC CHURCH

Since 1933, this immaculately kept Spanish-style church in the La Playa area of Point Loma has been the center of San Diego's Portuguese community. The surrounding neighborhood, with perfectly maintained homes and neatly manicured lawns, is still very much alive with Portuguese culture, which has been a part of the city's life since the 1880s, when the first fishermen from the Azores sailed into San Diego Bay. ♦ 1145 Evergreen St (at Ave de Portugal). 223.2200

34 Pt. Loma Camera

If you're into underwater photography, this is the place to check out the latest gear and get straight answers from knowledgeable clerk-shutterbugs. The selection of all types of cameras is excellent, and the staff can often fix small problems without having to send your camera out for costly repairs. ♦ M-Sa. 1310 Rosecrans St (between Carleton and Dickens Sts). 224.2719

35 West Marine

This outfit is one of the largest boating retailers in the world, with a successful Internet catalogue sales business. You'll find everything for the boating life here—from clothing and calendars to hats and hardware. ♦ Daily. 1250 Rosecrans St (at Carleton St). 225.8844

36 Seabreeze Nautical Books and Charts

This shop caters to every nautical need and whim and is bound to warm the cockles of any old salt's heart. You'll find every type of boating gadget, clothes, trinkets, nautical art, videos, and books. Salespeople are friendly, accommodating, and knowledgeable about the boating life. ♦ Daily. 1254 Scott St (at Carleton St). 223.8989

37 Hook, Line & Sinker

Jigs with neon pink tassels for attracting dorado, rods and reels for the mightiest marlin, and all the latest info on the local fishing scene can be picked up here. ♦ Daily. 1224 Scott St (between Carleton St and Shelter Island Dr). 224.1336.

38 Miguel's Cocina

★$ Brightly painted wooden masks and balsa-wood parrots create a party atmosphere in this lively restaurant, although the TV in the bar can be distracting. The menu features Mexican food with a flair for seafood—try the calamari *relleno* (stuffed), topped with jalapeño white sauce. Children and light eaters benefit from the extensive à la carte menu. The pleasant second-floor patio is heated on cool evenings. ♦ Mexican/seafood ♦ M-Sa, lunch and dinner; Su, brunch and dinner. 2912 Shelter Island Dr (at Scott St). 224.2401. www.brigantine.com

39 Con Pane Rustic Breads & Cafe

$ The lines outside this fragrant bakery don't discourage loyal patrons craving fresh sourdough, whole-grain, and specialty breads. There are tables indoors and out for feasting on sandwiches, or take your lunch to go and eat down by the waterfront. ♦ Coffeehouse/bakery ♦ Th-Tu. 1110 Rosecrans St (at Cañon St). 224.4344

40 Living Room Coffeehouse

★$ What was once the **Jennings House**, built in 1886, is now a comfy coffeehouse. Sandwiches, soup, quiche, and individual pizzas are served throughout the day for a light lunch or dinner. Thai coffee and Italian sodas bring an exotic touch to the California cuisine. Business bunches up during breakfast, lunch, and the after-dinner hours; the rest of the day, customers settle in for hours over local newspapers and the hippest magazines. ♦ Coffeehouse ♦ Daily. 1018 Rosecrans St (between Talbot and Upshur Sts). 222.6852. www.livingroomcafe.com

41 Old Venice

★★★$ The pizzas are so good at this Point Loma institution that the recipe was part of the deal when the business changed hands in the 1980s. Try the Greek Goddess pizza (with feta cheese and olives) or a veal Parmesan sandwich. If you've got a sweet tooth, save room for the "monster cookie," loaded with chocolate chips and pecans and topped with gelato. Ambience is informal; every table has butcher paper and felt pens to amuse the little ones and their adult companions. Jazz tapes play in the background as patrons unwind over wine and focaccia with fresh pesto, or Magic Mushrooms (mushrooms stuffed with shrimp and crabmeat). Adjacent to the dining room is a cozy bar, with stools along its green marble counter and upholstered chairs by the fireplace. ♦ Italian ♦ M-Sa, lunch and dinner; Su, dinner. 2910 Cañon St (at Scott St). 222.5888

42 The Brigantine

★★$$$ Lunch and dinner specials are changed each month but typically offer a selection of seafood and meats, including catch of the day and marinated jumbo shrimp, and fresh veggies, all basted in butter and charbroiled. The décor is nautical with lots of unfinished wood and shiny black booths for privacy. Outdoor tables on a narrow second-floor balcony are nice, but the view involves more parking lot than water. The bar fills up in late afternoon with deckhands and yacht owners. The Brig Burger is popular, and the Cobb salad is a winner. ◆ Seafood/steak ◆ M-Sa, lunch and dinner; Sa, Su, dinner. 2725 Shelter Island Dr (between Anchorage La and Shafter St). 224.2871. www.brigantine.com

43 RED SAILS INN

★$ This old-line waterfront seafood house (since 1935) is a bit musty inside, but it's still a favorite with the locals—particularly the sailors and boaters, who can get pretty boisterous in the bar. Nautical décor with bay windows overlooking a marina, and fast, no-frills service with plastic plates and paper napkins, add to the salty atmosphere. Try the good basic omelettes in the morning; later in the day, order some great shrimp or crab Louis, or breaded jumbo shrimp with fries. Head for the waterfront deck with shaded tables on a sunny day. ◆ Seafood ◆ Daily, breakfast, lunch, and dinner. 2614 Shelter Island Dr (near Anchorage La). 223.3030. www.theredsails.com

44 SAN DIEGO YACHT CLUB

The peaked red roof of the clubhouse rises above a seascape of masts and sails. From the water, the building looks cool, inviting, and important, conjuring images of blue blazers, jaunty caps, and ever-so-refined cordiality. When architect **Frederick Liebhardt** designed the building in 1964, he aimed for a classic seaworthy boathouse, not a clubhouse that could be perched at the edge of a golf course. In the end, the building reflected the image of the old **Coronado Boathouse**, which in turn echoes the towers and terraces of the **Hotel del Coronado**. When construction began, the existing house, an old navy barracks, was lifted and set in the parking lot, giving members a built-in reviewing stand for critiquing their emerging home, which weathered the gusts of opinion with aplomb to become the landmark of sailing in San Diego. Since its inception in 1885, the club has boasted a stellar roster of world-class sailing champions. This is a private club. ◆ 1011 Anchorage La (near Tarbot St). 221.8400. www.sdyc.org

45 HUMPHREY'S HALF MOON INN & SUITES

$$$ Take a trip to the islands without leaving the mainland. Surrounded by palm trees, sun-dappled decks, and poolside wet bars, this retro-Polynesian retreat is the island's original resort hotel. The owners also run the adjacent **Humphrey's** restaurant (see below), as well as an outdoor amphitheater famous for its summertime Concerts by the Bay series. Many of the 182 rooms and suites have views of either the marina or bay, and though they're far from spectacular, they do have carpeting and ceiling fans, hair dryers, and coffeemakers. Room service from Humphrey's is available. The low-key ambience and overgrown tropical isle landscaping make this a pleasant change from the more sterile high-rises. Opinions vary widely as to the hotel's quality. If you've been here before and love it, everything will be fine. If you're expecting modern facilities and fabulous beds and linens, go elsewhere. Special room rates are offered during slow times, but rooms are in big demand during the concert season. ◆ 2303 Shelter Island Dr. 224.3411, 800/542.7400; fax 224.3478. www.halfmooninn.com

Near Humphrey's Half Moon Inn & Suites:

HUMPHREY'S

★★$$$ The quintessential tropical décor is a bit dated, but the food—tasty mesquite-grilled fish, good lobster, excellent Cajun shrimp and corn chowder—is consistently good. The adjoining **Backstage Lounge** cocktail lounge has live music nightly. While away a Sunday at the lavish champagne brunch. ◆ Seafood ◆ M-Sa, breakfast, lunch, and dinner; Su, brunch and dinner. Reservations recommended for dinner. 2241 Shelter Island Dr. 224.3577. www.humphreysbythebay.com

MISSION BAY AND BEACHES

First, a word about dress codes. Shoes are out; rubber flip-flops are in. Shades (preferably name brands like Ray Ban, Oakley, or Vuarnet) are a must. Leave your cut-off jeans at home. Stock up on flimsy nylon runner's shorts and the briefest of tank tops in neon orange or pink. Cultivate a fondness for the aroma of coconut oil; tune your muscles until they're clearly defined. Practice catching a Frisbee and serving a volleyball. Assume a fun-comes-first attitude. Balance your beautiful bod atop skates or a bike and cruise like a pro.

Start at **Mission Bay Park**, a 4,236-acre panorama of Southern California at play. Spanish explorers called the area **False Bay** because the beautiful body of water they saw sometimes became swampy marshland with the fickle flow of the **San Diego River**. Channels were built to guide the river toward the open sea, but it wasn't until after World War II that San Diegans got serious about capitalizing on this area between the ocean and the **Clairemont Hills**. With public bonds and the Army Corps of Engineers, the river was successfully diverted to the sea by means of a channel that was deep enough for boats to travel in and out of the bay. The tidelands were dredged to create deep coves and sloping sandy beaches. The result was a park that was half land and half water, with two bridges linking 90 acres of developed public parks, 7,000 parking spaces, and slips for 2,500 boats. Seventy-five percent of Mission Bay is devoted to public parks and beaches; the remaining lands are leased to hotels, sportfishing companies, boatyards, and **Sea World**. To thousands of picnickers, joggers, water-skiers, and kite flyers, Mission Bay is where to go for company picnics and family reunions, marathon training and maximum relaxation, predawn fishing expeditions and sunset bonfires. The bay is also home to the newest trend in water sports: kiteboarding, which combines elements of windsurfing and kite flying. As you bike the winding cement sidewalks curving along the water's edge, let your mind go, soak in the sun's warmth and the sea's salty smell, and imagine being able to come to the bay every day after work to unwind. Seems San Diego's developers had some good ideas after all.

To the south, **Ocean Beach**, or OB, as it's called, is a small town at the end of I-8, where all roads lead to the beach. OB developed gradually, with a main street **Newport Avenue**, running toward the ocean, postwar tracts of California bungalows and Mission-style homes set in orderly straight lines up the hills toward Point Loma, and an abiding sense of neighborhood. Although fast-food chains and minimalls have been kept out, for the most part, antiques dealers have moved in setting up shop after shop along Newport Avenue. OB is neither gentrified nor yuppified, with just enough drawbacks to keep it from being "discovered." Proximity to the airport is perhaps the biggest flaw—visitors are usually blasted from their beds at 7AM when the first jets take off overhead with reverberations that set off the neighbors' car alarms. Then there's the OB reputation, distorted and magnified by legend and lore. Outsiders hear that the place is seamy and unsafe, a magnet for drifters and derelicts, where community standards are entirely too tolerant. It's true that eccentricities are encouraged here, but so is responsibility and civic involvement. OB is just like any other small town—it just happens to be at the beach with some of the best surfing waves in the county and the unparalleled vistas at **Sunset Cliffs**.

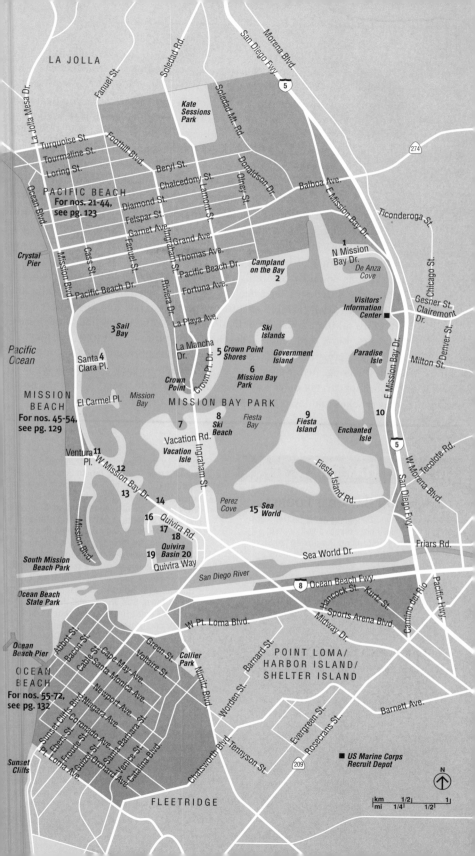

Just to the north, **Mission Beach** is a tourist attraction in search of a community. Its heart is a 2-mile-long peninsula, between the waters of Mission Bay and the Pacific Ocean, that's only a quarter-mile across at its widest point. The main drag, **Mission Boulevard**, runs from the southern tip of the peninsula to **Pacific Beach**. It becomes so overcrowded on summer weekends that the police close it to incoming traffic by noon and get real serious about parking tickets. Forget side streets—the peninsula only has two narrow, one-way streets that run parallel to the boulevard, with alleys and walkways squeezed between beat-up bungalows that abut futuristic condos. Every inch of Mission Beach is covered by bodies, buildings, and sand. The noise level is intense: In addition to boom boxes and shouted conversations, there are the screams from the **Belmont Park** roller coaster, the whirring of police and Coast Guard choppers overhead, and, faintly, the constant pounding of the surf. The boardwalk is action central, the epitome of the SoCal beach scene, a Hieronymus Bosch–type confluence of humanity hanging it *all* out in the sun.

The madness calms down considerably when you head north to Pacific Beach and the **Crystal Pier**. The daredevils on wheels are more considerate of pedestrians, the boardwalk is bordered with jasmine shrubs and pretty parks, and the loiterers are likely to be families taking a break from hauling coolers and umbrellas to the beach. Trendy restaurants, bars, and shops line **Garnet Avenue**, attracting outsiders in search of the hippest hangouts. Pacific Beach still has the horrendous Mission Boulevard traffic, but the congested system of alleys and back-to-back housing is replaced by wide neighborhood streets shaded by towering palms. Side streets lead to the area's least congested beaches and lawns, along **Sail Bay** and **Crown Point Shores**.

MISSION BAY PARK

1 MISSION BAY GOLF COURSE

You can get in a sunset game on the night-lighted, 18-hole executive golf course; practice your form on the driving range; or meet up with friends for a game in the sunshine. Watch for errant balls when you're playing 18 holes; this low-key course attracts more than its share of novice golfers. ♦ Admission. Daily. 2702 N Mission Bay Dr (between Clairemont Dr and Grand Ave). 858/581.7880

2 CAMPLAND ON THE BAY

Tucked away from the major thoroughfares of the bay is this 42-acre campground with 500 full-hookup spaces for RVs and 150 dirt spaces with fire rings. This is definitely the most scenic spot to park your motor home in the central San Diego area. Facilities include catamaran rentals, boat slips, pool, park areas, a barbecue café, and an ice-cream parlor. Pets are allowed, and there's a 2-night minimum stay on summer weekends. The grounds are full much of the time; make reservations at least 6 months in advance for the spring and summer months. The

spots by the marshlands (designated a wildlife reserve and a fabulous spot for bird-watching) are the most scenic; the view from the spots near the sandy bay beach and playground are also good, but you can count on noise and lots of kids running around. Spaces for RVs come in a variety of comfort levels; one site includes a private Jacuzzi and washer-dryer. Tent camping is much more primitive and can be far from idyllic for those seeking to really get away from it all. The campground runs an inexpensive shuttle to **Old Town, Sea World**, and the **Zoo**. ♦ 2211 Pacific Beach Dr (between E Mission Bay Dr and Olney St). fax number for reservations, 858/581.4260, 800/4BAY-FUN. www.campland.com

3 SAIL BAY

Private marinas, condos, and homes line the edges of this large inland bay formed by Santa Clara and Crown Points. When the bay was first developed in 1926, homeowners were offered 50-year leases allowing them to create private beaches by extending their patios, fences, and retaining walls onto the sand. When the leases ran out in 1976, the city forced homeowners—after lengthy battles—to remove some 25 private docks from the beach, and by 1986 the private

SURF LINGO

Bottom turn: turn back into the wave after riding atop it

Floater: riding off the tip of the wave into the air and landing back on the wave

Hang ten: hang your toes over the edge of the surfboard while riding a wave

The kind: the ultimate, as in *I bought the kind board today.*

Off the lip: a bottom turn on top of the wave

Tube: the hollow part of the wave, also called "barrel" or "green room"

---

fences, walls, and patios were also outlawed. This bay is now like a park, with a walkway running along its edges and an ever-growing lineup of sailboats beached on the sand. ♦ Pacific Beach Dr (between Riviera Dr and Mission Blvd)

4 MISSION BAY SPORTCENTER

You can reach this isolated haven only via a boat through the bay or a drive through the congestion and madness of **Mission Beach**. For dedicated windsurfers, water-skiers, or sailors, the hassle of the journey is rewarded by the prime breezes along the cove forming **Sail Bay**. You say you don't know the difference between a keel and a kayak? You can learn as much as you want to know about sailing, water-skiing, or surfing here, then rent a boat and wet suit and practice until your burned skin and weary muscles demand relief. Paddlers can rent kayaks, canoes, and rowboats; wave riders can try out surfboards and boogie boards at the nearby ocean beaches. Windsurfers, pro and amateur, rent their gear here, then stop in the sailing center next door for tips on the affairs of the wind and a browse through the gear and slick boards for sale. ♦ Daily. 1010 Santa Clara Pl (at Mission Blvd). 858/488.1004. www.missionbaysportcenter.com

Within Mission Bay SportCenter:

YOUTH CAMPS

If you're bringing along a water-child who is addicted to the wind and sea, you might consider signing him or her up for a weeklong intensive summer camp in the bay. Children aged 6 to 16 learn sailing, kayaking, boogie-boarding, water safety, water-skiing, windsurfing, and ocean surfing. ♦ 858/488.1004

5 CROWN POINT SHORES

One of the best spots for group gatherings, the shores face **Fiesta Island** and **Sea World**, with a spectacular view of the fireworks and the thunderboats that roar through the bay during the hydroplane races. This spot boasts fire rings, lifeguards, rest rooms, playgrounds, and best of all, a large parking lot. ♦ Crown Point Dr (between Lamont and Ingraham Sts)

6 MISSION BAY PARK

You've got to look at a map to grasp the immensity of this 4,236-acre park, an aquatic buffer zone between the beach towns and I-5. First-timers should pull into a parking lot by the **Visitors' Information Center** (see page 118) and consult their maps. Mission Bay's layout can be very overwhelming, and even locals get confused by the sheer number of channels, coves, islands, and bays along the curving 27-mile shoreline. I-5 runs along the park's eastern strip of lawns and rolling hills to Sea World Drive at the south. The Ingraham Street Bridge (aka the Glenn Rick Bridge, named for the park's builder) bisects the park about midway between the freeway and the ocean and leads to Pacific Beach. West Mission Bay Drive connects the park with Sea World Drive and Mission Beach. The entire area east of the Ingraham Street Bridge is open to water-skiing, except in the coves and channels marked with 5-mph buoys. The entire Northwest Bay is allocated for sailing. Fishing is permitted anyplace in the bay except official swimming, waterskiing, and personal watercraft areas including Bonita Cove, Ventura Cove, Crown Point Shores, De Anza Cove, Playa Pacifica, and Tecolote Shores. Fishing is not allowed from any bridge. In recent years the swimming areas have been affected by pollution—heed the signs. Playa Pacifica and Tecolote Shores along the bay's eastern edge entice families with their calm waters, playground equipment, and wide expanses of lawns for picnicking and kite flying. By the way, kite flying is a performance art here—red, yellow, blue, and green boxes, tails, and triangles guided by professional crews swirl against

---

Restaurants/Clubs: Red | Hotels: Purple | Shops: Orange | Outdoors/Parks: Green | Sights/Culture: Blue

the blue sky. This is the land of joggers, boaters, swimmers, picnickers, loungers, and loafers. Don't try to figure it all out in one trip. ♦ Bounded by Mission Bay and Sea World Drs and by I-5. www.sandiego.gov/park-and-recreation

Within Mission Bay Park:

VISITORS' INFORMATION CENTER

Brochure collectors, get out your knapsacks to handle all the slick handouts from hotels, tour operators, restaurants, and other businesses. The desk clerks have good maps, advice on navigating your way about, and answers for most reasonable questions. Spread your finds out on a lawn by the water and soak in the bay's coconut-oil-scented ambience. There's a big playground between the center and the water. ♦ Daily. 2688 E Mission Bay Dr (between Sea World and Clairemont Drs). 276.8200

7 PARADISE POINT RESORT AND SPA

$$$$ In the early 1960s, Hollywood producer Jack Skirball visited **Vacation Isle**, a 44-acre artificial island in the middle of Mission Bay, and decided to transform it into his own version of paradise. Skirball and architect **Eldridge Spencer** turned the barren island into the **Vacation Village South Seas Paradise**, with lagoons filled with water lilies, waterfalls, an abundance of palm trees and fragrant flowers, and a natural setting that can't be beat. Today, Noble House Hotels and Resorts owns the resort, with 462 rooms nestled among palm trees and tropical flowers and foliage. A true all-in-one resort, the facilities include three restaurants (including **Baleen**; see opposite); five swimming pools; five tennis courts; basketball and volleyball courts; bike and boat rentals; an 18-hole putting green; jogging paths; and children's summer programs. One of the highlights of the property is the luxurious Balinese-style **SpaTerre**, which offers body treatments,

---

Legendary mountain man Jedediah Smith arrived in San Diego in the late 1880s, after establishing the overland trail that would become a wagon-train freeway for the westward bound.

A farmers' market is held in Pacific Beach every Saturday 8AM to noon. Located on the first floor of the Promenade, the event offers fresh produce and flowers as well as specialty products such as honey and preserves.

---

massages, facials, and salon services. Accommodations are in single-story bungalows (a refreshing change from all the high-rise hotels around town), many overlooking the bay, with comfortable country-casual furnishings. Several suites are available with private patios. It's an ideal destination for families, and spacious enough for honeymoon couples to retain a sense of privacy. Rates are lowest between September and May. ♦ 1404 W Vacation Rd (between Ingraham St and W Mission Bay Dr). 858/274.4630, 800/344.2626; fax 858/581.5929. ₺ www.paradisepoint.com

Within Paradise Point Resort and Spa:

BALEEN RESTAURANT & BAR

★★★$$$ With its gorgeous bayside setting and whimsical tropical décor with lots of wicker monkeys hanging about, Baleen is one of the prettiest restaurants in town. The cuisine and setting have garnered much recognition of late, and locals think of it as a secret getaway for a special night out. The menu focuses on fresh seafood, including sublime ahi tartare and tempura crab cakes, but there are also steaks, lamb chops, and duck confit. The aptly named Chocolate Hangover dessert is a must, though you might want to stick with the monkey theme and go for the banana split. A children's menu includes small portions of shrimp scampi, a petit filet, and roast chicken. ♦ Californian/seafood ♦ Daily, dinner. 1404 W Vacation Rd (between Ingraham St and W Mission Bay Dr). 858/490.6363. ₺

BAREFOOT BAR & GRILL

★★$$ An institution among locals in flip-flops and aloha shirts, this casual open-air bar is a great escape for an after-work mango mai tai or margarita with cheesy nachos. Grab a table beside the water for great sunset views; you just might spot a white egret or blue heron perched on the grassy shores. The menu suits the setting, with an emphasis on tropical flavors including spicy jerked chicken and blackened salmon. Live bands play Jimmy Buffet–style tunes Friday through Sunday nights. ♦ American ♦ Daily, breakfast, lunch, and dinner. 858/581.5960. ₺

8 SKI BEACH

It's amazing that all those bodies dangling from tow ropes don't end up in a huge tangle as amateur and pro water-skiers dodge, twist, and leap in the water, swooshing through one another's wakes. There's a continuous line of customized trucks and jeeps at the launch ramp, and an occasional incredible bottleneck in the parking lot. Thunderboats take over the course during

SAN DIEGO BY BIKE

San Diego, one of the most bicycle-friendly cities in the nation, offers more than 800 miles of bike paths, lanes, and routes and ideal weather for cycling year round. Beach cruisers with thick tires are the latest fashion, although you'll see everything from sleek racing bikes to clunkers. Even police officers patrol the beach communities on two wheels. There are rows of bike racks (which fill quickly) in front of government buildings, shopping malls, tourist attractions, and park-and-ride trolley and bus stops; there are even bike racks on public buses. Drivers used to be more considerate of bicyclists than you'd expect in a big city, but times have changed. Now drivers distracted by cell phones or other multi-tasking activities have a tendency to weave into designated bike lanes, and accidents have become far too common. Be acutely aware of traffic when riding on busy streets.

Bicyclists seem to outnumber pedestrians on the **Mission Beach** boardwalk, where cyclists in bikinis and the briefest of bathing trunks cruise happily alongside in-line skaters. The boardwalk has become such a speedway that officials have instituted a speed limit of 8 mph—hard to enforce because few bikes sport speedometers. The pace is far calmer along the shores of **Mission Bay**, but if you ride along the sidewalks by the water, keep an eye out for stairs that seem to appear just when you've gained speed. Traffic is a bit of a problem along **San Diego Bay**, but you can follow a combination of bike paths and lanes from the **Embarcadero** to **Seaport Village** and the **San Diego Convention Center**, then take your bike on the ferry to **Coronado**, where the streets are flat and wide. The most challenging and rewarding routes travel through **Ocean Beach** and **Point Loma** to **Cabrillo**

National Monument, and along **Highway 101** from **La Jolla** to **Solana Beach**. Both involve hills and long stretches of spectacular scenery. Back-country cyclists with strong legs can make it up the 3,000-foot grade to the top of **Mount Palomar**; those with less energy can stick to the sea-level highways through the **Anza-Borrego Desert**. Off-road mountain bikes are restricted to certain trails in California state parks and are not allowed on the **Pacific Crest Trail**; for specific rules, contact the **California State Parks Department** (800/777.0369, 916/653.6995) and **San Diego County Parks Department** (858/694.3049). A free map of San Diego County bike routes is available online at www.ridelink.org or at various bike shops. For more in-depth information and directions on specific biking routes, get a copy of *Cycling San Diego* by Jerry Schad (Centra Publications, P.O. Box 191029, San Diego, CA 92159 or through online booksellers).

Free bike racks are available on several public bus routes. Bikes are also allowed on the trolley. For information on bus and trolley bike services, contact the **Transit Store** (449 Broadway, at Fifth Ave; 234.1060). Bikes are also allowed on the **San Diego Bay Ferry** (1050 N Harbor Dr, at Broadway; 234.4111, 800/442.7847). Organized bike tours are available through the **Sierra Club** (3820 Ray St, near 30th St in North Park; 299.1743). You can rent bikes, locks, and helmets (required by law for riders under 18 years of age) at **Bikes and Beyond** (1201 First St, at the Ferry Landing Marketplace, Coronado; 435.7180) and the **Beach Club** (704 Ventura Pl, between Mission Blvd and the boardwalk, Mission Beach; 858/488.5050).

the annual **San Diego Thunderboat Regatta** each September; their roar can be heard clear to the Ocean Beach Pier.
♦ Ingraham St (between Sunset Cliffs Blvd and Crown Point Dr)

9 FIESTA ISLAND

Ⓟ Water-skiers and jet-skiers do their dervish whirls in the waters off this 465-acre man-made sandlot, and dogs of all breeds are allowed to cavort along the shore without leashes any time of day or night. The island's most infamous regulars are the players of Over-the-Line, an oddball (in more ways than one) game played by teams with indecent names and a general tendency toward rowdiness. The annual July **Over-the-Line Tournament** attracts groupies by the hordes. Beer and bikinis are the norm. ♦ Fiesta

Island Rd (between E Mission Bay and Sea World Drs)

10 HILTON SAN DIEGO RESORT

$$$$ This resort came on the bay scene in 1963, when the hillsides framing the park were just starting to sprout homes. The property was completely renovated in 2007, with a complete refurbishment of all 357 rooms and suites. A tan and wine color scheme complements the Mission-style furnishings in the rooms, which all feature floor-to-ceiling windows. Some suites have expansive patios with fire pits. The grounds were also renovated and a relaxation garden was added, with chaises and couches for quiet reading and napping. The new **Essence Spa** also has an outdoor relaxation and meditation area, along with top-notch fitness

Restaurants/Clubs: Red | Hotels: Purple | Shops: Orange | Outdoors/Parks: Green | Sights/Culture: Blue

The Best

Jan Heying

Owner, Heying & Associates Public Relations and Advertising

Living in Paradise

Food first:

Breakfast—Kono's at the entrance to **Crystal Pier** in **Pacific Beach**, where the real surfers hang out and where you fit in with a pair of shorts and Pure Juice flops. Be sure to get there before 10AM unless you want to wait. People-watching is half the fun.

Lunch—has to be **Pt. Loma Seafood** on **Shelter Island**—the freshest fish sandwiches in town. Sit outside and watch the half-day boats bring in their hauls.

Drinks—no better view of the city skyline than from either the fourth floor of the **Hotel Solamar** on Sixth Street downtown or the outside deck atop the award-winning **Bertrand at Mr. A's** on Bankers Hill.

Dinner—favorite all-around—**George's at the Cove** in **La Jolla**. Casual outside ocean-view dining that is the closest thing to being on the Amalfi coast without having to leave the States.

While in **La Jolla**, take a walk around the cove and up to **La Valencia Hotel** for a nightcap in the famous **Whaling Bar**, frequented by many a Hollywood celeb. Ask for their signature after dinner drink, The Whaler—this counts as dessert as well with the magical ingredient of Häagen Dazs vanilla ice cream. Yum!

Fun stuff to do:

Stroll along the **Boardwalk**, starting at the foot of **Pacific Beach Drive** south along **Ocean Front Walk** down to **Belmont Park** (home of the wooden roller coaster). Cross over past the **Jack in the Box** for a walk back; head north along **Bayside Walk**. Cut through the **Catamaran Hotel**, cross over **Mission Boulevard**, and head for the **Green Flash** on the outside patio for a margarita and a chance of seeing the green flash right at sunset. Rollerblades or a bike

rented at the **Mission Beach Club** near the roller coaster are also acceptable modes of transportation. Be sure to keep under 8 mph.

Just a 1.5-hour drive away, head to **Julian** for a Sunday-afternoon stroll through this quaint mountain community famous for its homemade apple pie, cider, and clean air. In winter, it actually gets snow, so bring your sled.

An afternoon of walking and museum gazing in **Balboa Park**—a picnic on the lawn and taking in the latest original hit or soon-to-be hit Broadway show at the **Old Globe Theatre**.

If you're lucky enough to be here in the summer during **Humphrey's Concerts by the Bay** on **Shelter Island**, don't miss a chance to see top-name musical artists and comics perform live in this venue under the stars. If you can round up a boat, tie up and listen on the bay—for free!

Pub crawling starts at the **Turf Supper Club** in **Golden Hill**, where you can start out with the best Long Island iced tea in town while grilling your own $5 steak right in the middle of the bar. Just north of Golden Hill is the newly awakened South Park neighborhood with new restaurants and bars springing up almost daily. The best of the lot is **Vagabond**, offering delightful cuisine from all over the world in a French-bistro setting, filled with locals and people "in the know."

Head into the **Gaslamp Quarter** for just about anything you can think of, from **Martini Ranch** (you can guess their specialty) to the **Field**, an authentic Irish pub, for some Guinness on tap. **Petco Park**, home to the San Diego Padres baseball team is, worth seeing, but you can catch part of a game atop the Gaslamp Marriott's hip **Altitude Sky Bar**, 22 floors above it all.

Just 45 minutes south gets you to **Rosarito Beach** in Mexico. For a relaxing weekend or even for the day, make an appointment for a hot-rock massage or hydro-bath at the spa at **Las Rocas**, a beautiful, American-owned hotel overlooking the Pacific. While you're there, stop by **Puerto Nuevo** for a traditional lobster feast, complete with all the trimmings, rice, beans, guacamole, tortillas, and of course, margaritas—all for under $15. Olé!

---

gear and elaborate Vichy showers. Within steps of the guest rooms are plenty of attractions and distractions: a clean, half-mile-long beach; five tennis courts and a health club; rental catamarans, Windsurf-ers, Aqua Cycles, bicycles, and other land and sea toys; a beyond-Olympic-size pool; several restaurants and bars; and easy access to the picnic areas, playgrounds, and miles of trails through the park. ◆ 1775 E Mission Bay Dr (between Sea World and Clairemont Drs). 276.4010, 800/HILTONS; fax 275.8944. ᕼ www.sandiegohilton.com

11 Bayside Walk

The best overall view of the Mission Bay neighborhoods is from a bike cruising this concrete pathway from **Mission Point**, the southwest tip of the bay, to **Santa Clara Point** at the north. Residents of the bay-front homes along the path somehow carry on normal lives in the midst of a 24-hour-a-day playground. Windsurfer boards are the most popular toys to the south; sailboats abound to the north. ◆ Bayside Walk (between Mission Pt and Santa Clara Pl)

12 BAHIA RESORT HOTEL

$$$ This 14-acre resort on a sandy peninsula curves into sheltering Mission Beach's inner bay, where sailboats nearly obliterate the sky on sunny days. The location is ideal if you want easy access to the frenetic party action at Mission Beach; the roller coaster is just across the street, and shrieks pierce the drone of traffic and police helicopters. Despite its proximity to the beach, the hotel is usually peaceful. The one- and five-story buildings with their 320 rooms are laid out in a loop along the peninsula's outer edges, encircling pools, tennis courts, and pansy-striped gardens. There is also a casual restaurant serving continental fare for breakfast, lunch, and dinner. The general décor is pretty basic; rooms on the west side have the best views. It's a mainstream sort of place, good for families. Special rates are available in winter; weekend rates, throughout the year. ◆ 998 W Mission Bay Dr (at Mission Blvd). 858/488.0551, 800/576.4229; fax 858/488.7055. www.bahiahotel.com

12 *BAHIA BELLE*

The sunset and night lights of **Mission** and **Pacific Beaches** are more romantic when viewed from the white curlicue railings of this Victorian-style sternwheeler, which has been cruising the bay between the **Bahia** and **Catamaran** resorts since the 1960s. The *Belle*, boasting warm mahogany paneling, red velvet curtains, brass railings, and a stained-glass skylight, is understandably popular as a wedding site. Her sister ship, the **William D. Evans**, is even more luxurious, with a 42-foot-long stained-glass skylight, formal dining rooms, and teak trimmings. Both ships are available for charters, and the *Bahia Belle* is used for drinking and dancing cruises open to the public. Admission. ◆ Cruises nightly, July–Labor Day; F, Sa, Feb-1 Nov. The Bahia Resort, 998 W Mission Bay Dr (at Mission Blvd). 858/539.7779, 858/488.0551, 800/576.4229

13 BONITA COVE AND MARINERS POINT

◑ Across the water and directly south of **Belmont Park**, this sandy peninsula is used for Over-the-Line and volleyball tournaments. The parking lots here fill up quickly because it's an easy walk through the lawns of the park to the boardwalk and ocean across Mission Boulevard. ◆ Mariner's Way (at W Mission Bay Dr)

14 THE DANA ON MISSION BAY

$$$ One of Mission Bay's great hotels is now a delightful full-scale resort with 270 rooms and suites, a conference center, marina and boat launch, fitness center, two pools, water sport and bicycle rentals, and a bayside wedding site. Teak and mahogany furnishings have replaced the sturdy plastic and faux-wood accoutrements of old, and the hotel attracts business travelers as well as families. The casual **Blue Pearl** restaurant serves all meals and has children's menus; the **Firefly Bar and Grill** has a hipper ambience for grown-up cocktails. With **Sea World** on one side, acres of lawns on the other, and a bay and marina in front, the hotel is immensely popular and an ideal getaway. ◆ 1710 W Mission Bay Dr (entrance on Dana Landing Rd). 222.6440, 800/445.3339; fax 222.5916. & www.thedana.com

15 SEA WORLD

The bay's largest attraction is this 150-acre marine park. Four University of California, Los Angeles (UCLA) fraternity brothers opened the park in 1964 on just 22 acres. Now owned by Anheuser-Busch, Sea World has gradually expanded along the bay's southern shores and has seemingly endless parking lots and attractions to keep its guests amused. Once you've paid the steep entrance price, make sure you don't miss **Penguin Encounter**, completely renovated and reopened in 2007 as an ideal home for nearly 300 Antarctic penguins. Other must-sees include the **Shark Encounter**'s fierce inhabitants; the **Forbidden Reef** display of moray eels and bat rays; and the playful bottlenose dolphins and sea otters at **Rocky Point Preserve**. Let the kids run wild in **Shamu's Happy Harbor**, with its water maze, funship, and sand play area. When the sun gets high, load the whole family onto the **Shipwreck Rapids** ride for cool sprays from waterfalls or board a simulated helicopter ride through the **Wild Arctic**. The **Journey to Atlantis** ride, which looks like a garish space capsule sprouting tentacles, is like a roller coaster through water. You can't get away without going to see the sleek black-and-white killer whales leap from their 6.7-million-gallon pool to splash the crowd. ◆ Admission. Daily. 1720 S Shores Rd (between Sea World Dr and Ingraham St). 800/25-SHAMU (800/257.4268) www.seaworld.com

---

Restaurants/Clubs: Red | Hotels: Purple | Shops: Orange | Outdoors/Parks: Green | Sights/Culture: Blue

OVER-THE-LINE

People in San Diego are addicted to sports trends. For example, in-line skating long ago replaced ordinary roller skating on the **Mission Beach Boardwalk**. Frisbee golf tournaments draw pros bearing a half-dozen different-sized discs for a variety of challenging shots at **Balboa Park**'s **Frisbee Golf Course** in **Morley Field**.

But the oddest sport of all has got to be **Over-the-Line**. The game itself is a simple version of sandlot softball with three-person teams. But the spectacle is another

story. Hedonism, debauchery, and decadence reign during the annual world championships held every July on **Fiesta Island**. Not only do the players compete with a ball and bat but they also put untoward energy into composing raunchy and ridiculous team names that would make Andrew Dice Clay blush. Their team T-shirts set the mood for the ultimate party, a dawn-to-dusk sunbake where naked flesh is at a premium and inhibitions are ignored. Not for the faint of heart.

16 HYATT REGENCY MISSION BAY SPA AND MARINA

$$$$ Like many Mission Bay resorts, the Hyatt Regency underwent a multimillion-dollar renovation in 2006-2007. The 430 rooms and suites were tricked out with iPod docking stations, LCD-screen TVs, and wireless and high-speed Internet access. Pool areas and public spaces were all updated as well, and additional amenities including water taxi service in Mission Bay and shuttles to **Fashion Valley Center** mall are further enticements. The 17-story hotel tower seems out of place along the bay, but the tower rooms do have a top-notch view of the bay and ocean sides of Mission Beach. There's also a three-story section, with rooms right next to the marina, whose 150 slips are often filled with enviable private yachts. The hotel restaurant is best known for its lavish Sunday brunch, though the food has improved for dinners as well. ◆ 1441

Pacific Beach is one of San Diego County's oldest suburbs, dating back to the late 1880s. In 1902, oceanfront lots could be purchased for as little as $350.

Books aren't the only attraction at the Earl & Birdie Taylor Library, a branch of the public library at 4275 Cass Street (858/581.9934). The striking building is also home to numerous special events, including jazz concerts, art exhibits, and reading discussion groups.

In 1850, San Diego became both a city and a county, and California became the 31st US state.

The Glenn Curtiss Flying School, established on North Island in 1911, was the first military aviation school in the US.

Quivira Rd (between Sunset Cliffs Blvd and W Mission Bay Dr). 224.1234, 800/492.8804; fax 224.0348. www.missionbay.hyatt.com

17 SPORTSMEN'S SEAFOODS

★$ Fish and chips, fresh tuna burgers, and shrimp cocktails taste great when you're sitting at the small patio outside this self-service café by the rowboats and yachts moored in the bay. The adjacent fish market displays prize specimens from the daily catch. ◆ Seafood ◆ Daily, lunch and early dinner. 1617 Quivira Rd (between Sunset Cliffs Blvd and W Mission Bay Dr). 224.3551. www.sportsmensseafood.com

17 SEAFORTH BOAT RENTALS

Sailboats, water-ski boats, jet skis, kayaks, and even low-tech rowboats are for rent here. ◆ Daily (closed Christmas Day). 1641 Quivira Rd (off W Mission Bay Dr). 223.1681, 888/834.2628. www.seaforthboatrental.com

18 SEAFORTH SPORTFISHING

Bag an albacore, yellowtail, dorado, or snapper, depending on the season and your expertise (or luck). Seaforth and its predecessor, **Mission Bay Sportfishing**, started fishing charters out of the bay in the early 1960s, when there actually were fish worth catching not far from shore. Most of today's anglers are headed for the banks off Point Loma or the Coronado Islands (in Mexican waters). Half- and full-day trips are offered, and scuba-diving charters are also available. ◆ Daily, from 4:30AM. Daily, dinner in summer. 1717 Quivira Rd (between Sunset Cliffs Blvd and W Mission Bay Dr). 224.3383. www.seaforthlanding.com

18 THE LANDING

★★★$ The crew members at this waterside coffee shop cheerfully begin their workday

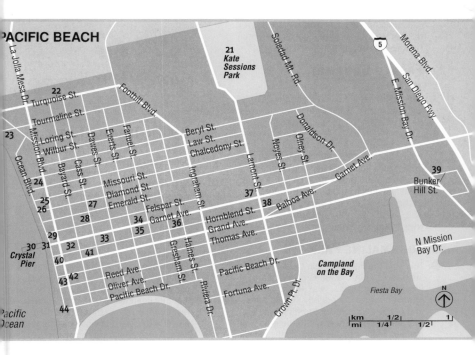

PACIFIC BEACH

at 5AM, serving coffee and eggs to hyped-up or half-asleep anglers. At the more humane hour of 9 or 10AM, they're still quick with a quip and coffeepot, and enough discarded newspapers have piled up that you don't have to purchase your own. Settle into a heavy wooden captain's chair to devour your flaky golden hash browns with a melted-cheese-and-Ortega-chili omelette with spicy homemade salsa, raisin-bread French toast, or oatmeal with walnuts and brown sugar. Lunch at the counter, where you can watch the grill master flip your burger, fry your shrimp, and slice your fresh-baked turkey. The food all tastes expertly homemade. ◆ Coffee shop ◆ Daily, breakfast and lunch. 1729 Quivira Rd (between Sunset Cliffs Blvd and W Mission Bay Dr). 222.3317

19 MISSION BAY PARK HEADQUARTERS

A wood-shake-and-shingle South Seas–style bungalow serves as action central for park activities and development; maps, brochures, and permits for group functions are dispensed efficiently. ◆ M-F. 2581 Quivira Ct (between Sunset Cliffs Blvd and W Mission Bay Dr). Offices, 221.8910

20 QUIVIRA BASIN

Sportfishers, boaters, and waterfront browsers roam these shores facing the Mission Bay Channel, which leads into the bay and open sea. The port office and park headquarters are located here, along with several boat sales and rental yards, marinas, a small shopping and dining center, sportfishing and whale-watching boats, and uncrowded picnic grounds. There's a fine view of Ocean and Mission Beaches from the rocky outcroppings along the channel mouth. ◆ Quivira Rd (between Sunset Cliffs Blvd and W Mission Bay Dr)

PACIFIC BEACH

21 KATE SESSIONS PARK

Here is another tribute to the indomitable **Kate Sessions**, who created much of San Diego's natural beauty with her early 1900s landscaping. Kate was a Pacific Beach resident and cherished the hillside of Soledad Mountain. In 1933, the city acquired 79 acres north of Lamont Street for this park, which wasn't landscaped and properly dedicated until 1957, on Sessions's 100th birthday. Don't miss the view from the

---

Restaurants/Clubs: Red | Hotels: Purple | Shops: Orange | Outdoors/Parks: Green | Sights/Culture: Blue

flagpole atop the hill looking out south over the bay to Point Loma and beyond. ◆ Park Dr (between Soledad Mt and Soledad Rds)

22 FRENCH GOURMET

★$$$ This neighborhood bistro is delightfully serene and a great place for lunching on classics including salade Niçoise, savory onion soup, or a simple quiche. The pastry case facing the doorway is unavoidable and irresistible. Choose an array of pastries (the almond croissants are divine) as a house gift and you're sure to receive a warm welcome. ◆ French ◆ Daily, breakfast, lunch, and dinner. 960 Turquoise St (between Cass and Bayard Sts). 858/488.1725, 800/929.1984. www.thefrenchgourmet.com

23 TOURMALINE PARK

ⓟ This small rocky beach isn't great for sunbathing, but the winds offshore are ideal for windsurfers, who balance on their narrow boards with brightly striped sails and capture the breeze seemingly effortlessly. Surfers gravitate here as well, and you're sure to see some flashy moves when the surf's up. The park has rest rooms and precious few parking spots. ◆ Tourmaline St (between Mission Blvd and Pacific View Dr)

24 PACIFIC SHORES INN

$$ Retirees and others looking for an escape from the sun and sounds of merriment find peace and shade at this small two-story inn. Many of the 59 rooms and suites have refrigerators and kitchenettes. The quiet northern beaches are just a block west; restaurants and shops are a few more blocks south. Facilities include a laundry room, a heated pool, and free continental breakfast; there is no restaurant. ◆ 4802 Mission Blvd (between Chalcedony and Law Sts). 858/483.6300,888/GR8.STAY; fax 858/483.9276. www.pacificshoresinn.com

25 BEACH HAVEN INN

$$$ Canadian families escaping the winter's cold and Arizona families racing from the summer's heat return annually to this small motel for clean, moderately priced accommodations near the beach yet away from the noisiest sections of Mission Boulevard. The heated pool and hot tub are enclosed with white metal gates and wooden fences that block the traffic noise. There is a washer and dryer on the premises, and several of the 23 units (18 with kitchenettes) have refrigerators. There is no restaurant. Rates drop significantly in winter. ◆ 4740 Mission Blvd (between Diamond and Missouri Sts). 858/272.3812, 800/831.6323; fax 858/272.3532. www.beachhaveninn.com

26 PACIFIC TERRACE HOTEL

$$$$ This sand-colored condolike hotel boasts two layers of balconies, encircled with cranberry-colored metal railings that jut past each other for the most advantageous views. The 73 rooms have small refrigerators, TVs, and phones; some of the units have kitchenettes. The complimentary cosmetics include a soothing aloe lotion (good for sunburn); soft terry-cloth robes and hair dryers are standard in all rooms. Guests have access to a washer and dryer, underground parking, massage service, complimentary wine from 4-5PM, and complimentary continental breakfast. There's no restaurant on the premises, but there are plenty within walking distance. The pool and hot tub face a relatively quiet stretch of beach with fire rings. Although trendier hotels have opened at the beach, it's still a winner. ◆ 610 Diamond St (between Mission and Ocean Blvds). 858/581.3500, 800/344.3370; fax 858/274.2534. ♿ www.pacificterrace.com

27 CREAM OF THE CROP

A prime destination for smart shoppers on a budget, this resale boutique specializes in high-quality, gently used women's clothing and shoes. You'll find a number of top designers represented, along with department-store brands and items from local boutiques. There's a particularly good selection of evening wear and accessories such as scarves, purses, and belts. Tu-Sa. 4683 Cass St (at Diamond St). 858/272.6601

28 CAFE 976

Tables and chairs are set about in the brick patio, screened porch, and dining and living rooms of this Victorian-style beach house, which has been turned into a coffeehouse. It's far more peaceful than the coffeehouses along Garnet Avenue. ◆ Coffeehouse ◆ Daily. 976 Felspar St (at Cass St). 858/272.0976. www.cafe976.com

28 CASS STREET BAR & GRILL

★$ Neighbors literally hang out from the street-side counters of this bar-café, shouting out greetings to friends parking their bikes and heading in for a cold one. Pictures of regulars with their favorite catches (marlin, tuna, and the like) decorate the walls, and the crowd has a sports-fan attitude. Several counters with bar stools line the walls and windows and surround two pool tables. You can't miss the wall-size mural of a tropical sunset. The burgers and chicken sandwiches are messy, flavorful, and guaranteed crowd pleasers. Also worth ordering: any of the fish specials of the day. ♦ American ♦ Daily, breakfast, lunch, and dinner (kitchen closes at 10PM). 4612 Cass St (between Felspar and Emerald Sts). 858/270.1320

28 ISABEL'S CANTINA

★★★$$ Chef Isabel Cruz combines her Puerto Rican roots with the influences from her upbringing in a multi-ethnic Los Angeles neighborhood to create an exciting Latin-Asian cuisine. She combines ingredients common in Thai, Mexican, and Japanese cooking, including cilantro, lime, tropical fruits, and chilies, in unusual ways, preparing healthy tofu tamales, brown rice and black bean burritos, and rice bowls topped with papaya mango salsa. Not everything's low-cal and healthy, however. Her Bananas Cantina, flambéed with spiced rum and served with ice cream, adds more than a few calories to a meal. Her first book, *Isabel's Cantina: Bold Latin Flavors from the New California Kitchen*, was published in 2007, and the Isabel's restaurant empire has grown to include five locations in California and Oregon. Don't be surprised if she pops up on the Food Network soon. ♦ Latin/Asian ♦ Daily, breakfast, lunch, and dinner. 966 Felspar St (between Cass and Bayard Sts). 858/272.8400 & www.isabelscantina.com

29 TOWER 23

$$$$ Named for the lifeguard tower it faces, this ultra-hip hotel has definitely upped the chic quotient in Pacific Beach. The 44 rooms have cutesy categories—Spirit Pad, Sky Pad, Surf Pad, Sanctuary Suite—and a sleek style with rainshowers, Egyptian cotton bedding, LCD-screen TVs, and H2O toiletries. Some suites overlook the boardwalk and beach and have private balconies. Wi-Fi is available throughout the property—checking your e-mail from a café table by the sand is just about as SoCal techie as you can get. ♦ 723 Felspar St (at the boardwalk). 858/270.5736, 866/TOWER23; fax 858/274.2333. & www.tower23hotel.com

JRDN

★★★★$$$$ The setting is ever so stimulating, with a wavy-patterned glass wall that casts a purple and blue hue over the dining room and another glass wall that encases the wine cellar. The mostly 20-to 30-something crowd practically pulses with high-spirited energy fueled by classy cocktails and the proximity to sea and sand. And the food is downright exceptional, from the salty Pacific oysters on the half-shell to the meaty Dungeness crab cakes and sensational sushi. Meyer's Ranch natural beef is the main event; steaks come with a variety of rubs, sauces, and sides. Go for the simple garlic salt rub or the sensational Chef's Thunder steak with Vidalia onions and blue cheese. Dinner is pricey; if you're on a strict budget, come by for a breakfast of flatiron steak and eggs or stick with the sushi bar. Yes, the name is pronounced Jordan. ♦ Steak/seafood ♦ Daily, breakfast, lunch, and dinner (brunch on Sa and Su). 858/270.JRDN &

30 CRYSTAL PIER

At first glance, the pier appears to be closed, but there is a chain-link gate that's open for pedestrians daily from dawn until sunset. Blue-and-white hotel cottages line both sides of the 400-foot-long pier's entrance; the rest is operated by the city during daylight hours as a fishing pier, with a small bait-and-tackle shop and a cluster of craggy-faced anglers who dangle their lines for halibut, perch, mackerel, and the occasional lobster. Surfers line the break where the waves form on both sides of the pilings, and gulls swarm about, squawking and swooping after trashy tidbits. The hotel's operators keep a close eye on the goings-on along the pier and prohibit alcohol, profanity, and boom boxes on the premises. The present-day scenario is far more natural than its first incarnation as **Pickering's Pleasure Pier**, an aborted attempt to capitalize on the building boom brought to Mission Beach by the **Mission Beach Amusement Center** in 1925. The initial plan was designed by **Ernest Pickering**, who had built several amusement center piers in Los Angeles but failed to see the San Diego project through. The investors pushed on, with **Neil Nettleship** and **Ben Tye** as designers, and in 1927 opened their Crystal Pier and the **Crystal Ballroom**, with a cork

---

Glass bottles are not allowed on most beaches.

To tell whether the tide is coming in or going out, check the color of the sand near the water's edge. If there is a distinct dark band of sand, the tide is coming in and you'd better move your towels. If the sand is uniform in color, the tide is going out and it's a good time to look for sea critters in tide pools.

Restaurants/Clubs: **Red** | Hotels: **Purple** | Shops: **Orange** | Outdoors/Parks: **Green** | Sights/Culture: **Blue**

dance floor that drove the flappers wild. Unfortunately, the pilings quickly became infested with marine borers and started swaying within 3 months, and the pier was condemned within a year. It was widened and reopened in 1935, then nearly destroyed by high tides and waves in 1982. After lengthy and costly renovations, including replacing the T-shaped fishing area at its far end, the pier reopened in time for the Pacific Beach Centennial in 1987. ◆ Daily, sunrise to sunset. Garnet Ave (at Ocean Blvd)

On Crystal Pier:

CRYSTAL PIER HOTEL & COTTAGES

$$$ You can't sleep any closer to the water than in these blue-and-white cottages, where the surf literally rocks you to sleep as it pounds the pier's pilings. Guests drive their cars right onto the pier and park in front of their doors. The wooden cottages are adorned with pink geraniums growing in window boxes under blue shutters. The 23 cottages and four second-story suites have full kitchens with large refrigerators, microwaves, and stovetops; separate bedrooms with queen beds covered in quilts; living rooms with TVs, futon couches, and wicker chairs; and patios looking almost straight down at the sea. The pier is closed to the public at sunset, giving the hotel's guests the privacy to quietly soak in the salty night air and dream above the pounding waves. The cottages are available at daily, weekly, and monthly rates (with a 2-night minimum stay) between 1 October and 14 June, although in the winter months the air can be damp and the sea rough. The daily rate soars (with a 3-night minimum stay) between 15 June and 15 September, with no special rates for longer stays. ◆ Reservations essential in summer. 4500 Ocean Blvd (at the foot of Garnet Ave past Mission Blvd). 858/483.6983, 800/748.5894; fax 858/483.6811. www.crystalpier.com

31 KONO'S CAFE

★★$ It's the food that packs the crowds into this tiny café, where the breakfast potatoes alone—laden with onions, green peppers, and cheese—warrant a visit. Surf movies play on TV, and gorgeous photos of great waves around the world line the walls. Be prepared to wait in line on weekend mornings. ◆ American ◆ Daily, breakfast and lunch. 704 Garnet Ave (at Ocean Blvd). 858/483.1669

32 KARINYA

★★$$ To accommodate wimpy American palates, dishes at this popular neighborhood Thai restaurant are prepared mild, medium, or hot, but be forewarned that medium is about as hot as the seeds of a jalapeño. Try the *nuah pad ped* (beef with sweet basil, garlic, chilies, and mint) and *gang ped* (chicken in red curry with coconut milk and bamboo shoots). ◆ Thai ◆ Daily, lunch and dinner. 825 Garnet Ave (between Bayard St and Mission Blvd). 858/270.5050. www.karinyathaicuisine.com

33 SOCIETY BILLIARD CAFE

Players line up to pay major bucks to play at the 15 pool tables in an industrial-chic setting with drainpipes as lighting columns and other heavy metal parts strewn about. Beer, wine, gourmet pizzas, and sandwiches are served. There are special day rates for die-hard players, and there's no minimum play time. The tables are in need of refurbishment. ◆ Daily. 1051 Garnet Ave (between Dawes and Cass Sts). 858/272.7665

34 HENRY'S MARKET PLACE

Expand your picnic spread with impeccably fresh avocados, breads, tortillas, oranges, brie, and goat cheese, and basics like environmentally correct paper towels. The market also offers freshly made sandwiches and has a nice selection of wines for sale. ◆ Daily. 1260 Garnet Ave (between Fanuel and Everts Sts). 858/270.8200. www.henrysmarkets.com

35 TRADER JOE'S

Stock up your hotel room, condo, or cooler with discount wines (but remember, no glass bottles on the beach), imported beers, and exotic flavors of sparkling water, as well as reasonably priced gourmet treats such as pretzels stuffed with peanut butter or chocolate-covered macadamia nuts. ◆ Daily. 1211 Garnet Ave (between Fanuel and Everts Sts). 858/272.7235. www.traderjoes.com

36 WORLD CURRY

★★$ With a selection of curries from Thailand, India, the Caribbean, and Japan, this informal eatery offers flavors to please just about everyone. The generous portions of curries range in strength from mild to fiery and can be ordered with either a choice of meats or strictly vegetarian. Side dishes include jasmine rice, fresh Indian breads, chicken skewers, and refreshing salads. Eat in the vibrantly painted dining room or order to go. ◆ International ◆ Daily, lunch and dinner. 1433 Garnet Ave (between Haines and Gresham Sts). 858/270.4455. www.worldcurry.com

37 CAFE ATHENA

★★$ Step into this pretty blue-and-white Greek taverna, redolent of olive oil, and feel your taste buds come alive. Dine with friends so you can split several dips—*tzatziki* (yogurt with cucumbers, garlic, and dill), *taramasalata* (caviar blended with olive oil and lemon juice), and *spanaki salata* (spinach blended with feta cheese and water chestnuts)—served with warm pita bread. Move on to the great salads, *tyropites* (feta and mozzarella in phyllo pastry), and cream of roasted eggplant soup. If you still have room, try the tender chicken souvlaki, the lamb meatballs (called *keftedes*), or the swordfish brochettes, and force yourself to sample at least one bite of the baklava. Takeout is available. ♦ Greek ♦ Daily, lunch and dinner. 1846 Garnet Ave (at Lamont St). 858/274.1140. ♿ www.cafeathena.com

38 Lamont Street Grill

★★$$$ Pacific Beach's loveliest dining room is located in a converted beach bungalow in a partly residential neighborhood. Outside, tables surround a fireplace on the small patio; inside, there are several little dining rooms. Chef/owner Robert Marnul is so confident in his skills he's written a cookbook called *The Soups of Lamont Street Grill*. Naturally, you're well advised to start with his soup of the day, perhaps followed by shrimp sautéed with green-chili pesto, or the mélange of Italian sausage, chicken, and pork over pasta with spicy beurre blanc. All meals are followed with fresh fruits dipped in chocolate. ♦ Californian ♦ Daily, dinner. Reservations recommended. 4445 Lamont St (at Hornblend St). 858/270.3060. www.lamontstreetgrill.com

39 Rubio's Deli-Mex

★★★$ Owner Ralph Rubio relished the fish tacos he devoured at sidewalk stands in the Mexican fishing village of San Felipe year after year, finally securing a vendor's secret recipe in 1978. In 1983, he opened his first fish taco stand on this bustling boulevard, and gradually his beloved fish tacos caught on in a big way. Now Rubio has restaurants and take-out stands scattered throughout San Diego County, even at the airport. The original eatery isn't exactly conveniently located, but it's worth a visit if you're curious about this culinary creation that now appears on trendy menus all around town. The classic fish taco is made of a battered and deep-fried strip of fresh fish wrapped in a soft corn tortilla with shredded cabbage, a squeeze of lime juice, and a spicy secret sauce; for the seafood-shy, Rubio's also serves terrific *carnitas* (marinated pork) and tame

chicken tacos. Look for outlets of this popular franchise at shopping malls and the airport. ♦ Mexican ♦ Daily, breakfast, lunch, and dinner. 4504 E Mission Bay Dr (at Bunker Hill St). 858/272.2801. Also at 3555 Rosecrans St (between Midway Dr and Sports Arena Blvd), Point Loma. 223.2631. www.rubios.com

OCEAN PARK INN

40 Ocean Park Inn

$$$ Earth-toned stucco helps this three-story hotel blend in with the surroundings; underground parking makes it convenient. The outdoor pool is heated (a plus in winter), and each of the rooms offers a patio or balcony with chairs and a small table. Other bonuses include kitchenettes in the suites, a coin-operated laundry, complimentary continental breakfast, and refrigerators in all of the 73 rooms and suites, which are well maintained and large. There's no restaurant in the hotel, but several are within easy walking distance. ♦ 710 Grand Ave (between Mission and Ocean Blvds). 858/483.5858, 800/231.7735; fax 858/274.0823. ♿ www.oceanparkinn.com

41 Bar West

★$$$$ Downtown's glam scene migrated to the beach with the 2007 opening of this eye-popping bar and restaurant from the owners of **Stingaree** and **Sidebar**. The action revolves around the "dj circle," where resident and guest DJs perform beneath a round ceiling with a chandelier that looks like floating bubbles. Executive chef Larry Abrams (formerly of **Thee Bungalow**) created a trendy menu featuring boneless organic chicken wings, truffle pommes frites, and duck confit with braised leeks to accompany Pears Hilton cocktails and Sunburn Martinis. The restaurant is open nightly, but the club's hours are restricted to Thursday through Saturday—though that may change if the beach crowd appreciates such an upscale venue. ♦ Californian ♦ Daily, dinner. Club Th-Sa, 9PM-2AM. 959 Hornblend Street (between Bayard and Cass Sts). 858/273.4800. www.barwestsd.com

42 Nick's at the Beach

★★$$ There's a lot to like about this two-story restaurant and bar, which attracts a merry young crowd along with middle-aged regulars. The eclectic menu satisfies varied appetites, but the cooking is less than stellar these days. The baked, broiled, or blackened fresh fish entrées, the grilled veggie salad, and the steamed mussels flavored with cilantro and lime are good bets. To wash it all down in style, Nick's offers a reasonably priced wine list, more than a dozen draft beers, and a full liquor selection. Upstairs, the lively bar area draws the 21-and-over crowd with pool tables, TVs, a CD jukebox, and plenty of ocean-view seating indoors and on the adjacent sun deck. Night owls will appreciate the fact that food is served until 1AM nightly. ♦ Seafood/American ♦ Daily, lunch and dinner; Su, brunch. 809 Thomas Ave (at Mission Blvd). 858/270.1730. www.nicksatthebeach.com

43 THE PROMENADE

This two-block-long shopping and dining complex has a wonderful underground parking lot—a real find in these crowded streets. Parking for a limited time period is free with validation from businesses in the complex, which include T-shirt and beachwear shops, take-out food stands, and mainstream restaurants. ♦ Daily. Mission Blvd (between Pacific Beach Dr and Thomas Ave)

Within the Promenade:

EGGERY ETC.

★$ Quantity is as important as quality among this crowd, who wolf down *chorizo* omelettes smothered in hot salsa as a hangover cure, or piles of syrupy pancakes and French toast for that first sugar rush of the day. ♦ American ♦ Daily, breakfast and lunch. 4130 Mission Blvd (between Pacific Beach Dr and Reed Ave). 858/274.3122

Randy Strunk
Owner

PACIFIC BEACH SURF SHOP

If you need it to surf, they've got it here: wet suits, bodyboards, surfboards and wax, along with skateboards, skimboards, clothing, and sunscreen. The shop also offers rentals on bikes, swim fins, beach chairs, and in-line or roller skates. Surfing lessons are offered by appointment year-round. ♦ Daily. 4150 Mission Blvd (between Pacific Beach Dr and Reed Ave). 858/373.1139. www.pacificbeachsurfshop.com

43 GREEN FLASH

★$ The glassed-in patio is the perfect spot for a sunset dinner (salads, fish, pastas), whereas the dining room and bar inside are great places to meet locals. This is one of the nicest eateries on the boardwalk. ♦ Continental ♦ Daily, breakfast, lunch, and dinner. 701 Thomas Ave (at Ocean Blvd). 858/270.7715. & www.greenflashrestaurant.com

World Famous
california coastal cuisine

44 WORLD FAMOUS

★★$$$ Set right on the boardwalk, this beachy restaurant features "California coastal cuisine," which can be anything from lobster bisque and grilled fresh fish to seafood salads, fish and chips, or prime rib. The food is generally quite good, not to mention filling, and service is informal but pleasant. Both the bar and dining room offer ocean views, but the best seating (if you want to view the nonstop boardwalk action) is out on the patio. ♦ American/continental ♦ Daily, breakfast, lunch, and dinner. 711 Pacific Beach Dr (at Ocean Blvd). 858/272.3100

MISSION BEACH

45 CATAMARAN

$$$ The South Seas theme is taken to the max at this tropical resort hidden behind Polynesian pagoda-style green copper roofs facing the pandemonium on Mission Boulevard. The two-story atrium lobby is a misty green oasis of ferns and waterfalls, and streams run through the grounds between the tower and two-story buildings facing Sail Bay. The 315 rooms and suites are decorated in earth tones and greens;

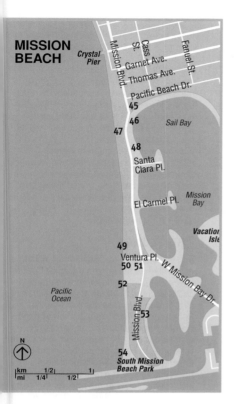

MISSION BEACH

Crystal Pier
Cass St.
Mission Blvd
Garnet Ave.
Thomas Ave.
Fanuel St.
Pacific Beach Dr.
45
46
47
Sail Bay
48
Santa Clara Pl.
El Carmel Pl.
Mission Bay
Vacation Isle
49
Ventura Pl.
50 51
W Mission Bay Dr.
52
Pacific Ocean
Mission Blvd.
53
54
South Mission Beach Park
N
km 1/2 1
mi 1/4 1/2

spicy "Chino-Latino" fare such as Baja shrimp wraps, along with imaginative sandwiches and salads. No need to dress up. Because reservations aren't accepted, expect to wait for a table on the weekends. ♦ American/international ♦ Daily, breakfast and lunch. 3795 Mission Blvd (between Santa Clara Pl and San Jose Pl). 858/488.9060

47 SASKA'S

★★$$$ This place started out as a decent, reasonably priced steak and seafood restaurant with dependable grilled fresh catches, uninspired but fresh salads, and gigantic baked potatoes. The restaurant is a godsend at 1AM when everywhere else is closed. Saska's updated its image with the help of architect **Tom Grondona**, known for his wacky, playful designs. Grondona added an arch, a fish market, and an upstairs open-air café, with neon stripes and cut-out palm trees. An adjacent storefront serves as a popular sushi bar. ♦ Steak/seafood ♦ Daily, lunch and dinner until 1AM. 3768 Mission Blvd (between Pismo and Redondo Cts). 858/488.7311. www.saskas.com

48 PILAR'S BEACH WEAR

Every female body must someday encounter the bathing suit. At this shop, the choice is wide enough to camouflage most flaws and help make the best of what you've got. The shop is mostly devoted to women's swimwear, but there are also a few pairs of swim trunks in stock. ♦ Daily. 3745 Mission Blvd (between Portsmouth and Queenstown Cts). 858/488.3056

49 MISSION BEACH CLUB

Brothers Dan and Ray Hamel opened their bike shop, formerly known as **Hamel's**, back in 1966. Things have changed a lot since then—the façade has been rebuilt to resemble a Gothic castle, the bike shop has expanded to include lots of other sporting equipment, and the brothers sold the place a few years ago. But bathing beauties in string bikinis and briefs still wait in line to rent bikes, boogie boards, roller skates, and in-line skates. Tourists and locals drop by to

some have refrigerators and balconies. Facilities include a restaurant that is well-regarded for its Sunday brunch, a fitness room, pool (not as lavish as you would expect), and bike and water-sports equipment rental. The hotel is owned by the William Evans family, who also own the **Bahia** in Mission Bay and the *Bahia Belle* sternwheeler (see page 121), which offers nighttime cruises between the two hotels. Check on weekend rates, family packages, and other discounts. ♦ 3999 Mission Blvd (between Zanzibar Ct and Pacific Beach Dr). 858/488.1081, 800/422.8386; fax 858/488.1387. &
www.catamaranresort.com

46 MISSION CAFÉ

★★$ Breakfast is the featured meal of the day at this funky neighborhood hangout. Waffles, breakfast burritos, eggs (in various incarnations), and French toast are standouts on the wide-ranging menu, and the pancakes are simply some of the best in town (check out the strawberry-granola and the banana-blackberry versions). Lunch offers plenty of satisfaction too, with

San Diego's first health club was established downtown in 1924. It was an elaborate affair, with 96 sleeping rooms, 2 solariums, 4 handball courts, a gymnasium, and pool. There was also a separate dining room, lounge, and entrance for women.

Restaurants/Clubs: Red | Hotels: Purple | Shops: Orange | Outdoors/Parks: Green | Sights/Culture: Blue

peruse the selection of clothing, accessories, and beach gear on sale. Daring skateboarders perform nearby, entertaining the crowd. A cautionary note: first-time skaters should practice their skills south of **Belmont Park** before attempting to blend with the boardwalk crowd. ♦ Daily. 704 Ventura Pl (between Mission Blvd and Boardwalk). 858/488.8889

50 BELMONT PARK

Belmont Park is the closest San Diego comes to the Jersey shore approach, replete with screams from the roller coaster, the aroma of hot dogs and cotton candy, and a toned-down, carnival-like ambience. The Mission Beach scene received a much-needed commercial boost when this 18-acre shopping-dining-amusement complex opened in 1990, ending nearly a decade of acrimonious discourse about the future of the priceless chunk of real estate between Mission Boulevard and the beach. After a burst of fun and popularity, the park once again became run-down, but it's scheduled for a major redo soon. The park had been Mission Beach's centerpiece since 1925, through prosperous highs and seedy lows. When first developed by John D. Spreckels as a distraction from the raging success of his Coronado Tent City, it was a fanciful, elaborate amusement park with a **Natorium** (now called **The Plunge**), a dance hall, and a roller rink. The midway rides and arcades were contained in **Luna Park**, which was fenced in by the wooden trestles of the **Giant Dipper**. The park survived the ravages of the Depression and peaked in popularity during World War II, when sailors and their dates escaped reality and partied hearty before being parted by the war. By 1976, the park had deteriorated to the point where the city was forced to close it. Gradually the roller coaster's frame became home to a growing huddle of drifters, and the neighbors grew more anxious. In the end, the interests of commerce and nature were integrated into this controversial complex that still hasn't quite caught on. Restaurants and shops have a tendency to disappear after a few months of high rents and low returns. Still, its impact can hardly be ignored, as the **Giant Dipper**'s passengers echo the screams of all roller coaster riders through history. Other attractions here include a merry-go-round and a games arcade. ♦ Daily. 3126 Mission Blvd (between San Fernando and Ventura Pls). 858/488.0668. www.belmontpark.com

Within Belmont Park:

GIANT DIPPER ROLLER COASTER

The retro mint green and cotton-candy pink color scheme of this 1925 coaster seems out of place against the blue summer sky and takes away a bit of the charm of the half-mile of wooden tracks swooping and dipping on the horizon. But at night the 1,600 twinkling white lights outlining its curves are downright romantic. Thanks to the volunteer efforts of the Save the Coaster Foundation, the Giant Dipper became a National Historic Landmark on its 65th birthday (4 July 1990). Nearly one third of the wooden framework and all the tracks were replaced, along with all the nuts and bolts, as restorers faithfully followed the 1925 Frank Prior and Frederick Church design. Granted, there are far more exciting roller coasters around today, but nothing beats this one for nostalgia. ♦ Admission. M-Th, 11AM-8PM; F-Su, 11AM-10PM. 488.1549

THE PLUNGE

If you like swimming pools, don't miss this one, billed as the largest indoor saltwater swimming pool in the world when built in 1925. Architect **Lincoln Rogers** housed the 175-foot-long pool in a grand Spanish-Renaissance palace reminiscent of the **Balboa Park** buildings from the 1915 exposition. The pool was inlaid with painted tiles brought by horse and buggy from Ensenada, Mexico, and both the building and tiles were at the heart of all controversies over changes in the park for the next 65 years. Unlike other **Belmont Park** landmarks, this one has remained open to the public since 1925, and its preservation became a condition of later development. Lap swimmers who were addicted to 60-foot lanes were bereft when the building was closed for renovations in 1987 and had a hard time coping with its transformation from a slightly seedy, mildewy hideaway into a gorgeous showplace at the heart of an upscale fitness club that opened in 1988. The second-story mezzanine that once overlooked the pool was replaced with a two-story-high mural of orca whales. ♦ Admission. 3115 Ocean Front Walk (between San Fernando and Ventura Pls). 858/228.9300

WAVE HOUSE

Should the real-world ocean not provide sufficient thrills, check out the man-made waves at this combo athletic club, beach bar and grill, and new-wave water park. Owner Tom Lochtefeld, a native of La Jolla and co-founder of Raging Waters theme parks, has received lots of praise and attention from pro surfers practicing their acrobatic feats at Bruticus Maximus, a ten-foot wave created by a burst of 100,000 gallons of fresh water per minute crashing at up to 30 miles an hour onto a soft-foam surface. Riders beware—the velocity of the wave machine can spit you out like a sunflower seed. Surfer wannabes enjoy the Flow Rider, a continuous wave that you can ride on with one of their flow boards. Riders pay by the hour and lessons are available. The athletic club offers state-of-the-art equipment, fitness classes, water polo, and personal trainers. The aquatic center offers lifeguard training, summer camps, and various water exercise classes at **The Plunge**. ♦ Daily. 3125 Mission Blvd (between San Fernando and Ventura Pls). 858/228.WAVE, 858/228.9300. www.wavehouse.com

51 CANES BAR AND GRILL

★★$$ The beach scene is in full view from the upstairs deck at this combo restaurant/nightclub on the boardwalk. The *carne asada torta* (Mexican marinated steak sandwich served on a soft roll) goes down well with a chilled margarita; the *carnitas* (roasted pork) plate is a bountiful meal. Burgers and pizzas are available for those with tamer taste buds. But the food isn't really the issue. The draw here is music and fun. Come nightfall, Canes becomes the best outdoor music venue around, with DJs spinning the latest beat when live bands aren't scheduled. If you're not into music, check out the bar's 25 TVs blaring out sporting events. ♦ Mexican/American ♦ M-F, 11AM-2AM; Sa, Su, 9AM-2AM. 3150 Mission Blvd (at Belmont Park). 858/488.1780. www.canesbarandgrill.com

52 BOARDWALK

To attempt a peaceful Sunday-afternoon stroll down the 3-mile boardwalk from **Belmont Park** to **Pacific Beach** is to definitely risk life and limb. Bicyclists with beer-can holders on their handlebars whip through clusters of pedestrians as if determined to win an obstacle-course race, though their exuberance has been somewhat tempered by the addition of designated lanes for walking and riding. At the same time, roller skaters in string bikinis charge oncoming traffic with fearless abandon, passing the males loitering on the wall between the boardwalk and sand, who respond with whistles and catcalls. In 1994, the city instituted an 8-mph speed limit on the boardwalk; because bikes and skates don't typically have speedometers, the law is difficult to enforce, but it does give the cops a chance to nab the worst offenders. It's difficult to imagine how anyone over the age of 25 could bear to spend the night in any of the rental houses along this stretch, which is patrolled frequently by police officers wearing tan shorts, riding herd on

the crowd from their beach-cruiser bicycles. Fortunately, weekdays are much calmer, except at summer's height. Unless you're determined to witness beach life at its rowdiest, stick with the boardwalk's northern stretches near the **Crystal Pier** (see page 125). ♦ South Mission Beach Park to Palisades Park. ♿

53 THE PENNANT

This classic beach bar is popular with the members of OMBAC (the Old Mission Beach Athletic Club)—including police officers, postal workers, and teachers—who thrive on sports and beer. Spend an hour or two on the second-story open-air deck quaffing pitchers of beer and take in yet another view of the beach scene. ♦ Daily, 8AM-2AM in summer; 11AM-2AM in winter. 2893 Mission Blvd (between San Gabriel La and Deal Ct). 488.1671

54 SOUTH MISSION BEACH PARK

Ⓟ This spit of land at the south end of the park has beaches facing both the bay and the open sea. The neighborhood's streets are far less crowded than in central Mission Beach, and the homes far more luxurious. There are several sand volleyball courts and fire rings on the ocean side of South Mission Beach and bicycle paths on the bay side. ♦ Ocean Front Walk (between Belmont Park and San Luis Rey Pl)

OCEAN BEACH

55 DOG BEACH

Ⓟ Rover and Spot can frolic in the waves without leashes here, where the San Diego River flows (or rather trickles) into the sea. It's obviously paradise for dogs, who race in and out of the waves with glee. Dog owners are required to clean up after their pets; compliance, however, can be very spotty. Their territory is separated from the rest of OB by the rock jetty that forms the flood channel; another jetty to the north blocks the river's natural course into the bay. The river floodway is a fertile feeding ground for mussels, clams, egrets, herons, and countless other creatures who appear and disappear with the tides, and the jetty is a popular courseway for bicyclists and joggers heading from the beach to **Robb Field** (see opposite). ♦ W Point Loma Blvd (at Abbott St)

56 THEE BUNGALOW

★★★$$$$ Owner-chef Ed Moore startled longtime customers when he sold this

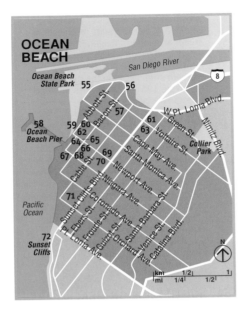

OCEAN BEACH

dinner. Reservations recommended. 4996 W Point Loma Blvd (near Bacon St). 224.2884. www.theebungalow.com

Seafood with a Mediterranean Flair

56 THE 3RD CORNER

★★★$$$ Just across the street from **Thee Bungalow**, the **3rd Corner** restaurant was formerly the site of the **Belgian Lion**. When the Coulon family (longtime owners of the much-missed Belgian Lion) decided to sell, Ed Moore purchased the space, extensively remodeled it, and created an eye-pleasing wine bar with dining rooms separated by stacks of wine crates and shelves of reasonably priced wines. Guests are welcome to dine at the bar counter or simply savor a glass or two of imported beer or fine wine. The menu, a blend of Southern French and Mediterranean influences, features sampler-size "small plates" of Stilton terrines with warm fruit breads, steamed mussels, and scallops niçoise, as well as full-size classic entrées, such as cassoulet and bouillabaisse. An offbeat wine list eschews familiar Chardonnays and Merlots in favor of an international lineup of whites and reds from Italy, Spain, Argentina, France, and Chile. The interior is chic yet inviting, with faux-finished walls, flattering lighting (with lots of candles), and a small fireplace in the bar. ◆ French/Mediterranean ◆ Daily, dinner. Reservations recommended. 2265 Bacon St (at W Point Loma Blvd). 223.2700 ⚐ www.thethirdcorner.com

56 ROBB FIELD

Rugby players collide over leather balls on the playing fields beside the flood channel, in full view of the cars streaming into OB off I-8. On spring and fall weekends, the field is packed with players and fans, and there's a steady stream of joggers passing by. The vast grass fields are also home to soccer leagues, softball teams, model-plane enthusiasts, dog walkers, bird watchers, and picnickers and sunbathers. Bicyclists favor the asphalt path that runs east from **Dog Beach** along the floodway and over Sunset Cliffs Boulevard Bridge to Mission Bay. ◆ W Point Loma Blvd (between Sunset Cliffs Blvd and Bacon St)

Within Robb Field:

ROBB FIELD SKATE PARK

Young boarders flock to this 40,000-square-foot park from throughout the county, attracted by bowls, rails, quarter pipes, and other features of this all-concrete facility.

venerable French restaurant to the Cohn group, owners of several popular eateries around San Diego. The new owners wisely retained the restaurant's character and subtly updated the menu. The small converted bungalow at the edge of **Robb Field** has four intimate dining rooms that glow with candlelight and warmth from the fireplaces, as well as a sheltered patio. Guests dine on pâté; lobster bisque served with fresh Maine lobster meat; roast duck (the house specialty) with cumberland sauce, orange sauce, or pepper-rum glaze; or game specials such as venison, pheasant, and goose. The wine list features more than 1,000 selections and is revered by connoisseurs for its fair pricing and depth. For bargain hunters, there's an early-bird special, including soup or salad and entrée, nightly. ◆ French/continental ◆ Daily,

John D. Spreckels developed much of early San Diego by building spectacular gardens, amusement parks, and other tourist attractions such as Coronado's Tent City, the Mission Beach Amusement Park, and the Mission Cliff Gardens above Mission Valley at the end of his rail lines, where investors were needed to establish new communities.

Ocean Beach's Wednesday evening Farmers' Market (4PM-7PM, until 8PM during the summer) draws crowds to Newport Avenue for fresh produce and flowers, along with baked goods, potted plants, jellies and salsas, and live music. Kids especially enjoy the enclosed trampoline and the rides on real llamas.

Guests must be 6 or older, and pads are required. The fenced park is at the north end of Robb Field, near the bridge over the San Diego River. ♦ Admission (daily, three-month, and annual passes are sold). Daily (closes at sunset). 525.8486

PENINSULA TENNIS CLUB

This club has well-maintained courts and is open to both members and the general public. Members play for free; there's a daily fee for nonmembers. ♦ Daily. 2525 Bacon St (in Robb Field). 226.3407

DOG W🐾SH

57 DOG BEACH DOG WASH

Dogs of all shapes and sizes (and their owners) abound at this bright, friendly establishment devoted to the do-it-yourself washing, grooming, and general pampering of canines. The large elevated tubs (with warm water, towels, and shampoo included in the price) are the centerpiece of the operation, but you can also rent training videos; sign up for various classes; and purchase a variety of shampoos, toys, collars, bandannas, and treats for your best friend. The helpful and enthusiastic staff keeps the place clean and running smoothly. ♦ Daily. 4933 Voltaire St (between Cable and Bacon Sts). 523.1700. www.dogwash.com

58 OCEAN BEACH PIER

The walk to the T at the end of the pier relaxes both body and mind, blowing away tensions in salty breezes. The air seems 10 degrees cooler no matter what time of day, and the waves seem ever more powerful as they pound against the concrete pilings. At the peak of summer's heat, the sun's glare leaves wrinkles around your eyes and sand leaves a fine white crust on your broiled skin. And when the fog of winter rolls in, your body disappears into a cool gray cocoon. The pier has its ardent admirers who barely pass a day without strolling its length. Fishing is part of the daily routine for a few, who dangle their lines from carefully calculated perches for their dinner of mackerel, halibut, or bass. You won't need a fishing license (though catch regulations are enforced) to join the pier anglers, but you will need squid, hooks, and advice from the crusty characters at the small bait-and-tackle shop near the far end of the pier. Be prepared to dodge dive-bombing seagulls that brazenly swarm along the rails, snatching any even remotely edible snacks. Beneath the pier's boardwalk daredevil surfers dodge past the pilings atop curling waves, performing for wanderers who loiter mindlessly, soaking in the scene. The view is even more spectacular on summer nights, when the fireworks from **Sea World** explode on the midnight-blue horizon. ♦ Daily, 8AM–8PM. Park in the lot at the foot of Newport and Abbott Sts. Niagara Ave (at Bacon St)

On Ocean Beach Pier:

OCEAN BEACH PIER CAFE

$ Welcome to the latest of several restaurants/cafés whose main distinction is an enviable setting. Think of it as a resting spot, a place to write postcards with the sea pounding at your feet. The fish tacos, clam chowder, and burgers are all good, though not exceptional. ♦ American ♦ Daily, breakfast, lunch, and early dinner. Almost one-half mile beyond the foot of Niagara (at the end of the pier). 226.3474

59 OCEAN BEACH

These sands are known for their volleyball courts, playgrounds, fire rings, and crowds; the waves are legendary among board and body surfers. North of the pier, oceanfront cliffs crumble into rocky shores, creating tide pools for starfish and hermit crabs. As the rock piles give way to sand south of the pier, the beach widens and surfers congregate at the foot of Newport Avenue, territory also popular with clientele familiar to the police officers on the beach beat. The main lifeguard tower is at the foot of Santa Monica Avenue, and six outposts are scattered north to the end of Voltaire Street and the beginning of **Dog Beach** (see page 131). The lifeguards post flags noting safe swimming areas. Pay attention to them: OB is known for its rip currents that can sweep an unsuspecting swimmer out to sea. Large groups of revelers tend to congregate early around the fire rings, where they bake their bodies in the sun, roast hot dogs over the coals, and burn wooden pallets in an orange blaze against the darkening sky. Lifeguards are on duty at the beach from 9AM until sunset, 365 days a year; they can see you on the beach, even if you can't see them. Parking lots at Abbott Street and Newport Avenue and Abbott Street and West Point Loma Boulevard. ♦ Abbott St (between Newport Ave and W Point Loma Blvd)

60 SHADES

★★$$ This popular spot offers a dynamite location across from the beach and consistently top-notch food. The small dining room is framed with full-length windows, and the tables are judiciously placed for optimum views. Breakfast fare includes the usual bacon and eggs along with pancakes, huge bowls of granola, and bowls of fruit. The fish-and-chips lunch is the star of the menu, with crunchy strips of perfectly battered and fried fish and piles of fries. Even the salads are bountiful, literally spilling out of their bowls. Dinners include fresh fish and pastas. ◆ Californian ◆ Daily, breakfast, lunch, and dinner. 5083 Santa Monica Ave (between Bacon and Abbott Sts). 222.0501. ♿ www.shadesob.com

60 NICK'S AT THE PIER

★$$ Few Ocean Beach restaurants actually overlook the sand and sea. This location at the foot of Santa Monica was hugely controversial when first built in 1985. OBceans didn't look fondly upon fancy digs and fern bars in that era, but grew to love the food and setting at Qwiigs restaurant, which claimed the space for two decades. It took more than a year for new owners (including Ed Moore from the **3rd Corner**) to remodel the dining room and reopen the space as a branch of the popular Pacific Beach Nick's. The restaurant was still in its infancy at press time, and the food was less than stellar. The menu meanders through salad, seafood, pasta, and ethnic cuisine; the chef is most successful with simple fish tacos, burgers, and pastas. Food is served until 1AM—a novelty in OB that's sure to please patrons of the vastly enlarged bar. ◆ American ◆ Daily, lunch and dinner; Sa, Su, brunch and dinner. 5083 Santa Monica Ave (between Bacon and Abbott Sts). 222.7437. ♿

60 TOWER TWO BEACH CAFE

★$ Completing the dining triad at OB's ocean-facing minimall is this totally casual outdoor eatery where dogs lap cool water from communal bowls, kids play with crayons, and grownups quaff chilled beer. The food is of the mainstream burger, hot dog, fish sandwich genre, but the scene is far more fascinating than at any fast-food joint. ◆ American ◆ Daily, breakfast, lunch, and dinner. 5083 Santa Monica Ave (between Bacon and Abbott Sts). 223.4059. ♿

61 KAISERHOF

★★$$ San Diego's best German restaurant, Kaiserhof is a favored destination for anyone who loves a good beef *rouladen* or wiener schnitzel. Entrée portions are enormous, and just to make sure no one leaves hungry, dinners include soup or salad, two side dishes, and lots of hearty breads. As befits a *biergarten*, there's a sizable collection of German beers on tap. In addition to the covered patio (the best place to sit on sunny days and balmy evenings), there's seating in the cozy bar area and the dining room with a fireplace. Come here with a big appetite and don't be afraid to request a doggie bag. ◆ German ◆ Tu-Su, dinner; F-Su, lunch. 2253 Sunset Cliffs Blvd (between Voltaire St and W Point Loma Blvd). 224.0606. www.kaiserhofrestaurant.com

62 HODAD'S

★★$ Lunch at this burger joint is a true OB experience. Surfing and cartoon memorabilia cover every wall; you can even dine inside a VW bus. The menu is simple: big greasy burgers, steak fries, and thick shakes and malts. ◆ American ◆ Daily, lunch and dinner. 5010 Newport Ave (between Bacon and Abbott Sts). 224.4623

63 OB PEOPLE'S ORGANIC FOODS MARKET

Flash into the past as you select your kefir of choice to the sounds of Joni Mitchell or the Grateful Dead. This 1970s food co-op entered the 21st century with an award-winning, sustainable "green" building designed by **hannah gabriel wells architects.** The two-story structure was built with recycled and sustainably harvested materials, and windows are located for maximum use of daylight for indoor lighting. Energy-efficient strategies are used throughout—down to shoppers bringing their own bags (they do have free bags in case you forget yours). It remains one of the precious few markets with organic veggies and fruits; bins of granola and brown rice; coolers with carrot juice and rennetless cheese; and shelves filled with herbal and nonchemical lotions, shampoos, and soaps. Members get a 10-percent discount on purchases. ◆ Daily. 4765 Voltaire St (between Ebers St and Sunset Cliffs Blvd). 224.1387. www.obpeoplesfood.coop

64 SOUTH BEACH BAR & GRILL

★★$ The windows by the bar look out across the parking lot to the ocean and right onto the sidewalk, allowing patrons to visit with friends passing by without even leaving their stools. The fish tacos and oyster shooters are good and popular with the beach crowd. ◆ American ◆ Daily, lunch and dinner. 5059 Newport Ave (between Bacon and Abbott Sts). 226.4577. ♿

Nature's Calendar

San Diego's seasonal changes are subtle and even invisible to the untrained eye until a few years have gone by. Then, it slowly sinks in. Winter means whales; spring brings flowers and showers; summer belongs to the beach. Check out these signs when you visit.

January

Over 10,000 gray whales migrate past San Diego on their way from the Bering Strait to **Baja California**. Whales' spouts can be spotted from **Point Loma**, **Sunset Cliffs**, and whale-watching boats.

February

More whales, rough seas, and cold nights—sometimes as low as 50 degrees! There's the possibility of snow in the mountains, which causes bumper-to-bumper traffic on mountain roads as San Diego natives race to get a peek at winter.

March

If it's going to rain, this is the most likely time. In March 1991, the city got 7 inches of precipitation all at once—that's almost the normal annual rainfall.

April

Ocotillo and other cacti bloom in the **Anza-Borrego Desert**.

May

Wild lilacs bloom along mountain roads; tulip and daffodil bulbs are coaxed into production; orange blossoms fill the air with their heady perfume.

June

Jacaranda trees cast a feathery purple haze over neighborhood streets; June Gloom descends, covering the skies with gray clouds through most of the day; June bugs attack windows, lamp shades, and walls with their brittle shells; grunion season begins.

July

Skies clear for the fireworks; the ocean temperature reaches the high 60s; brush and forest fires fill the skies with smoke and soot.

August

The Perseid meteor showers fill the back-country skies with streaks of shooting stars; drive to **Sunrise Highway** near **Mount Laguna** and set out your beach chair in an empty field for the show.

September

Ocean temperatures hit the mid-70s; the kids are back in school, and the beaches are nearly empty; hot, dry Santa Ana winds blow at 40–50 mph, challenging drivers to stay in their lanes; apples ripen in **Julian**.

October

Golden leaves and bushels of acorns fall from the oak trees in the **Cuyamaca**, **Palomar**, and **Laguna Mountains**; coastal fogs are so thick you can hear the foghorns for miles.

November

Expect the Taurid meteor showers (see August); red and white poinsettias bloom in front yards all over town.

December

Ocean waves are whipped by the winds into whitecaps, and wool sweaters actually get some wear.

---

65 Southcoast Surf Shop

This is possibly the best shop in San Diego for surfboards, boogie boards, wet suits, and all the appropriate gear for the hang-ten set; there's also a great selection of beach wear and T-shirts. ◆ Daily. 5023 Newport Ave (between Bacon and Abbott Sts). 223.7017. www.southcoast.com

65 The Black

The 1960s are alive and well in this head shop reeking of incense and patchouli oil. Drug paraphernalia is *verboten* in San Diego these days, but this shop still has an impressive collection of bongs, pipes, roach clips, and rolling papers—presumably for use by tobacco smokers. There's lots of other merchandise as well, ranging from clothing and jewelry to posters, magazines, and a huge selection of beads (for creating your own jewelry). ◆ Daily. 5017 Newport Ave (between Bacon and Abbott Sts). 222.5498

66 Golden Seashell

The selection of silver and gold charms at this small jewelry shop is worth perusing, especially if you're looking for a sea-motif gift, like a sterling silver manta ray or a marlin in 14-karat gold. ◆ M-Su. 4920 Newport Ave (between Cable and Bacon Sts). 225.0481

Restaurants/Clubs: Red | **Hotels: Purple** | **Shops: Orange** | **Outdoors/Parks: Green** | **Sights/Culture: Blue**

66 OCEAN BEACH INTERNATIONAL HOSTEL

$ Also called the OBI Hostel, this is the latest incarnation of the old **Newport Hotel**. The hostel has 60 dorm beds, a kitchen and lounge for guests' use, and a great front porch for watching the street action. Passports or other ID are required, to keep out the riffraff tired of sleeping on the beach. Also, only international travelers are accepted; you'll need to have proof of travel, such as current visas, international travel tickets, or foreign ID cards. Reservations are available by phone, fax, or Internet. ◆ 4961 Newport Ave (between Cable and Bacon Sts). 223.SURF, 800/339.7263; 243.0093. www.californiahostel.com

66 PACIFIC SHORES BAR

Aficionados of dive beach bars need look no farther than the kidney-shaped table embedded with seashells and kelp near the front door. Order a round of Schlitz and shots of Rock & Rye, punch up a Johnny Cash tune on the jukebox, and pretend you're a beach bum circa 1950. For a change of flavor, arrive late at night on a weekend and mingle with a young crowd more into martinis, multiple piercings, and modern music. ◆ Daily. 4927 Newport Ave (between Cable and Bacon Sts). 223.7549

67 POMA'S

★★$ Leonard Poma tried to give up his sub shop and retire to Hawaii, but he couldn't stay away from OB. When he returned, the word spread quickly—aided by enormous signs hanging from the small shop proclaiming "Leonard's Back!" Soon the hungry hordes clamored for Leonard's subs: the Newport packed with cold cuts and cheese, the hot roast beef, the salami, the pastrami, and the mortadella. Thick-crusted pizzas are piled high with toppings, and the antipasto has plenty of marinated vegetables, oil-cured olives, and lip-puckering peppers. There are tables and a TV inside and a few sidewalk tables, but you're much better off taking your lunch to the pier or beach. ◆ Subs/pizza ◆ Daily, lunch and dinner. 1846 Bacon St (at Niagara Ave). 223.3027

67 NATI'S MEXICAN RESTAURANT

$$ A couple of generations of OB residents have grown up on **Nati's** Americanized Mexican fare. No, the cheese crisps and ground-beef tacos aren't particularly authentic, but prices are reasonable and the atmosphere is ultra casual, making it a popular spot for families with kids. Indoor and patio seating. ◆ Mexican ◆ Daily, lunch and dinner. 1852 Bacon St (at Niagara Ave). 224.3369

68 IN HARMONY HERBS AND SPICES

Stop in this unusual little shop for an incredible selection of spices, seeds, herbs (for cooking or medicinal purposes), aromatherapy products, herbal extracts, and books. Live herb plants, some of them rare or hard to find, are also available for gardeners. Definitely an OB treasure, with savvy staffers and some fun and unusual gift items. ◆ M-Su. 1862½ Bacon St (between Niagara and Newport Aves). 223.8051. www.inharmonyherbs.com

68 SWOOZY'S

OB has lots of trendy shops selling swimwear and sexy clothing for perfect young bods. Swoozy's is perfectly in touch with all that, but also sells Dickies pants and shoes that fit and befit grown-ups. The selection changes constantly and the sales staff is consistently helpful and friendly. Bring the teens here—they'll love you for it. ◆ Daily. 1857 Bacon St (between Niagara and Newport Aves). 523.5801

69 NEWPORT AVENUE ANTIQUE CENTER

Locals mourned the demise of **Coronet**, the classic five-and-dime store that closed on this spot in 1993. Its place was soon taken by yet another antiques emporium, this one divided into sections for dozens of different vendors, some selling treasures and some selling junk. ◆ Daily. 4864 Newport Ave (between Sunset Cliffs Blvd and Cable St). 222.8686

69 ORTEGA'S

★★$$ One of the best Mexican restaurants in all San Diego, this family-run place is usually packed. With only a handful of tables and a small counter, expect a wait during peak hours—then dig into excellent dishes such as tamales, enchiladas, *huevos rancheros*, *tortas* (sandwiches), and daily fresh fish specials. Unless the chef is frantically busy frying fresh chips and creating special causes, he'll whip up breakfast any time of the day. Though it may sound bizarre, one of the best menu items is the Fries Asada, a pile of freshly cut french fries covered with cheese, carne asada, pico de gallo (a fresh salsa of chopped onions, cilantro, chilies, and tomatoes), and dollops of sour cream and guacamole. Calories be damned! ◆ Mexican ◆ W-M, breakfast, lunch, and dinner. 4888 Newport Ave (between Sunset Cliffs Blvd and Cable St). 222.4205. Also at 4993 Niagara St (at Bacon St). 222.1722

70 GARY GILMORE GOLDSMITH

Gorgeous emeralds and freshwater pearls grace the display windows outside this elegant jewelry shop. The jewelers will willingly indulge your fantasies with their trays of minerals and gems—everything from turquoise to fine diamonds—and their inspirations in jewelry design. ♦ Tu-Sa. 4857 Newport Ave (between Sunset Cliffs Blvd and Cable St). 225.1137. www.gggoldsmith.com

70 OCEAN BEACH ANTIQUE MALL

The displays alone are worth a visit, making you long for items you couldn't possibly adapt to your décor: gorgeous furniture, holiday ornaments, and plenty of objets d'art and vintage jewelry. ♦ Daily. 4847 Newport Ave (between Sunset Cliffs Blvd and Cable St). 223.6170

71 O.B. DONUTS

Local food critics always include this shop in their lists of San Diego's best doughnut makers, and with good cause. From the basic cake to the airy twists and rich buttermilk bars, these are some darn good doughnuts. The cheerful, hardworking family who runs the place also makes croissants, scones, and other pastries. ♦ Doughnuts/coffeehouse ♦ Daily. 1830 Sunset Cliffs Blvd (between Narragansett and Coronado Aves). 222.0298. www.obdonuts.com

72 SUNSET CLIFFS

Guess what you're supposed to do here? Focus your lens, brace your sandal-clad feet a few steps away from the crumbly edge of the cliffs, and press the shutter studiously as the orange ball sinks into the golden sea. Most town residents have a hefty portfolio of sunset shots. And it's pretty hard to resist. The setting is pure drama—the ragged edge of the continent battered by the spray of the wild sea. Since the turn of the 19th century, speculators and developers have coveted the cliffs. Albert Goodwill Spalding, the sporting-goods magnate, attempted to tame them with studied civility in 1910 when he bought a dramatic chunk of hillside facing the cliffs and the sea. When the **1915-1916 Panama California Exposition** opened, so did Spaulding's Japanese gardens, with arched bridges across canyons dug by the surf, palm-thatch umbrellas shading benches on rocky points above the water's foam, and pebbled paths curving through gardens of serenity. Nature scoffed at the $2 million investment and blew the plantings away like shredded dollar bills. Be careful here: Don't become so entranced by the beauty that you forget your personal safety. The cliffs' edges are as unpredictable as the surge of water below and can crumble all too easily. Cliff rescues, complete with screaming sirens, whirring helicopters, and tragic consequences, are common—and largely unnecessary. Pay attention to signs warning you to stay away from the edges, and stick to populated paths. ♦ Sunset Cliffs Blvd (between Hill St and Point Loma Ave)

72 MILLS MANOR

You would expect the homes closest to **Sunset Cliffs** to be particularly elegant and grand, given the breathtaking view. John P. Mills, real estate salesman extraordinaire, certainly thought so in the early 1920s, when he hustled a lot for his imaginary residential community of winding paved streets and red-roofed, white-stucco homes staggering up the hillside above the Japanese gardens. Mills and his partners bought the land from Spalding's widow, gave their new streets Italian and Spanish names, and hosted lavish gatherings to entice potential buyers. The centerpiece of Mills's development scheme is still an attention grabber. The 1926 pink-stucco, red-tile-roofed, 12-bedroom mansion was meant to rival any similar estate along the California coast. A wall partially hides the Corinthian columns and arched stained-glass windows of the main house; the adjoining 19-horse stable has been converted to a four-car garage with apartments on the second floor. Mills didn't have a lot of time to enjoy his palace (equipped with a $40,000 chinchilla rug, polished rosewood paneling, and hand-carved Italian furnishings): His development company ran smack up against the Great Depression. By 1929, Mills was destitute, and his development was never revived. The manor has had several owners since then; when last sold, it went for several million. It remains a private residence. ♦ Sunset Cliffs Blvd (at Osprey St)

LA JOLLA

La Jolla can be thought of as a series of snapshots: a panorama of green palms and pines, turquoise sky and amethyst sea, white domes and red-tile roofs adorned with bougainvillea; an underwater closeup of an orange garibaldi surrounded by iridescent neon fish; a formal wedding portrait on the lawn of a seaside park; an action shot of a Frisbee in flight; a wide-angle view of surfers gliding on white foam toward a wall of sun-baked bodies on hazy brown sand.

It's an understatement to say that La Jolla is a wealthy community. It's hard to keep the dollar signs out of your mind as you stroll through the tony, eucalyptus-lined streets. La Jollans motor in Mercedes, Range Rovers, and BMWs. Their sweats are by Polo, their suits by Armani, their dresses by Yves Saint Laurent. Homes nestled in foliage line the coast and punctuate the palm-studded hills, boasting columned terraces and tiled swimming pools in glistening shades of blue. Much of La Jolla's character can be attributed to its founders, who understood the potential of the rugged coastline and chaparral-covered hills. Frank Bosford and George Heald of the 1887 Pacific Coast Land Bureau had the sense to lay out the streets of their new town along its natural lines, following the curve of the coastline with boulevards 80 feet wide. They planted 2,000 eucalyptus, cedar, and palm trees from the waterfront into the hills.

Ellen Browning Scripps gave La Jolla its soul. Scripps, who amassed a small fortune in the newspaper business, started buying land here in 1896, moved into her La Jolla cottage a year later, and immediately assumed the role of benefactor. Over the next 50 years, she gave the village a bounty of lasting gifts. With her brother and half sister, she funded the **Scripps Institution of Oceanography (SIO)**. She created the **Children's Pool** south of **La Jolla Bay** and donated much of **Torrey Pines Park** to the city. Employing architect **Irving Gill**, she started **Bishop's School** and **La Jolla Recreation Center**, the Wisteria Cottage, and LaJolla Woman's Club. With **Louis Gill** (Irving's nephew), she added a bell tower to **St. James-by-the-Sea Episcopal Church**. This cluster of Gill buildings and vast, undisturbed lawns is a treasured cultural zone, protected by Scripps's wise investments and good taste. In 1927 La Jollans gratefully dedicated their most picturesque park to Ellen Scripps on her 91st birthday. The Monterey cypress that twists and bends around the simple brick marker bearing her name was planted in 1936 in a posthumous celebration of her 100th birthday.

La Jolla's heart is the **Village**, roughly delineated by **Pearl Street** to the south, **Prospect Street** to the north, **Torrey Pines Road** to the east, and the rugged coast to the west. Within these boundaries are **La Jolla Cove** and **Scripps Park**, and the restaurants, shops, galleries, and glamour that entrance visitors and make this such a perfect neighborhood for simply strolling about. North of the cove is **La Jolla Shores**, a long stretch of waves on sand. Early La Jollans dreamed of establishing a yacht club here, but F.W. Kellogg realized the folly of the scheme (boats couldn't moor along the open coast) and established **La Jolla Beach & Tennis Club** in 1935, a members-only establishment now run by his descendants. In 1951 Florence Scripps Kellogg donated a large park north of the club to the city; **Kellogg Park** now borders a long beach unequaled by any other in San Diego. **Scripps Pier** is the shore's northern boundary, where the sandstone cliffs prevent further coastline development.

spread throughout the 1,200-acre campus—in eucalyptus groves and lawns and even atop buildings. The 16 pieces of sculpture include Terry Allen's *Trees*, three lead-covered eucalyptus trees that stand initially unnoticeable near the library. Passersby are more likely to hear the trees before they see them, and the sound of a tree "reciting" Aztec poetry or country-western songs startles the unsuspecting. Sculptor Robert Irwin wrapped sections of another eucalyptus grove with blue-violet, plastic-coated, small-gauge chain-link fencing atop 25-foot-high stainless steel poles; the late French artist Niki de Saint- Phalle built a 14-foot fiberglass *Sun God* that stands on top of a 15-foot ivy-laced arch in a grassy park near the **Mandeville Auditorium**. The Scottish avant-garde gardener Hamilton Finlay created a park with chiseled stone benches and birdbaths shaped like aircraft carriers, and Jenny Holzer engraved a massive green granite table with thought-provoking quotes. ◆ For a map of the collection, call 534.2117. www.stuartcollection.ucsd.edu

10 SCRIPPS INSTITUTION OF OCEANOGRAPHY (SIO)

The **Scripps Pier**, where biologists have run all sorts of unusual experiments, has been a local landmark since 1916, when Ellen Browning Scripps established an endowment fund for the institution. The pier was replaced by a new one in 1987–1988 and renamed the **Ellen Browning Scripps Memorial Pier**—yet another testament to a beloved benefactor. Currently the largest and oldest oceanographic institution in the world, **SIO** began as the Marine Biological Association of San Diego in 1903, when scientists led by Berkeley professor William E. Ritter worked out of a boathouse and a wooden shack that they called the "little green laboratory." By 1910, the scientists had a permanent laboratory overlooking the Pacific. In 1912, the institute became part of the **University of California** system and was the first college to award doctorates in oceanography. It now has a staff of more than 1,300 biologists, oceanographers, geologists, and other scientists and support personnel researching the greenhouse effect, global warming, earthquake prediction, the marine food chain, pharmaceuticals derived from sea life, and other subjects. The campus on both sides of La Jolla Shores Drive includes one of the original 1910 **Irving Gill** buildings, a library by **Liebhardt & Weston**, and a library by **Lloyd Ruocco**. ◆ 8602 La Jolla Shores Dr

(off El Paseo Grande, a mile north of Torrey Pines Rd). 534.3624. www.sio.ucsd.edu

11 BIRCH AQUARIUM

Opened in 1992, this 64,157-square-foot, $14 million facility replaced the beloved, ramshackle **Scripps Aquarium** that had entertained and educated hundreds of thousands of visitors since 1950. The current museum, designed by San Diego architects **Wheeler, Wimer, Blackman & Associates**, sits on a bluff above La Jolla Shores and has more than 60 tanks filled with lobsters, octopus, eels, sharks, and all the colorful creatures that keep us fascinated with underwater realms. An outdoor tide pool displays the starfish, urchins, anemones, and crabs like those found on San Diego's beaches during low tide, and the museum includes interactive displays explaining tides, waves, and earthquakes. The museum runs educational programs and great field trips, including visits to tide pools, snorkeling excursions, and specimen collecting in Mission Bay. The bookshop has an imaginative collection of sea-life–oriented gifts. ◆ Admission. Daily. 2300 Expedition Way (at N Torrey Pines Rd). 534.3474. & www.aquarium.ucsd.edu

12 LA JOLLA PLAYHOUSE

San Diego's reputation as a center for theater has been bolstered by this playhouse, formally called the **Mandell Weiss Center for the Performing Arts**. The summer season has become nationally known for its elaborate and innovative sets and its eclectic selection of plays. It was established in 1947 by the **Actors Company**, a repertory company founded by San Diegan Gregory Peck and Hollywood friends Dorothy McGuire and Mel Ferrer, using a high school auditorium on Nautilus Street. Peck and company staged a series of acclaimed plays for 17 years; then, in 1964, the theater closed down. It wasn't until 1983 that it reopened under the aegis of **UCSD**. Since then, several of its productions have moved east, to Broadway, including the rock musical *Tommy* and Randy Newman's *Faust*. After two extensions of sold-out performances in 2004 and 2005, *Jersey Boys*, based on the life story of Frankie Valli and the Four Seasons, became the Playhouse's biggest draw since the West Coast premiere of *Rent* in 1997. The **Joan and Irwin Jacobs Center** opened in 2005, adding the **Potiker Theatre** to the Playhouse's compound of three theaters and various workshop spaces. The season generally runs from May through October; call ahead for exact schedule.

Restaurants/Clubs: Red | Hotels: Purple | Shops: Orange | Outdoors/Parks: Green | Sights/Culture: Blue

♦ Admission. 2910 La Jolla Village Dr N (between Gilman Dr and Torrey Pines Rd). 550.1010. www.lajollaplayhouse.com

13 ELIJAH'S

$ Given the scarcity of Jewish delis in San Diego, this is a blessing, albeit an overpriced one. A Hollywood theme prevails, with the walls covered in celebrity photos and movie stills. The menu is traditionally lengthy—a dozen omelettes; lox and whitefish platters; eight soups including matzo ball and borscht; and mammoth pastrami, chopped liver, knockwurst, and kosher bologna sandwiches. A trip to the adjoining bakery for chocolate-chip *rugelach*, pumpernickel bagels, and lox should clean out your wallet. ♦ Deli ♦ Daily, breakfast, lunch, and dinner. 8861 Villa La Jolla Dr (between Nobel and La Jolla Village Drs). 455.1461. www.elijahsrestaurant.com

14 THE AVENTINE

People either love or hate architect **Michael Graves**'s monumental attention-grabber on a hillside, rising above I-5 (and anything else in its way). Named after one of Rome's seven hills, it has been criticized for lack of harmony with its neighbors. The complex, which includes a 419-room **Hyatt Regency** hotel, an office building, an upscale health club, and a restaurant court, is an architectural landmark—one often compared to an Art Deco radio, a monstrous piece of whole-wheat toast, or a modernistic tombstone. Parking can be confusing: There is one enclosed lot on La Jolla Village Drive and another on Executive Way, and the hike from either lot to the restaurants can be lengthy. ♦ 3777 La Jolla Village Dr (between Regents Rd and I-5)

Within The Aventine:

HYATT REGENCY LA JOLLA AT AVENTINE

$$$ You can't miss the golden-ochre, crescent-shaped roof of this 16-story hotel looming on the horizon, surrounded by rust-colored pillars and imposing lawns. **Michael**

Graves went far beyond designing the façade, also acting as interior design and art consultant and even including his own paintings and sketches on the walls. Graves responded to developer Jack Naiman's challenge for a romantic designer hotel by blending neoclassical, Mediterranean, and Postmodern elements, using towers, campaniles, colonnades, and a collection of classical sculptures. The earth-toned stucco walls and rose, gray, and red Italian marble floors add warmth to the massive public spaces; white harem tents and terra-cotta pillars shade sunbathers by the pool; and palms are used inside and out. The 419 guest rooms and suites have cherry wood furnishings with black lacquered designs that repeat the pattern of square glass panes on the hotel's exterior. The adjacent 32,000-square-foot health club was renovated in 2007 and has basketball and tennis courts (there is an extra charge for guests to use the facility). Business travelers are far more prevalent than families. ♦ 3777 La Jolla Village Dr (between Lebon Dr and University Center La). 552.1234, 888/552.1234; fax 552.6066. www.lajollahyatt.com

CAFÉ JAPENGO

★★★$$$$ This sleek and sophisticated dining room attracts office workers from the Golden Triangle, lots of good-looking singles from all over town, and the theater crowd headed for the **La Jolla Playhouse**. The most popular seats in the house are at the sushi bar, where everything is prepared to order. Other entrées include a succulent slow-roasted duckling, several different grilled fish dishes, and a filling 10-ingredient fried rice. The sushi bar is open until 11PM Monday through Saturday. ♦ Asian ♦ M-F, lunch and dinner; Sa, Su, dinner. 8960 University Center La (between Nobel and La Jolla Village Drs). 450.3355

15 DONOVAN'S STEAK & CHOP HOUSE

★★★★$$$$ Calling Donovan's a steak house is doing it a disservice, as surely it will be compared with all the other beef palaces charging upwards of $35 for a simple steak. Donovan's certainly serves a mean USDA prime porterhouse and, unlike other self-important spots, the restaurant doesn't skimp on sides (go for the crispy skillet-fried potatoes with onions) included in the price. The classic shrimp cocktail and crab cakes are perfect starters for the occasion, and a light cheesecake makes a fine ending. There's an outdoor patio lounge that caters specifically to cigar smokers for that final cognac. ♦ Steak house ♦ M-Sa, dinner. Reservations recommended. 4340 La Jolla

Theodor Seuss Geisel—better known as Dr. Seuss, author of *The Cat in the Hat* and *The Grinch Who Stole Christmas*, among other books—lived in La Jolla from the late 1940s until his death in 1991. He won a Pulitzer Prize in 1984 for his contributions to children's literature.

Author Raymond Chandler lived in La Jolla between 1949-1959. His novel *Playback* is set in La Jolla (called Esmeralda in the book).

AVIATION IN SAN DIEGO

1883 The first controlled-wing flight is performed on 9 August by John and James Montgomery, who carry their soaring machine on a hay wagon to its first test flight in what is now known as **Otay Mesa**. John sits in the bicycle saddle between two 20-foot muslin-covered wings while James stands on the crest of a hill with the 40-foot towrope. At the signal, he runs downhill, pulling the 40-foot glider behind him. John glides to a graceful landing 600 feet away.

1922 The first airplane manufacturing plant is started by Claude Ryan on **Dutch Flats**.

1925 The first daily scheduled year-round passenger airline is inaugurated when **Ryan Airlines** starts operating the **San Diego–Los Angeles Air Line**.

1926 San Diego becomes the first city to establish a municipal board of air control and issue a complete set of air ordinances.

1927 Colonel Charles A. Lindbergh starts his historic flight on 10 May in the *Spirit of St. Louis* from a small private landing strip adjacent to the **Ryan Aircraft Company**. Lindbergh flies over **San Diego Bay** to **North Island** to refuel, then flies to New York and eventually across the Atlantic to Paris.

Village Dr (at Genesee Ave). 450.6666. ♿ www.donovanssteakhouse.com

16 EMBASSY SUITES

$$$ The Golden Triangle's most reasonably priced rooms are to be found at this chain hotel. All 335 suites have separate living rooms with separate televisions and wet bars with refrigerators and microwaves and are as popular with business travelers as with families. Complimentary full breakfast and afternoon cocktails are served in the atrium lounge, and the **Coast Cafe** restaurant is open for lunch and dinner. Facilities include a fitness center and indoor pool. Ask about special weekend and family rates. ♦ 4550 La Jolla Village Dr (between I-805 and Genesee Ave). 453.0400, 800/EMBASSY; fax 453.4226. ♿ www.eslajolla.com

17 COSTA VERDE CENTER

Another in the series of shopping malls that serve as the Golden Triangle's neighborhood centers, this one is significant for its wide range of great restaurants. The multilevel complex can be confusing, as it is completely oriented to the automobile and various parking lots. Shop and restaurant hours vary. ♦ Daily. Genesee Ave (at La Jolla Village Dr). www.costaverdecenter.com

Within Costa Verde Center:

APOLLONIA GREEK BISTRO

★★★$$ Whether you dine in or order your dinner to go, you'll be delighted with the results at this café; the owners of popular **Café Athena** in Pacific Beach took over the spot in 2007 and have made it better than ever. The Greek salads are legendary, and anchovy lovers will want to order the *horiatiki* salad, with chunks of tomato, cucumber, red onion, artichoke hearts, feta, olives, and salty anchovies. The gyros, souvlaki, *spanakopita* (spinach pie), and moussaka are all first rate, and the chef also prepares specials such as lamb shanks or fish stew. Don't miss the baklava for dessert. Several small dining rooms opening toward a deli area and the open kitchen give a sense of privacy. ♦ Greek ♦ M-Sa, lunch and dinner; Su, dinner. Lower level. 455.1535. ♿

18 WESTFIELD SHOPPINGTOWN UTC

Developer Ernest Hahn turned the shopping center of the 1960s into a faux center city when he built UTC on 90 acres of barren hillsides in the late 1970s. His mall begat the Golden Triangle, and ultimately became the commercial district for the sprawling, red-roofed condo communities and spiraling office towers that now fill the rolling hills between Interstates 5 and 805. But UTC is far more than a shopping mall. Its tenants include an indoor ice-skating rink surrounded by a video-game arcade and a food court with take-out delicacies from egg rolls to *spanakopita*; a child-care center; the **Well Being Center**, with health education and exercise classes; a full-scale fitness center; a bank; four major department stores (**Macy's, Nordstrom, Sport Chalet**, and **Sears**); and enough clothing and specialty shops to keep those plastic cards shuffled. It's a great spot for mall browsers, and those who know the layout well enough to park near their destination get in and out quickly. Developer Hahn went on to build downtown's

Restaurants/Clubs: Red | Hotels: Purple | Shops: Orange | Outdoors/Parks: Green | Sights/Culture: Blue

fantastical **Horton Plaza** and the blessedly cool, indoor **North County Fair** in Escondido. ♦ Daily. 4545 La Jolla Village Dr (between Towne Centre Dr and Genesee Ave). 546.8858

19 LA JOLLA SHORES

The mile-long beach from the **La Jolla Beach & Tennis Club** to the 1,000-foot-long **Scripps Pier** is one of the most popular playgrounds in San Diego, offering plenty of room for scuba divers, surfers, boogie boarders, body surfers, swimmers, and toddlers running from the surf. **Kellogg Park**, the grassy lawn at the south end of the shores, was donated to the city by Florence Scripps Kellogg, niece of Ellen Browning Scripps and wife of William Kellogg, creator of the **Beach & Tennis Club**. Scuba divers enter the water here, headed for the underwater canyons offshore, and kids are quite happy at the playground by the sand. Lifeguards patrol the beach during the summer months, performing hundreds of rescues of unwary swimmers caught in riptides, unruly surfers in over their heads, and lost children wandering the shoreline. There are rest rooms, showers, and parking lots, all of which are full from dawn until dusk in the summertime. The best areas for solitude and tide pools are at the far north end of the beach, toward the **Scripps Pier** (see page 143). Keep an eye on the tides; you can easily lose your strip of sand and watch your towels get washed away when the tide comes in. ♦ La Jolla Shores Dr (between Camino del Sol and Scripps Pier)

20 LA JOLLA VILLAGE SQUARE

When it opened in 1979, the mall was the only enclosed shopping center in San Diego—an idea that never took off. New owners took over the mall in 1991 and literally turned it inside out, updating the exterior façades and placing all shop entrances outside, close to the parking lots. High-priced tenants moved out and were

---

My first impulse was to get out in the street at high noon and shout four-letter words.

—Raymond Chandler, on arriving in the genteel village of La Jolla

---

Scuba divers used to pry green and red abalone from under algae-encrusted rocks off La Jolla's shores. The meat itself is wonderful, but more beautiful are the insides of the shells, with opalescent bands of turquoise, rose, and green. Unfortunately, the abalone are now endangered and divers are forbidden to collect them.

---

replaced by low-priced megastores: a **Cost Plus**, **World Market**, **Trader Joe's** liquor and specialty food market, along with an **AMC** movie theater, **Ralph's Grocery**, and **PetSmart**, and numerous take-out food stands and restaurants. The mall has become a popular destination for neighborhood residents running errands and picking up dinner. Store and restaurant hours vary. ♦ Daily. 8657 Villa La Jolla Dr (south of Nobel Dr). 455.7550. &

Within La Jolla Village Square:

CALIFORNIA PIZZA KITCHEN

★$ This is a family favorite because of its hefty portions, inexpensive prices, and eclectic menu sure to please everyone. Finicky eaters can have pasta with plain tomato sauce; more adventurous types might like the jambalaya pasta and Thai chicken pizza. Thin-crust pizzas for two have toppings ranging from pepperoni to pineapple, and the desserts get rave reviews from all ages. ♦ Californian/Italian ♦ Daily, lunch and dinner. 457.4222. Also at 437 S Hwy 101 (near Lomas Santa Fe), Solana Beach. 793.0999. www.cpk.com

21 SAN DIEGO, CALIFORNIA, TEMPLE FOR THE CHURCH OF JESUS CHRIST OF LATTER-DAY SAINTS

Motorists on I-5 can be expected to gawk when they first see the 10 alabaster spires of this Gothic temple. A 10-foot gold-leaf statue of Moroni (the angel who spoke with the church's founder, Joseph Smith) tops the temple, designed by **Deems Lewis McKinley Architects**. When it opened in 1993, outsiders were allowed to tour its interior; now the temple is used only for special religious occasions and is closed to the public. ♦ 7474 Charmant Dr (off Lebon Dr)

22 LA JOLLA SHORES HOTEL

$$$ Smack up against the sidewalk at the southern end of La Jolla Shores beach is an ocean lover's delight. The hotel, designed by **Liebhardt, Weston and Goldman**, opened in 1970; renovations have repaired any aging caused by the sun and salt air. The hotel retains a peaceful, colonial Mexican ambience, with three-story, tile-roofed buildings encircling courtyards and fountains and open-air walkways offering sudden glimpses of the waves. The 128 rooms come in a variety of shapes and sizes. All have refrigerators, irons and ironing boards, hair dryers, and coffeemakers; some have full kitchens and high-speed Internet. Ocean-front rooms have wooden balconies as big as porches. Families check in for weeks at a

time in the summer; the children's pool, beach, and nearby playground are big draws. But there's also a large contingent of business travelers combining work with time on the two tennis courts, in the fitness center, or on the beach. Book summer reservations early. ♦ 8110 Camino del Oro (at Ave de la Playa). 459.8271, 800/640.7702; fax 456.9346. ♿ www.ljshoreshotel.com

Within La Jolla Shores Hotel:

THE SHORES RESTAURANT

★★$$ Even if you're not staying at the hotel, stop in the oceanfront restaurant for inexpensive happy hour munchies, the daily breakfast buffet, Friday-night seafood buffets, Sunday brunch, or the early-bird dinner specials. The menu's been beefed up a bit—literally. Steaks are the dinner special, and the wine list has been upgraded to fit the fare. The setting can't be beat, with a series of arched windows facing the surf, and the service is friendly, cheerful, and rapid. ♦ American ♦ Daily, breakfast, lunch, and dinner. 866/644.2630. www.theshoresrestaurant.com

23 SURF DIVA

Even if you cringe at the thought of perching atop a wave, stop by this fun, Hawaiian-inspired surf shop, well-known among beginners and pros for its excellent classes and surf forays to Costa Rica. Surfer chicks abound, most (but not all) tanned and buff. The shop is stocked with bathing suits and beach and surf gear, and there's plenty of space to chat about waves. ♦ 2160 Ave de la Playa (between El Paseo Grande and Camino del Oro). 454.8273. www.surfdiva.com

24 BARBARELLA

★★★$$ Converting a run-down taco shop into a charming cottage café was owner Barbara Beltaire's first hurdle. Developing a fanatically loyal local clientele was the other. She jumped both with ease, and now La Jollans show up unfashionably early to claim a table on the patio beside the see-through fireplace or resign themselves to waiting with friends at the bar. They don't mind. Barbarella's décor is so imaginative and the food so satisfying, a little inconvenience becomes an opportunity to catch up with neighbors and friends. The menu roams the globe, from silky risotto and crisp pizzas to savory French onion soup and steamed black mussels to a tender brisket sandwich and crisp fries. It's like a gaggle of grandmas

are preparing their favorite comfort foods for family and friends. ♦ Eclectic ♦ Daily, lunch and dinner. 2171 Ave de la Playa (between El Paseo Grande and Calle de la Plata). 454.7373

25 THE MARINE ROOM

★★★★$$$$ If you happen to be in town during high tide (the highest are in December and January), by all means stop here at least for a drink and the literally smashing view of the waves crashing against the restaurant's windows. This spot opened in 1941, and in 1944 guests were treated to a startling show of windows shattering against the force of the waves. In 1948 tempered glass was installed and withstood every storm for 34 years, until the window frames caved in during a 1982 storm. Thus far, the latest windows are holding strong. It's part of the **La Jolla Beach & Tennis Club** (see below) and is open to the public. The view even on calm days can't be beat, and the food—an artful mix of Pacific Rim, French, Mediterranean, and California influences—is consistently pleasing. Chef Bernard Guillas is such a local star he has his own web site. Out-of-town fans make reservations before they arrive in San Diego to make sure they get a chance to sample his latest creations. The menu changes frequently, and Guillas enjoys playing with unusual combinations. Consider the goat cheese brûlée, or the elk tenderloin. Enamored with Australia, Guillas has wattle seed–rubbed ostrich and barramundi. You don't often see an artisan cheese plate on local dessert menus; this one is always intriguing. Best bets include fresh fish and seafood, steaks, and the occasional wild-game specials. The service is courtly and gracious. All in all, a good spot for a romantic dinner or a special occasion. In addition to the main dining rooms, where just about every table has an ocean view, there's a cozy bar just right for sipping martinis at sunset. ♦ Californian/continental ♦ Daily, dinner. Reservations recommended. 2000 Spindrift Dr (on the loop off of Paseo Dorado). 459.7222, 866/644.2351. www.marineroom.com

26 LA JOLLA BEACH & TENNIS CLUB

$$$ Stately palm trees gracefully outline the 14-acre oceanfront spread where the elite hobnob on 12 championship tennis courts and an immaculate quarter-mile beach. The club's facilities (including a heated 25-yard-long tiled pool and a pitch-and-putt course

around a tropical lagoon) are closed to the public. The only way for nonmembers to use them is to rent one of the club's 98 hotel rooms. Back when cattle roamed free on this beach, some enterprising La Jollans decided to establish a yacht club and laid its cornerstone in 1927. The yacht harbor never materialized. In 1935, Frederick William (F. W.) Kellogg, a retired newspaper publisher from Pasadena who often summered in La Jolla, bought the property, envisioning a beach and tennis club. His son, W.S. Kellogg, took over in 1940, planted the palms along the club's entrance, donated 800 more palms to the La Jolla Shores community, and commenced to create a picturesque private enclave that remains the pride of La Jolla. ◆ 2000 Spindrift Dr (on the loop off of Paseo Dorado). 454.7126, 800/640.7702; fax 456.3805. www.ljbtc.com.

27 RISTORANTE PIATTI

★★$$$ You should definitely make reservations for dinner at this little Italian café, where trompe l'oeil murals enliven the Mexican-style rough-wood and tile décor of the dining rooms. It's so popular with the locals, there's rarely an open table. In addition to the attractive dining rooms, there's a plant-filled patio shaded by an enormous tree; it's a choice spot among La Jollans for an alfresco lunch or dinner. The open kitchen stimulates the appetite for pizza margherita, assorted panini, herbed bruschetta, and perfect rotisserie chicken. ◆ Italian/Californian ◆ Daily, lunch and dinner. Reservations highly recommended. 2182 Ave de la Playa (between El Paseo Grande and Calle de la Plata). 454.1589. &. www.piatti.com

28 LA JOLLA COVE

Craggy sandstone cliffs edge this pocket of aquamarine water where bright orange garibaldi, iridescent pink and blue neons, and silvery swarms of smelt swim in an underwater preserve. On sunny afternoons when the underwater visibility reaches 10 to 15 feet, the sea's surface seems to be composed of human bodies, snorkels, and fins. The tiny beach fills quickly, and nearby parking spots are claimed by 10AM. Scuba divers hang out at the patch of grass above the stairs to the beach, near the showers and rest rooms. The flat-topped rocky ledges framing the south side of the cove are popular spots for photographers, sunset worshipers, and explorers examining pools of water for a glimpse of a sea anemone or hermit crab. Youngsters are often tempted to dive from the top of the cliffs to the water below—a very dangerous prospect which may lead to serious injury. ◆ S Coast Blvd (between Prospect St and Girard Ave)

29 LA JOLLA COVE SUITES

$$$$ It's a miracle this 1950s-style motel hasn't been replaced by a $500-a-night penthouse palace. It's literally across the street from the cove. There are 154 rooms and suites spread throughout several squat cement buildings, furnished in a mishmash of colors and styles. There's a wide range of prices and amenities, from wood-shingled terrace condos with full kitchens and living rooms on a hill at the back of the complex to small studios toward the back of the complex. The oceanfront rooms on the top floors are the most expensive and desirable. All suites have kitchen facilities. The long, narrow pool, sundeck, and putting green sit on a strip of cement between the condos and hotel. A good-size, clean-looking launderette is available for guests. There's no restaurant, but a continental breakfast is served on the rooftop terrace and in the fifth-floor entertainment center every morning. This is one of the best places to stay if you're into sleeping to the sound of pounding surf and don't mind the less-than-palatial atmosphere. Book early for summer stays. ◆ 1155 S Coast Blvd (between Prospect St and Girard Ave). 888/LA-JOLLA, 800/248.2683; fax 551.3405. & www.lajollacove.com

30 BROCKTON VILLA RESTAURANT

★★$$ The tables on the front porch face the sea and are almost never empty. Breakfast selections include steamed eggs with feta or Jarlsberg cheese and famed soufflé-like French toast; lunch items range from light salads to stacked-high sandwiches filled with turkey, meat loaf, or other fresh choices. If the café is full, order a coffee and muffin to go and take them to the cove. ◆ Coffeehouse ◆ Tu-Su, breakfast, lunch, and dinner; M, breakfast and lunch. 1235 S Coast Blvd (between Prospect St and Girard Ave). 454.7393

31 RED ROOST AND RED REST

These two run-down brown-and-red cottages are smack across the street from the cove. Less romantic types might exclaim, "What a prime piece of turf!" Ongoing legal struggles over the cottages' historic status (they were built in 1894) have prevented the owner from replacing them, so instead they accumulate "No Trespassing" signs and continue to disintegrate. ◆ 1179 and 1187 S Coast Blvd (between Prospect St and Girard Ave)

32 THE CAVE STORE

Claustrophobes, beware! To visit **Sunny Jim Cave**, you must creep down 145 dark, narrow stairs—or you could swim a quarter-mile or so

LA JOLLA

Pacific Ocean

Pt. La Jolla

Alligator Head

28 *La Jolla Cove*

Boomer Beach

S Coast Blvd. 32

La Jolla Bay

29 30 31

Ellen Browning Scripps Park 33

38 39

La Jolla Caves

40 41

34 36 37

35

Roslyn La.

Seal Rock

Shell Beach

Ocean La. 44

Girard Ave.

Cave St.

Pt. Mencinger

42

Coast Blvd. 43

45 46

Jenner St.

47 48 49

Ivanhoe Ave.

Silverado Pl.

Exchange Pl.

Prospect St.

Casa Beach

50

Wall St.

51 52

Herschel Ave.

Park Row

Union Pl.

Wipeout Beach

Eads Ave. 53 54

S Girard Ave.

55 56

Coast Blvd.

Silverado St.

61 62

Ivanhoe Ave. E

Coast Blvd. Park

60

58 59

Fay Ave.

66

Drury La.

68

Bluebird La.

Whale View Pt.

57

63 64

65

67

69

Kline St.

S Coast Blvd.

Curier St.

La Jolla Recreation Center

70

Eads Ave.

Bishops La.

71 72

Torrey Pines Rd.

Virginia Way

High Ave.

Cabrillo Ave.

Prospect St.

75

76

Silver St.

74

77

Herschel Ave.

81

Rhoda Dr.

73

La Jolla Blvd.

80

82 83

Ravina St.

78

Pearl St. 79

Curier St.

Draper Ave.

Olivetas Ave.

Marine St.

La Jolla Country Club (Private)

Genter St.

N

km
mi

1/8   1/4

1/4   1/2

north from the cove. La Jolla has seven natural caves along the coastline, the largest of which is Sunny Jim. The land entrance to the cave is through this funky little store, which has assorted knickknacks and paintings for sale but no longer the extensive shell collection of years past. If you're wearing walking shoes, be sure to wander along the **Coast Walk Trail**, a dirt path which starts just past the entrance to the shop (it's marked with a Historical Landmark sign). Along the way, you'll get spectacular views of the ocean (and the multimillion-dollar homes nestled on the cliffs), as well as the shores north past La

Jolla to Del Mar, Encinitas, and beyond.
♦ Admission to cave. Daily. 1325 S Coast Blvd (between Prospect St and Girard Ave). 459.0746. www.cavestore.com

33 ELLEN BROWNING SCRIPPS PARK

Washington palms nearly 100 years old stretch from **La Jolla Cove** to the **Children's Pool** (see page 152), curving in harmony with the bay's natural outline and framing lush lawns that cool bare feet. Walter Lieber, who first visited La Jolla in 1904, is credited

Restaurants/Clubs: Red | Hotels: Purple | Shops: Orange | Outdoors/Parks: Green | Sights/Culture: Blue

with convincing his neighbors to clean up the area around the cove (which was littered with tents, bottles, and cans) and plant the palms. But the park that eventually developed within the palms was named for Ellen Browning Scripps in 1927, on her 91st birthday. A Monterey cypress that has been twisted into dramatic contortions by the force of the sea winds was planted at the corner of Girard and Coast in 1936, again in honor of Scripps. A walk through this park is an essential part of any visit to San Diego.
♦ Coast Blvd (at Girard Ave)

34 LA JOLLA INN

$$ This European-style inn, next door to the posh **La Valencia** (see opposite), finished a $1 million remodel in 2007, adding Wi-Fi, TV, kitchen facilities, and new bedding to the 23 rooms and suites. Smoking is not allowed in the inn but is tolerated on the sundeck. Some rooms and suites have narrow balconies looking out to Girard Street and **Scripps Park**. Kitchenettes and weekly and monthly rates are available. Many of the guests are Europeans who return for their annual La Jolla vacations. Continental breakfast, afternoon beverages, and parking are included in the rate. ♦ 1110 Prospect St (at Herschel Ave). 454.0133, 800/855.7829; fax 454.2056. www.lajollainn.com

h o t e l p a r i s i

35 HOTEL PARISI

$$$ Sleek and contemporary without being cold, the Hotel Parisi is a hip alternative to La Jolla's older hotels. Situated just across from **La Valencia** (see opposite), the Hotel Parisi has 28 spacious rooms with soaring ceilings, restful neutral colors, and spare, sophisticated décor. Several of the rooms have balconies, and many offer delicious ocean views. Be aware that live music is often played on weekend evenings on the streetside courtyard under several of the rooms. The hotel is located over retail shops and galleries; climb the winding staircase to reach the inviting lobby centered by a fountain. Feng shui principles were used throughout the hotel; maybe that's why it feels so cool and comfortable. Complimentary parking and breakfast. Evening room service is available from **Fresh[er]** restaurant. ♦ 1111 Prospect St (at Herschel Ave). 454.1511; fax 454.1531. www.hotelparisi.com

36 LA VALENCIA

$$$$ Beauty, elegance, and charm live inside the pink stucco walls of this property, known colloquially as La V. It has been the centerpiece of Prospect Street since 1926, when **Reginald Johnson** designed the building. La Jolla brides and grooms pose in front of the many windows overlooking La Jolla Cove; neighborhood nabobs quaff martinis with their cronies in the woodsy **Whaling Bar**; stylish women lunch in the rosy glow on the patio. Summon your most refined attitude and walk through the wrought-iron gates, under the trellis, and into the lobby. Stunning views are everywhere: from the picture window in the richly appointed **La Sala** room (where ceviche martinis and other tapas are served in the evening) to the vistas from the main dining room overlooking the pool. Even the balcony in the women's rest room overlooks the sea. The hotel has undergone a complete remodel, refurbishing the 100-plus original guest rooms and adding a stunning collection of luxury villas just beyond the pool area. The 15 villas each boast an ocean view, whirlpool tub, and king-size bed, and range from 400 to 1,200 square feet. Several have fireplaces as well, and personalized butler service is included for the duration of your stay. Rooms at the back of the main building are built into the hillside and overlook the hotel's terraced gardens and pool and on to the sea. Don't try to find floors numbered 1 through 3, however; owing to the way the hotel was originally constructed, they simply don't exist.
♦ 1132 Prospect St (between Ivanhoe and Herschel Aves). 454.0771, 800/451.0772; fax 456.3921. & www.lavalencia.com

Within La Valencia:

THE SKY ROOM

★★★★$$$ Above it all, the penthouse Sky Room has long been one of the most elegant restaurants in town. After being closed for months for a complete remodel, it reopened in August 2007 with a totally new design. A kitchen was added (saving waiters the burden of rushing back and forth to the main kitchen 10 floors below) and designed so that guests can wander through a sliding glass door and watch executive chef Vaughan G. Mabee and sous-chef Thomas Gérard at work. A new menu includes garden vegetables with fresh black truffles, Japanese Kobe, Kona Kampachi with fava beans, and the "Stars" in the Sky signature dish with pearl point oysters, Beluga caviar, South Pacific genuine pearls, Cristal Champagne, and Baccarat crystal champagne flutes for guests to take home. The décor was updated with a fountain, an intimate five-seat bar, and designer tableware and linens. On Fridays and

Up, Up, and Away

Every evening near dusk (conditions permitting), the cloudless blue sky east of **Del Mar** is dotted with glowing hot-air balloons drifting toward the hills. One of the best views of this sky show is from **Interstate 5**, near the **Del Mar Fairgrounds** exit. Fortunately, traffic moves so slowly during rush hour that you'll have plenty of time to gawk and to dial the following companies on your cellular phone: **Skysurfer Balloon Company** (800/660.6809; www.skysurferballoon.com), and **Panorama Balloon Tours** (481.9561, 888/455.3592; www.gohotair.com).

Vintage biplanes, including an open-cockpit biplane, are the specialty of **Biplane, Air Combat, Warbird &**

Space Adventures (760/930.0903, 800/759.5667; www.barnstorming.com).

For an even greater rush, head to the **Torrey Pines Gliderport in La Jolla**, where hang gliders step ever so gracefully from atop a 300-foot cliff and fly above the ocean, suspended from multicolored wings.

The ultimate in soaring sans machinery is in a silent sailplane swooping over back country valleys and hills, under the expert guidance of a pilot from **Sky Sailing** (760/782.0404; www.skysailing.com) in **Warner Springs**. And should you care to do it totally alone, visit the parachute-jump range at **Skydive San Diego** (619/216.8416, 800/FREEFALL; www.skydivesandiego.com) on **Otay Lakes Road**.

Saturdays there are special seatings at 6:30PM and 8:30PM; other nights you can choose your time to dine (sunset is best, as the sky-high view of La Jolla Cove is fabulous). ◆ Californian. ◆ Dinner, nightly. Reservations required. 454.0771. ㅎ

37 POMEGRANATE

Women delight in the one-of-a-kind purses, jewelry, and dresses that make up the selection here. ◆ Daily. 1152 Prospect St (between Ivanhoe and Herschel Aves). 459.0629

38 TOP OF THE COVE

This beloved restaurant and bar overlooking the cove was purchased by downtown's hippest dining/entertainment team and will be closed until 2009. The company plans to put $10 million into a total makeover. Still, the building and restaurant bear strong memories for locals and visitors. Table 6 should have a brass plaque bearing the names of couples who have become engaged while watching the sunset over the cove. This wooden cliffside bungalow, originally built as a private home by **Thorpe and Kennedy** in 1893, has resisted the fate of its neighbors and remained intact. It became the **Top O' the Cove** in 1955 and immediately earned the title of "San Diego's most romantic restaurant." The second-story **Bar at the Top of the Cove** was constructed against formidable odds in 1990. A crane with a 200-foot reach had to be used to hoist steel beams and posts above the Morton Bay fig trees planted before the turn of the 19th century. You can be sure local

historians are closely watching the new developments. ◆ Continental/Californian ◆ Daily, lunch and dinner. Jacket requested. Reservations required. 1216 Prospect St (at Ivanhoe Ave). 454.7779. www.topofthecove.com

39 PROSPECT PLACE

The understated white arches and subdued signage at this shopping-dining-office complex designed by **William Lumpkins** in 1963 are far easier on the eye than the neon hype of the newer minimalls a few blocks away on Girard Avenue. Wander past the second-story galleries that overlook the coastline to La Jolla Shores. ◆ 1250 Prospect St (between S Coast Blvd and Ivanhoe Ave)

Within Prospect Place:

GEORGE'S

★★★★$$$ Gregarious host George Hauer greets old friends and initiates with the confidence of one who knows his guests will be more than satisfied with their dining experience. His two restaurants are consistent award winners for cordial service, gorgeous views of the cove, and innovative California cuisine. The original George's at the Cove underwent a complete renovation and reopened in 2007 as the hipper, more cosmopolitan **George's California Modern**. A sleek wine bar was added and the sleek décor takes advantage of the floor-to-ceiling view. Chef Trey Foshee's menu changes with the seasons. Order the octopus carpaccio and ricotta ravioli with Meyer lemon—if

---

Restaurants/Clubs: Red | Hotels: Purple | Shops: Orange | Outdoors/Parks: Green | Sights/Culture: Blue

available, or follow Foshee's recommendations on the set-price tasting menu. The warm chocolate cake with mandarin orange ice cream is sublime. The vibe upstairs at the informal, rooftop **Ocean Terrace** draws a more casual crowd for lengthy lunches (business or not) and sunset dinners. ◆ Californian ◆ Daily, lunch and dinner. Reservations recommended. 454.4244. www.georgesatthecove.com

AFRICA & BEYOND

This tiny shop is filled with wood carvings, beadwork, garish masks, woven baskets, tapestries, conga drums, and xylophones. ◆ Daily. 454.9983. www.africaandbeyond.com

AZUL LA JOLLA

★★$$$$ One of La Jolla's prettiest restaurants, indoors and out, Azul offers ocean-view dining and inventive California cuisine. In addition to the main dining room overlooking the sea, there's a sleek, inviting bar area and an outdoor patio complete with fireplace and additional views. Try the smoked king salmon or duet of Muscovy duckling, or, for a less expensive meal, chef Orion Balliet's Greek-style chicken flatbread. ◆ California/Mediterranean. ◆ Tu-Sa, lunch; daily, dinner; Su, brunch. 454.9616. www.azul-lajolla.com

40 ALFONSO'S

★★★$$ After you've window-shopped until you're ready to drop, plop your weary body down at one of the patio tables here and indulge in some of San Diego's best margaritas, corn chips, salsa, and marinated carrots. Still hungry? Try the *nachos con chorizo* (with sausage) lathered with sour cream, or the *carne asada* (grilled beef) burrito, a La Jolla tradition. The inside cantina and restaurant are dark and noisy, but the food is hearty and crowd-pleasing. And nothing beats a sidewalk table on a warm summer night for a real treat. ◆ Mexican ◆ Daily, lunch and dinner. 1251 Prospect St (between Roslyn La and Ivanhoe Ave). 454.2232

41 TRATTORIA ACQUA

★★$$ White-clothed tables are set in several dining rooms, along the patio, and in a separate gazebo overlooking the cove (views from here are the best in the restaurant) at this delightful trattoria.

Highlights of the Mediterranean-based menu include osso buco, lobster ravioli, and spicy seafood pasta. Panini sandwiches are both filling and inexpensive—try the excellent portobello mushroom version. The tiramisù is not to be missed, and the wine list is excellent. By the way, if you're not up to taking the stairs, there's an elevator that connects the street-level entrance to the subterranean restaurant and parking lot. ◆ Italian/Mediterranean ◆ M-F, lunch and dinner; Sa, Su, brunch and dinner. Reservations recommended. 1298 Prospect St (at S Coast Blvd). 454.0709. ♿ www.trattoriaacqua.com

42 CHILDREN'S POOL

Up until 1997, when it was closed to the public, this calm and sheltered cove was home to snorkelers, swimmers, and of course, lots of children. Now, however, it's home to scores of harbor seals, who have effectively taken over the beach and waters as their own. Environmental activists, marine biologists, and animal lovers screamed foul at the San Diego City Council's vote in September 2004 to remove the rope barrier separating beachgoers from a colony of approximately 200 harbor seals. Signs now prohibit humans from bothering the seals, though some swimmers still brave the water. Wildlife biologists are worried that interaction with beachgoers will disrupt the birthing habits of the seals. Lawsuits have been filed, and the battle between man and pinniped continues. You can still get a close-up view of the seals (which spend much of their time sleeping and sunning on the sand) from the breakwater wall and the sidewalks above the beach. ◆ Coast Blvd (between Jenner St and Eads Ave)

43 SHELL BEACH GUEST APARTMENTS

$$$ Regulars settle in for weeks and months at the 44 apartment-like units with kitchen facilities and comfortably worn furnishings. Studios are available as well as one-, two- and three-bedroom suites. Families and retirees are more common here than surfers or college kids. There's nothing pretty or elegant about the place, but the proximity to the water more than makes up for any shortcomings. Senior citizens and AAA members usually get a discount. ◆ 981 Coast Blvd (between Ocean La and Jenner St). 888/LA-JOLLA, 800/248.2683; fax 555.3405

44 LIVING ROOM COFFEEHOUSE

★★$ Appropriately named, the coffeehouse is furnished with an assortment of couches, tables, and chairs set about a large, sunny room facing the sea (though you can only glimpse it between the rooftops). The décor is a bit funky by La Jolla standards but utterly comfortable for students and writers as well as families with young children. Bonus: the sidewalk patio is a dog-friendly place to sit with your canine companions. Choose from steamed eggs or bagels for breakfast, quiche or croissant sandwiches for lunch or dinner, or any of the tempting sweets displayed throughout the day. ♦ Coffeehouse ♦ Daily, breakfast, lunch, and dinner (closes at midnight). 1010 Prospect St (at Girard Ave). 459.1187. www.livingroomcafe.com

45 THE GRANDE COLONIAL

$$$ The dark polished mahogany and brass fittings of this delightful 1913 hotel make it seem as if it should be in Georgetown or London rather than La Jolla. It grew a bit in 2007 with the acquisition and remodel of the adjacent **Little Hotel by the Sea** and Garden Terraces. The entire hotel now has 93 rooms and suites with many vintage touches, including antique furnishings, steam radiators, bathrooms with 1920s tile, and the original elevator. The best views are from the fourth-floor rooms at the back of the main building; the best setting is the 1913 wooden cottage surrounded by flowers and vines that's home to eight of the suites. All of the rooms have been designated as nonsmoking. Situated on a quiet block of Prospect Street, the yellow-and-white inn has a peaceful pool area in back, a genteel lobby and adjacent bar, and a bright, cheerful sunroom that can be reserved for meetings and banquets. ♦ 910 Prospect St (at Jenner St). 454.2181, 888/530.5766; fax 454.5679. ♿ www.thegrandecolonial.com

Within the Grande Colonial:

NINE-TEN

★★★$$$ Classy and comfortable, Nine-Ten is an excellent choice for foodies who want to sample expertly prepared Californian cuisine. Chef Jason Knibb, who has made several appearances at the James Beard House, has an "earth-to-table" approach to food. He uses fresh local ingredients and unusual fish flown in from Hawaii, France, and the East Coast. His Maine scallops are paired with roasted cauliflower and pine

nuts, and the salmon is smoked in-house. Knibb calls his five-course tasting menu "Mercy of the Chef." Don't worry—this chef is kind. In addition to the dramatic-looking dining room and bar, seating is available on the sidewalk patio and garden-view terrace. ♦ Californian ♦ Daily, breakfast, lunch, and dinner. Reservations recommended. 964.5400. www.nine-ten.com

46 JOSE'S COURT ROOM

★$ Casual, fun, and occasionally a bit rowdy, this place is a tradition among La Jolla's younger set, who gather for beers and great chicken burritos and *pollo asado* (grilled, marinated chicken breast) plates. ♦ Mexican ♦ M-F, lunch and dinner; Sa, Su, dinner. 1037 Prospect St (between Herschel and Girard Aves). 454.7655. www.joses.com

47 THE ATHENAEUM

The original **La Jolla Library**, designed by **William Templeton Johnson** in 1921, and this building, designed by **William Lumpkins** in 1957, were linked together in 1991 with an unobtrusive design by **David Raphael Singer**. The complex makes an incomparable setting for chamber concerts, lectures, and an impressive collection of rare books and manuscripts on music, architecture, design, and the arts. ♦ 10AM-5:30PM Tu-Sa; W, until 8:30PM. 1008 Wall St (at Girard Ave). 454.5872. ♿ www.ljathenaeum.org

48 FRESH[ER]

★★★$$$$ A seascape décor with billowing fabrics covering the ceiling and walls and metal sculptures reminiscent of flowing water enhance the experience of dining on seafood that lives up to the restaurant's name—which changed from Fresh to Fresh[er] in preparation for a late-2007 remodel. Chef Ryan Johnston has retained the restaurant's devotion to superb seafood and expanded the menu to include sweetbreads, flatiron steak, and a superb Humbolt Fog goat cheese and beet salad. Wines from Australia to Oregon complement the global scope of the menu. ♦ Seafood ♦ Daily, lunch and dinner. 1044 Wall St (between Herschel and Girard Aves). 551.7575. www.fresh-er.com

49 LA JOLLA POST OFFICE

Outlying areas may claim to be within La Jolla, but the postal service knows better, and only those living and doing business within the village can have the prestigious 92037 ZIP code. They pick up their packages at this simple stucco, red-tile–roofed office (built in 1935) fronted by eucalyptus trees. ♦ M-F; Sa, 8:30AM-1:30PM. 1140 Wall St

---

(between Ivanhoe and Herschel Aves). 800/ASK-USPS

50 CASA DE MAÑANA

If you have to retire, you'd couldn't do better than in the utterly magnificent style at this Spanish Colonial spread designed by **Edgar Ullrich** in 1924. Originally a coastal resort, the building was taken over by the Methodist church in 1953 and remodeled as a retirement home. It's a private facility. ◆ 849 Coast Blvd (entrance at Eads Ave and S Coast Blvd). 456.4256, 800/959.7010. www.casademanana.org

51 GIRARD AVENUE SHOPS

La Jolla is one of San Diego's greatest shopping centers, and much of the action takes place on this stretch of Girard Avenue. One-of-a-kind galleries and boutiques are gradually disappearing, replaced by chain stores, including **Talbot's**, **Chico's**, **Gap**, **Banana Republic**, **Polo Ralph Lauren**, and **A/X Armani Exchange** ◆ Daily. Girard Ave (between Pearl and Prospect Sts)

52 JACK'S LA JOLLA

★★★$$$$ Glitzy and as trendy as La Jolla could possibly get, Jack's is cleverly contrived to contain three restaurants and four bars with live music and dancing. The Dining Room is the most sophisticated space, with somewhat aloof waiters serving lychee martinis and foie gras. Chef Tony DiSalvo oversees the three distinctive dining rooms, two of which serve more casual Kobe burgers and sushi. ◆ Daily, lunch and dinner. Reservations recommended. 7863 Girard Ave (between Silverado and Wall Sts). 456.8111. www.jackslajolla.com

53 TASENDE GALLERY

Since the 1990s, Jose Tasende has made a bold imprint on the La Jolla art scene, staging dramatic exhibitions of sculpture and drawings by Henry Moore, Jose Luis Cuevas, Eduardo Chillida, Isamu Noguchi, and others in his visually understated gallery, designed by **Robert Mosher** in 1979. When Tasende first came to town in 1979, he attempted to influence local culture by installing a Henry Moore sculpture at La Jolla Cove, but the public reaction was virulent. Ten years later he got the community's approval and support for an anniversary exhibition with nine large sculptures installed on the grounds of some of Prospect Street's most beloved buildings. The gallery's exhibitions focus on art of the post–World War II era, with group shows by such artists as Giacomo Manzù, Andres Nagel, Fernando Botero, and Lynn Chadwick. ◆ Tu-Sa. 820 Prospect St

(between Eads Ave and Jenner St). 454.3691. www.tasendegallery.com

54 ROPPONGI RESTAURANT, BAR AND CAFE

★★$$$ Owned by Sami Ladeki, the successful restaurateur who also founded **Sammy's California Woodfired Pizza** (see page 159), Roppongi offers upmarket atmosphere and a trendy menu. The high-style dining room features booth and table seating (as well as a private room that can be reserved in advance) and is anchored by an eye-popping oversize 600-gallon aquarium. The fare is best described as Asian fusion meets tapas bar, with such dishes as kung pao calamari steak, a Polynesian crab stack with mango, and a Mongolian shredded duck quesadilla with spicy Asian guacamole. The menu veers toward Europe with the sticky English toffee pudding with caramel gelato. A sushi and sashimi bar adds to the wide-ranging selection. Out front, the patio centered by a fire pit is a favorite spot from which to watch the world go by. ◆ Asian/Pacific Rim ◆ Daily, lunch and dinner. 875 Prospect St (between Faye Ave and Bishops La). 551.5252. ら www.roppongiusa.com

55 GIRARD GOURMET

★★$ The crowds at the sidewalk tables and at the deli counter are a tipoff. In the morning, office workers stop by to pick up egg sandwiches and almond croissants, and the place really gets packed at lunchtime as regulars place their orders for gargantuan ham-and-cheese sandwiches, smoked salmon sandwiches, or BLTs; salad plates accompanied by homemade bread; or such hot specialties of the day as lamb stew, turkey stuffed with broccoli, eggplant stuffed with spinach and cheese, or tortellini marinara. The crowds pick up again in early evening as neighborhood folks stop by for gourmet dinners to take home. It's a great place to stock up on picnic supplies before a day at the cove. ◆ Deli ◆ Daily, breakfast, lunch, and takeout. 7837 Girard Ave (between Silverado and Wall Sts). 454.3321. www.girardgourmet.com

56 SANTE

★★★$$$ Two small California bungalows and a patio surrounding an old oak tree have been transformed into a romantic Italian eatery. Tony Buonsante operated Manhattan's posh La Fenice for 10 years before escaping to La Jolla with his recipe file. The homemade gnocchi are the house favorite. The host is very protective of his guests, and the dining room feels more like a private club than a public restaurant. ◆ Italian ◆ M-Sa, lunch; daily, dinner. Jacket requested. Reservations recommended. 7811 Herschel Ave (between Silverado and Wall Sts). 454.1315. www.santeristorante.com

57 SCRIPPS INN

$$$ It's easy to miss this quiet, dark brown, 14-room bed-and-breakfast tucked in a corner of Coast Boulevard. Many guests check in for a month or more each year, taking advantage of the reasonable rates, parklike setting, and kitchen facilities. The best rooms are **No. 6** and **No. 12**, each with a fireplace and ocean view. Croissants from the **French Gourmet**, a nearby bakery, are served every morning in the lobby. Reserve far in advance. ◆ 555 S Coast Blvd (near Cuvier St). 454.3391; fax 456.0389. www.scrippsinn.com

58 MUSEUM OF CONTEMPORARY ART SAN DIEGO

It seems fitting that the former estate of Ellen Browning Scripps, designed by **Irving Gill** in 1916, is now La Jolla's cultural centerpiece. Since its founding in 1941, the museum has become San Diego's resource for innovative exhibitions of post-1950s art, and for its music and film programs, including the annual Animation Film Festival. The museum has undergone several changes in name and appearance and was closed between 1992 and 1996 for a radical renovation and expansion. Architect **Robert Venturi**'s design restores and complements the original Gill arches and cubes while expanding the museum to incorporate additional exhibition space on the western side of the existing building, a large sculpture garden, more space for the excellent bookstore, and a café on Prospect Street. The museum's permanent collection includes works by Andy Warhol, Robert Rauschenberg, Frank Stella, Edward Ruscha, Edward Kienholz, John Baldessari, Kiki Smith, Robert Irwin, Richard Serra, Jasper Johns, Nancy Rubins, and Agnes Martin. A second location in downtown San Diego presents temporary exhibitions and film screenings and has a branch of the museum shop. An expansion of the downtown location was completed in January 2007. The expansion includes the renovated 1915 **Santa Fe Depot** baggage building now known as the **Joan and Irwin Jacobs Building** and the new three-story **David C. Copley Building**. ◆ Admission. Th-Tu; closed W. 700 Prospect St (at Silverado St). 454.3541. ♿ Also at 1001 Kettner Blvd (at Broadway). ♿ www.mcasd.org

59 LA JOLLA WOMAN'S CLUB

This elegant white building is one of architect **Irving Gill**'s purest designs, featuring simple arches and cubes framed by green lawns and modest shrubs. It was first called the **Reading Club**, then the **Literary Club**, and in 1902 joined the state and national federations of Women's Clubs. Ellen Browning Scripps donated the money for the building, joining with Gill in 1914 to create yet another lasting landmark in her neighborhood. The building is open during club events and is a popular site for weddings and receptions. ◆ 715 Silverado St (between Eads and Draper Aves). 454.2354. www.lajollawomansclub.com

60 ST. JAMES BY-THE-SEA EPISCOPAL CHURCH

Several angular tiers of red-tile roofs cast shadows across the pale pink stucco walls of this imposing structure, where Deagan chimes toll the hour from a brick bell tower. The original church on this site was designed by **Irving Gill** in 1907. In 1928, **Louis Gill** added the tower (modeled after one destroyed by Porfirio Díaz's forces in Campo Florida, Mexico) at the request and bequest of Elizabeth Scripps for her sister Virginia. Six months later, the first building was moved and an entire new compound designed. Although the original church was soft and rounded with white arches, the new one was far more elaborate, with a peaked roof and inset cloverleaf windows. The chapel was donated by relatives of Scripps, who followed her commitment to sharing their wealth with La Jolla. A gift shop, which is open daily, offers a surprisingly eclectic selection of objets d'art and children's toys along with books and devotional materials. The church building is open each day; hours vary. ◆ 743 Prospect St (between Eads and Draper Aves). 459.3421. www.stjamesbythesea.org

61 WARWICK'S

Faithful patrons mill around the display tables and shelves for lectures and signings by local writers Judith and Neil Morgan, and out-of-town best-selling authors like Thomas Keneally, Amy Tan, and George Will. The intelligentsia of La Jolla orders its more obscure tomes here, and mainstream readers get valuable advice and suggestions from a knowledgeable staff. The bookstore has been in the Warwick family since 1902. Part of the shop is devoted to stationery supplies, including a wonderful selection of inexpensive pens, calligraphy

---

Restaurants/Clubs: Red | Hotels: Purple | Shops: Orange | Outdoors/Parks: Green | Sights/Culture: Blue

supplies, and personalized stationery. ♦ Daily. 7812 Girard Ave (between Silverado and Wall Sts). 454.0347. www.warwicks.com

62 LA JOLLA VILLAGE LODGE

$$ This motor hotel, just a 10-minute walk from the cove, isn't fancy, but the rooms are worth checking out, especially if you're seeking reasonable rates. Good news for folks who travel with their dogs (or cats or parrots, etc.): It's a pet-friendly establishment. There's an extra fee of $20 (per stay, not per night), and owners are asked not to leave dogs alone in the rooms and to keep cats and birds caged. All 30 rooms have a tropical theme, many have refrigerators, and free parking is available right outside each room. Most of the accommodations are designated nonsmoking. There's no restaurant on the premises, but several are within easy walking distance. ♦ 1141 Silverado St (between Ivanhoe and Herschel Aves). 551.2001, 877/551.2001; fax 551.3277. www.lajollavillagelodge.com

63 LA JOLLA RECREATION CENTER

The junction of La Jolla Boulevard and Prospect Street is one of the prettiest stretches of land left in the city, thanks largely to the beneficence of Ellen Browning Scripps, who donated the land for a community center. Amateur painters, potters, and poets practice their skills in the center's classrooms, looking out through classic 1915 **Irving** and **Louis Gill** arches toward vast lawns and shaggy palms. Children climb aboard dragons and butterflies in the playground, and the constant plop of tennis balls keeps a rhythmic sound in the air. In 1926, the schoolchildren of La Jolla supposedly donated one penny apiece for a monument to Scripps on the southwest corner of Draper Street. Sculptor James Porter created a bronze child kneeling on the ground, cupping water from a silken pond. ♦ 615 Prospect St (between Draper Ave and Cuvier St). 552.1658

64 BED & BREAKFAST INN AT LA JOLLA

$$$ There is no better introduction to the **Irving Gill** era than this charming hideaway at the end of a flower-lined path. Gill designed the house in 1913 for George Kautz, and **Kate Sessions**, who designed much of early

San Diego's landscaping, planted the original gardens. Gill's signature nooks and crannies and arched passageways have been incorporated into each of the 15 enchanting guest rooms, each with private bath. The **Pacific View Room** has a fireplace beside an antique desk and wood-framed window that looks out to sea; the **Gill Penthouse** has an upstairs deck. Fresh fruit, a decanter of sherry, cut flowers, and terry robes are standard amenities; some rooms also have wonderful bathtubs perfect for a leisurely soak. Call for midweek specials. ♦ 7753 Draper Ave (between Kline and Silverado Sts). 456.2066, 800/582.2466. www.innlajolla.com

65 MANHATTAN

★★$$$ A throwback in time, this dependable standard for beef dinners in comfy banquettes is a favorite among those who would rather converse than shout. The live music Thursday through Saturday kicks things up a notch, but you can still dress casually and admire the tropical fish in several tanks. ♦ 7766 Fay Ave (between Kline and Silverado Sts). 858/459.0700

66 ADELAIDE'S FLOWERS AND GIFTS

White tulips, violet freesias, buttercup daffodils, and branches of lilacs, forsythia, and pussy willows herald the coming of spring from the fragrant sidewalk display. Inside, gorgeous orchids and bromeliads are tucked into crystal vases, bronze pots, and other attractive receptacles. Take a fragrant tuberose or two back to your hotel room. Or, for a souvenir that will last years instead of days, buy some of the gorgeous artificial flowers made with a variety of materials. Hint: A gift from this shop is always appreciated by San Diego hosts and hostesses. ♦ M-Sa; closed Su. 7766 Girard Ave (between Kline and Silverado Sts). 454.0146, 800/322.2771; fax 454.1474. www.adelaidesflowers.com

67 K. NATHAN GALLERY

California's own Impressionist period flourished in the early 1900s, giving rise to the gorgeous landscapes and ocean scenes featured at this small but fascinating gallery. Along with this selection of California plein-air paintings, the proprietor has a number of other pre-1950s American works. ♦ Daily. 7723 Fay Ave (between Kline and Silverado Sts). 459. 3490. www.knathangallery.com

68 J&S BEAUTY SUPPLY

Locals and tourists alike love browsing the product-packed aisles here. There's an incredible array of beauty supplies, including hair and skin-care products, aromatherapy potions, makeup and hair accessories, and discounted designer perfumes in both regular and miniature sizes. This is a great place to stock up on fun and unusual gift items or special treats for yourself. ♦ Daily. 7734 Girard Ave (between Kline and Silverado Sts). 551.4056

68 SUSHI ON THE ROCK

★★$$ This trendy sushi bar is *the* place to go for California rolls, smoked eel, and red tuna sashimi, as well as less-traditional concoctions such as Monkey Balls (mushrooms stuffed with spicy seafood) and a variety of cooked Asian dishes. It's lively, generally packed, and noisy, especially on the weekends, so don't come expecting a quiet dinner for two. ♦ Sushi ♦ M-F, lunch and dinner; Sa, Su, dinner. 7734 Girard Ave (between Kline and Silverado Sts). 456.1138

69 MARY STAR OF THE SEA

For ecclesiastical beauty, few local buildings are as impressive as this Catholic church. It reigns over the shops on Girard Avenue like a California version of St. Patrick's Cathedral. The church was designed in 1937 by **Carleton Winslow** as a tribute to the early missions, and it manages to be austere and elegant at the same time. A mural above the church's front door was painted by Alfredo Ramos Martinez in 1937; by 1960, it had faded and aged irreparably in the salt air. The image of the Virgin standing atop rippled blue waves was reproduced in a tile mosaic installed in 1967. ♦ 7727 Girard Ave (between Kline and Silverado Sts). 454.2631. www.marystarlajolla.com

70 ZENBU

★★$$ If you want impeccably fresh fish in your kitchen, you might as well have your own fishing boats. That's how avid fisherman Matt Rimel manages to serve fresh uni (sea urchin) sashimi and rosy pink ahi. Grab a stool at the sushi bar and order the catch of the day, preferably still raw and tasting of the sea. If you prefer your food cooked, go for the Lobster Dynamite or ginger panko-crusted salmon. Next door to the dining room, **Zenbu Lounge** has live DJs spinning Thursday through Saturday nights and offers signature cocktails and late-night dining. Reservations are not accepted, so be prepared to wait. ♦ Sushi/Asian ♦ Daily, lunch and dinner. 7660 Fay Ave (between Pearl and Kline Sts). 454.4540. www.zenbusushi.com

Encore OF LA JOLLA

71 ENCORE OF LA JOLLA

Treasured by fashion-conscious bargain hunters, Encore is one of the best consignment clothing stores in the county. This is the place to find gently used (or occasionally, never-worn) clothing and accessories from top designers. Although there's a small men's section, the two-story store (with discounted merchandise upstairs) is basically for women. The selection is incredible, as well as ever changing, as local socialites tend to drop off their party finery here after wearing it only once. Just about every designer imaginable is represented here, from Armani to Zegna. ♦ Daily. 7655 Girard Ave (between Torrey Pines Rd and Kline St). 454.7540. www.encorelajolla.com

72 PORKYLAND

★$ Yes, the name is strange, but the take-out Mexican food is *delicioso*. All you need is one taste of the *carnitas* or a tamale to forget such mundane concerns as fat and cholesterol. The fresh tortillas have replaced sliced bread in many a gringo household, and the *tacos al pastor* (pork with spices) will make you swear off burgers forever. Outdoor seating available in a tree-shaded courtyard adjacent to the parking lot. ♦ Mexican ♦ Daily, lunch and dinner. 1030 Torrey Pines Rd (between Herschel and Girard Aves). 459.1708. www.goporkyland.com

73 BISHOP'S SCHOOL

Ellen and Virginia Scripps donated much of the land and funds for this venerable private school, and successive benefactors, parents, and alumni have preserved the school's heritage. **Irving Gill** designed the first building in graceful Minimalist style. Then San Diegans became entranced with the more formal and decorative style used to create **Balboa Park**'s **El Prado** and hired **Carleton Winslow** to design a more ornate church and bell tower topped with a yellow-and-blue dome. The tower wasn't actually built until 1930, after **Louis Gill** had designed an addition to the original building, complete with a simple white dome, tying the two styles together and creating a picturesque landmark enhanced by blue skies and emerald green lawns. The school is an independent college prep school for grades 7 through 12. ♦ 7607 La Jolla Blvd (at Prospect St). 459.4021. www.bishops.com

Restaurants/Clubs: Red | Hotels: Purple | Shops: Orange | Outdoors/Parks: Green | Sights/Culture: Blue

74 LA JOLLA LIBRARY

The village's original library has been mated with the **Athenaeum** (see page 153), and this new facility, designed by **Robert Mosher** and **Roy Drew** in 1989, reflects some of the style of the old with its red-tile roof and stucco walls. The inside, though, is purely modern, with 25,000 square feet of space devoted to efficiency and curiosity. ♦ Daily; hours vary. 7555 Draper Ave (between Pearl and Silver Sts). 552.1657. www.lajollalibrary.org

75 TAPENADE

★★★★$$$$ Jean-Michel Diot made his name in New York when he opened the Park Bistro and Les Halles. He brought his style of French Provençal cuisine to La Jolla in 1998, opening an airy bistro on a side street, away from the village bustle. His homemade duck foie gras terrine alone is good reason to visit, and if you're craving a steak, his aged strip loin with *pommes frites* will more than satisfy. A two-course prix-fixe lunch menu and dinner tasting menu are reasonably priced (when compared with à la carte prices). Meals begin with an olive tapenade (of course) and end with divine desserts. ♦ French ♦ Daily, lunch and dinner. Reservations recommended. 7612 Fay Ave (between Pearl and Kline Sts). 551.7500; fax 551.9913. www.tapenaderestaurant.com

76 MICHELE COULON DESSERTIER

★★$$$ A gifted pastry chef, Michele Coulon makes some of the finest desserts and wedding cakes in Southern California. One bite of her Belgian chocolate torte, white chocolate mousse cake, or amareno cherry torte and you'll be hooked. Her cozy café, furnished with antiques, makes a lovely place to linger over a light salad or soup for lunch. There's also a tree-sheltered patio for alfresco coffee and a special treat. And of course, you'll want to bring something home for dessert. Beer and wine are served. ♦ M-Sa, lunch. 7556 Fay Ave in the Sycamore Ct square (between Pearl and Kline Sts). 456.5098. www.dessertier.com

77 HARRY'S COFFEE SHOP

★★$ This spot has been a popular breakfast institution since the early 1960s, and the banter behind the counter is heavily sprinkled with familiarity. The works of local artists are displayed and occasionally purchased. Your breakfast—banana pancakes, a bacon-and-cheese omelette, hot oatmeal with raisins—comes with an individual fresh-brewed pot of coffee (not included in food price). Lunch is served too, but people come for the breakfast dishes, which are served until closing. ♦ American ♦ Daily, breakfast and lunch. 7545 Girard Ave (between Pearl St and Virginia Way). 454.7381. www.harryscoffeeshop.com

78 MARRAKESH

★★$$$ Dining here is a night-long event. Guests sit on the floor or on low padded banquettes around enormous inlaid wooden tables. Multicourse Moroccan feasts are presented stylishly, augmented by belly dancers on weekends. Try the excellent lamb brochettes and kabobs, or pastry stuffed with chicken, raisins, and eggs. ♦ Moroccan ♦ Daily, lunch and dinner. Reservations recommended. 634 Pearl St (between Draper Ave and Cuvier St). 454.2500. www.marrakeshrestaurant.com

79 EL PESCADOR FISH MARKET

★$$ Fresh-from-the-sea snapper, tuna, halibut, and seasonal catches of the day are on display at this La Jolla institution, where locals have been showing up for lunch and early dinner (open 10AM to 8PM), ordering grilled fish plates, sandwiches, and salads. Of course, you can also get do-it-yourself shrimp and wild salmon (flown in from Alaska) for home cooking. ♦ Daily; 627 Pearl St (between Draper Ave and Cuvier St). 456.2526. www.elpescadorfishmarket.com

In 1927 San Diegans passed a $650,000 bond issue to deepen San Diego Bay, which built up the tidelands near downtown, making them suitable for airport runways. For decades, San Diegans have vehemently debated the wisdom of having an ever-growing international airport in one of the most congested areas of the county. But the airport has been expanded, and it seems destined to remain at the edge of downtown.

80 SAMMY'S CALIFORNIA WOODFIRED PIZZA

★★$ Try any of the 21 variations of gourmet pizza, including garlic chicken, spicy Italian sausage, and Hawaiian pineapple. Pasta lovers can opt for chicken tequila fettuccine flavored with cilantro or angel hair with sun-dried tomatoes. Salads are enormous and excellent; choose a half-order if you're sharing a pizza. For dessert, the signature "messy sundae" with chocolate and caramel sauce is big enough for two or more. La Jollans of all social persuasions come here for casual, inexpensive meals. ♦ Californian/pizza ♦ Daily, lunch and dinner. 702 Pearl St (between Eads and Draper Aves). 456.5222. ♿ Also at 770 Fourth Ave (between F and G Sts). 619/230.8888; 12925 El Camino Real (at Del Mar Heights Rd), Del Mar. 858/259.6600. www.sammyspizza.com

81 COMEDY STORE

Up-and-coming and famous comedians perfect their shticks here before easily amused audiences. ♦ Admission. Shows: nightly; call for specific acts. 916 Pearl St (between Drury La and Fay Ave). 454.9176. www.thecomedystore.com

82 GALLERY EIGHT

Prices here range from $10 to thousands of dollars for gorgeous contemporary crafts, including silver jewelry by Steven Brixner, ceramics by Patrick Crabb, and unique baskets woven with needles from the endangered Torrey pines by Neil and Fran Prince. ♦ M-Sa. 7464 Girard Ave (between Genter and Pearl Sts). 454.9781

83 D.G. WILLS BOOKS

Indulge your urge to browse among the new and used scholarly books in this appropriately musty setting. Book signings and poetry readings are held frequently. ♦ Daily. 7461 Girard Ave (between Genter and Pearl Sts). 456.1800. www.dgwillsbooks.com

84 MOUNT SOLEDAD

For a close-up look at a real earthquake fault (**Rose Canyon**) topped by a 43-foot-high cross, navigate the winding roads to the top of the 822-foot-high hill, which is grandly called **Mount Soledad** (Spanish for "solitude"). Several crosses (including a flaming one, courtesy of the Ku Klux Klan)

have stood atop the hill since 1913; the latest was designed by architect **Don Campbell** in 1954, as a memorial to servicepeople in the world wars and the Korean conflict. The cross itself is an ongoing subject of conflict and controversy over the separation of church and state. Million-dollar homes line Mount Soledad's winding streets in neighborhoods constructed on unstable lands that have shifted over the years. A major landslide in October 2007 destroyed two homes and left several others uninhabitable. Lawsuits between the homeowners and the city are ongoing. ♦ Soledad Rd (at La Jolla Scenic Dr)

85 WINDANSEA BEACH

If you're not accustomed to shooting the tube or riding the curl, you're best off staying on the sand at this serious surfer hangout. Strangers are barely tolerated on the waves but certainly welcome as admiring fans. Tom Wolfe memorialized the Windansea surfers of the 1960s in *The Pump House Gang*, graphically describing the shocking lifestyle of the Max Meda Destruction Company (MMDC), a group of surfers who hung out at a pink water-pump house facing the waves. Members were known to harass outsiders who attempted to set up their beach umbrellas on MMDC turf and were given to holding "conventions," or rowdy beer parties, and driving the neighbors mad. MMDC alumni and admirers still sport T-shirts and decals bearing the group's logo (though at the height of the group's notoriety, police were known to stop anyone who would so brazenly support the renegade tribe). The beach is much calmer now, but the waves are still wild. Parking is scarce, so be prepared for a hike to and from your car. ♦ Neptune Pl (south of Nautilus St)

86 LA JOLLA UNITED METHODIST CHURCH

These striking, cream-colored church buildings were once home to the San Carlos trolley depot (designed by **Eugene Hoffman**) and the **La Plaza** Mexican restaurant and **El Toro Bar**, favorite haunts of Raymond Chandler, Billy Wilder, and other La Jolla celebs. In 1959, church members remodeled the buildings into a sanctuary, library, and chapel (using the appropriate blessings to drive away any questionable spirits) and have since added on several buildings in faithful adherence to the original Mission-style lines and arches. ♦ 6063 La Jolla Blvd (north of La Cañada St). 454.7108

Restaurants/Clubs: Red | Hotels: Purple | Shops: Orange | Outdoors/Parks: Green | Sights/Culture: Blue

COASTAL NORTH COUNTY

The drive along **Coast Highway** (S21) from **Torrey Pines State Reserve** to **Oceanside** is a must for anyone who wants a real glimpse of life along the Pacific Coast. The locals' highway has four lanes in most places, and lots of traffic lights and stop signs. It meanders along the coast, changing names seemingly at will. In Del Mar, it's Camino del Mar. In Oceanside, signs proudly proclaim the road is part of US Highway 101, running from Southern California through Washington. This section of 101 is among the best, with long stretches of coastal scenery and several small towns worth exploring.

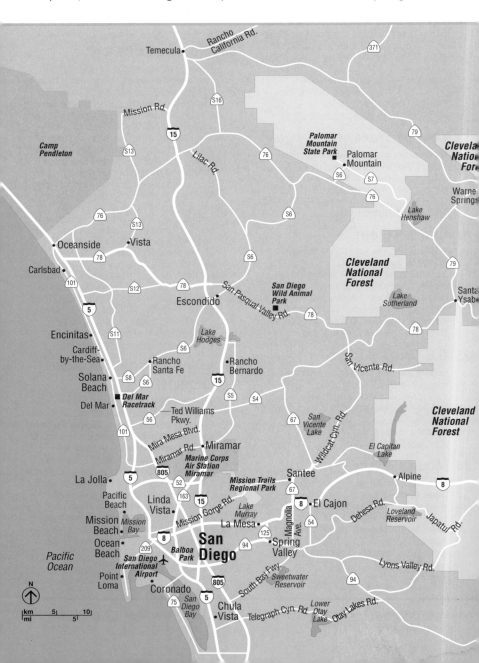

mountain streams and hiking paths. The road then passes through the mountain town of **Julian**, best known for its annual Apple Days Festival held in October, when San Diegans drive through town by the hundreds in search of homemade apple pies. **Santa Ysabel**, a few miles north, is famous because of **Dudley's** restaurant and bakery (30218 Hwy 78, at Hwy 79; 760/765.0488, 800/225.3348; www.dudleysbakery.com), and its selection of dozens of varieties of home-baked bread. The next town, **Warner Springs**, has an airfield where glider planes land soundlessly. Back west off **Highway 76** is **Palomar Mountain State Park** (760/742.3462) and the **Palomar Observatory** (760/742.2119), with the 200-inch Hale Telescope, one of the largest reflecting telescopes in the world. The white-domed observatory building is open to the public daily; admission is free. Although the wildfires of October 2007 burned nearly 30 percent of the 1,800-acre park, no buildings were destroyed, and the fire mainly burned away low-lying vegetation.

For an alternative mountain experience, take I-8 east from San Diego to **Pine Valley** and the turnoff for **Highway S1**, also called **Sunrise Highway**, through the **Laguna Mountains**. From the lookouts near the 5,975-foot-high **Mount Laguna** you can see east across the desert to the vast unknown beyond.

The **Anza-Borrego Desert State Park** comprises some 600,000 acres of parched, undeveloped land where cactus bloom in the spring and snowbirds in motor homes migrate in winter months. The park's **Visitor Information Center** (760/767.4205) is the best place to begin your desert explorations with a hike through the cactus gardens and museums. The town of **Borrego Springs** has several campgrounds and hotels; call the **Chamber of Commerce** (760/767.5555, 800/559.5524; www.borregosprings.info) for information. **La Casa del Zorro Resort** (3845 Yaqui Pass Rd, betweeen Borrego Springs Rd and Oleander La; 760/767.5323, 800/824.1884; fax 760/767.5963; www.lacasadelzorro.com) offers 82 rooms and suites in several two-story buildings and private casitas beside pools, gardens, and putting greens. Jazz concerts are held in the summer; book early during the spring wildflower season.

CHULA VISTA

Chula Vista, the second-largest city in San Diego County, is just 7 miles south of downtown and easily accessible by freeway

or the **San Diego Trolley**. Its greatest attraction, at least for nature lovers, is the **Sweetwater Marsh National Wildlife Refuge** and the **Chula Vista Nature Center** (1000 Gunpowder Point Dr, at E St; 619/409.5900). One of the few remaining salt marsh bird habitats on California's coast, the 316-acre plot of priceless waterfront property stretches along the southern end of **San Diego Bay**. Graceful blue and white herons glide above the glassy ponds and burrowing owls nest in simple cages; bird watchers have spotted more than 200 species of birds from the center's wooden lookout tower. Bat rays, sand sharks, and guitarfish populate an outdoor petting tank, and several indoor exhibits highlight the natural inhabitants of the coast. The park, which charges admission, is open Tuesday through Sunday.

Coors Amphitheatre (2050 Entertainment Circle; 619/671.3600) is an open-air concert venue with 10,000 seats and space for an additional 10,000 music lovers on the lawn. Its excellent acoustics makes it a favorite of top musical acts, including the Dixie Chicks, Sting, and Incubus. In 2007, it was chosen as the venue for San Diego's annual Street Scene, a massive music fest that's outgrown its origins in downtown.

The US Olympic Committee's **ARCO Training Center** (2800 Olympic Pkwy; 619/656.1500) is a state-of-the-art facility for athletes, many of whom live on-site and train in such sports as soccer, field hockey, cycling, rowing, and archery. Tours are offered Monday through Saturday (call ahead to make sure it's open), and sports memorabilia is available in the Spirit Store. Let the kids test their bravura on the water slides and rides at **Knott's Soak City USA** (2052 Entertainment Cir; 619/661.7373), a water park open during summer months.

One of the most traditional eateries in the area is **Anthony's Fish Grotto** (215 West Bay Blvd, at E St; 619/425.4200; www.gofishanthonys.com), one in a small chain of family restaurants. Crab, lobster, shrimp, and swordfish are all expertly prepared.

Nearby are the **Chula Vista Harbor** and **California Yacht Marina**, pleasant places for boat connoisseurs to stroll waterside pathways and admire the yachts. Chula Vista has managed to surpass San Diego City when it comes to public libraries, with its spectacular **South Chula Vista Library**, which opened in April 1994. Mexican architect **Ricardo Legorreta** designed the sunflower-yellow building with bright purple trim, which has received rave reviews from architectural organizations and a few pans from its neighbors.

TIJUANA

To really appreciate Tijuana, you've got to leave your timidity at the border. You'll have to see the blatant poverty and cope with the crush of the crowd. You'll have to consider the culture, customs, and laws of a foreign land, despite its proximity to your home. Then you'll see Tijuana for what it is: a young city, a little over 115 years old; the fourth largest city in Mexico; entryway to the 800-mile-long Baja California peninsula. Many of its inhabitants have come from throughout Latin America looking for opportunity along the border. City leaders boast that Tijuana's unemployment is among the lowest in the nation, owing to the large number of factory jobs at *maquiladoras*. These manufacturing plants, many foreign owned, are strung along the border in a region that casual travelers rarely see.

Avenida Revolución is the traditional tourist destination—a strip of restaurants, bars, and shopping arcades where gringos run wild, chasing bargains, cheap drinks and eats, and good times. It's been that way since the 1920s. Today's Avenida Revolución is largely the province of bands of college-age kids gone wild and wide-eyed tourists buying truckloads of trinkets. All that said, you absolutely must cruise Revolución for an hour or so. Check out the *pasajes* (shopping arcades), the restaurants, and the ornate façade of the former **Palacio Frontón**. Buy a paper flower, woven bracelet, or pack of gum from the children on the street. Then retreat to the **Centro Cultural** to see exhibits, films, and performances about Mexico's cultures and history.

Day-trippers have traditionally made up the bulk of Tijuana's guests, but there are reasons to spend the night. You can easily fill a weekend with shopping, golfing, restaurant hopping, and visiting cultural sights. The Centro Cultural features dance troupes, symphonies, and performers from throughout Latin America and Cuba, hosting those who never make it to the US—as well as those who do. The discos and clubs are nearly as extravagant and exciting as those in Acapulco, and they don't even begin to rock until after midnight. Rock, heavy metal, and ska bands play at trendy nightclubs. When it comes to nightlife, Tijuana is pure Mexican—vibrant, jazzy, dazzling, and inexhaustible.

The country code is 52. The area code is 664.

Getting to Tijuana

By Air

Travelers visiting from mainland Mexico arrive at the **Abelardo Rodríguez International Airport** in the **Otay Mesa** area, a 15-minute cab ride from downtown Tijuana. Airlines serving Tijuana include **Mexicana** (800/531.7921; www.mexicana.com); **Aeroméxico** (800/237.6639; www.aeromexico.com); and once daily from LAX, the small airline **Express Jet** (through Delta Airlines, 800/221.1212. www.delta.com)

By Bus

Greyhound (619/239.3266, 800/231.2222; www.greyhound.com) offers frequent bus service from downtown San Diego to downtown Tijuana: currently four round-trips per day. The Greyhound terminal (686.0695)

in Tijuana is at **Avenida México**, at Madero. **Five-Star Tours** (619/232.5049), at the **Santa Fe Depot** on Broadway at Kettner, offers expensive private bus service; it's $80 for one or two persons, one way, to the San Ysidro border crossing or wherever you want to go in Tijuana.

By Car

Many drivers prefer to leave their cars in the large parking lots in San Ysidro on the US side of the border and walk across rather than hassle with driving in Tijuana. If you must leave valuables in the car, at least stash them in the trunk, as large lots like these are vulnerable to theft. It's worth the extra money to leave your car in a guarded lot. And if you do take your car, it's essential to buy auto insurance, because most US policies do not cover driving in Mexico. Stop at one of

Azulejos (House of Tiles) but inside, it looks exactly like its 100-plus sister outlets, displaying a little bit of everything the consumer needs. The selection of folk art is impressive, with lacquered boxes from Guerrero, papier-mâché sculptures from Guanajuato, and silver filigree earrings from Taxco displayed tastefully. The chocolates counter and bakery are legendary: Be sure to pick up a sweet treat. The book and periodicals section has many classic books about Mexico in Spanish and English and a good selection of postcards. The restaurant is best at breakfast, when you can sit by the French doors in the sunlit room and feast on a bountiful buffet or order French toast, *huevos rancheros*, or fresh Danishes from the menu. Another bonus: an underground parking lot on Calle 9 (three hours free with validation). ♦ Daily, 8AM-10PM. Av Revolución 1102 (between Calles 9 and 8). 688.1462

13 TIJUANA CENTRO CULTURAL

The cultural center, designed in 1974 by **Pedro Ramírez Vázquez** and **Manuel Rosen**, is the centerpiece of Tijuana's art community and a must-see for those interested in exploring Mexico beyond Tijuana. An Omnimax theater rises above the low-profile museum buildings, looking like a sand-colored UFO. Films on space, travel, and science are shown in the theater throughout the day. Inaugurated in 1999, the **California Museum** (admission) houses a permanent display explaining life throughout the peninsula, from pre-Hispanic times to the modern era. Kids and adults will enjoy the variety of exhibits, from a massive gray whale skull to a series of old ships built to scale, models of early missions, and a Kumayaay Indian willow hut, as well as oil paintings and icons. The museum space itself is a pleasure to explore, with exposed metal beams and track lighting illuminating items in Lucite display cases; its café is a nice place to rejuvenate. Music, theater, film, and dance performances are held in the concert hall and courtyard; a schedule of upcoming performances is available at the museum's information desk or on their web site. The bookstore has a great collection of art books in Spanish, and a few postcards and souvenirs. ♦ Paseo de los Héroes 9350 (between Avs Independencia and Mina). 687.9600. www.cecut.gob.mx

14 MERCADO HIDALGO

For a touch of authentic Mexico, stop by this busy marketplace with stands displaying fresh flowers, produce, dried and fresh chilies, herbs, and beans. The large selection of piñatas, along with the candy to fill them, makes, if nothing else, an excellent photo opportunity. You'll find a few souvenirs ensconced among the household necessities, and they're sure to cost less than in the tourist shops. ♦ Daily. Av Independencia (at Av Sánchez Taboada). No phone

15 PLAZA RÍO TIJUANA

Comparable in size and selection to many US malls, this complex has several department stores, including **Sara's** and **Dorian's**, dozens of specialty shops, a **Sanborn's** restaurant and shop, and a multiplex movie theater (showing first-run US films in many of its 17 salons). ♦ Paseo de los Héroes (between Avs Cuauhtémoc and Independencia). 684.0402

16 L.A. CETTO WINERY

Mexico's best wines come from Baja California, and **Cetto** is one of Baja's premier wineries. Tours of the Tijuana facilities include visits to the aging room and bottling plant, a wine tasting ($2 for traditional vintages, $8 for reserve quality; four vintages of either), and plenty of time in the gift and wine shop. The winery is a short walk from Revolución, one block west on Calle 9 and two blocks south on Constitución. ♦ M-Sa, 9:30AM-6:30PM. Cañón Johnson 2108 (at Av Constitución). 685.3031. www.cettowines.com

17 PARROQUIA ESPÍRITU SANTO

The parish church is overwhelmingly beautiful. Legend has it that the pastor's mother dreamed of a church that appeared like a rainbow, with arcs of color changing in hue with the sun. The designer Jaime Sandoval Hernández (an engineer from Michoacán) relied on stained glass to cast a rainbow on the stark white arches, the colors changing in intensity with the movement of the sun. The effect is best seen from inside the building. As you look toward the altar, the arches appear to be softly washed in gold, green, lavender, and blue; as you look from the altar toward the pews, the series of stained-glass arcs come into sight, framing the stained-glass wall at the rear of the church. Additional ornamentation has been kept to a bare minimum. ♦ Avs Rosales and Cumpas. 621.8355

18 GRAND HOTEL

$$ The twin mirrored towers of the **Plaza Agua Caliente** and this hotel rise 18 stories above the clutter and congestion of the city, acting as landmarks for confused travelers

and hallmarks of a prosperous Tijuana at its height in the early 1980s. Architect **Alfredo Lauren** designed the hotel, which opened in 1982 as a **Fiesta Americana** and is still referred to by that name by many locals. This is a gathering spot for Tijuana society hosting charity balls, beauty contests, and fashion shows. The 422 rooms—all with minibars and direct-dial phones—are popular with business travelers, visiting celebrities, and tourists alike. Facilities include Wi-Fi throughout the hotel, a pool, two tennis courts, a health club, a shopping mall, three restaurants, a lively bar, and a branch of the **Caliente Race and Sports Book**. ♦ Blvd Agua Caliente 4500 (between Av 16 de Septiembre and Av Jalisco). 684.7000, 866/472.6385 from the US. www.grandhoteltj.com.mx

19 CORONA PLAZA

$ Don't be fooled by the understated officelike edifice of this hotel—the décor inside is quite sophisticated. It mimics the newer hotels in other parts of Mexico, where the landscaping and public spaces are arranged atrium-like in the center of the building, with its 100 rooms overlooking the open restaurant. For less noise and more light and fresh air, take a room on the second or third floor at the back near the swimming pool. The color scheme is a subdued gray, peach, and blue combo with bleached wood furnishings. There's a parking structure at the basement level; most sites of interest to travelers are within a short cab ride. ♦ Blvd Agua Caliente 1426 (between Av Río Yaqui and Av Cuauhtémoc). 681.8183; fax 681.8185

20 CASA DE LOS REMEDIOS

One of a chain with other outlets in Guadalajara and Puerto Vallarta, the "House of Remedies" is lively and fun, and feels halfway between a touristy restaurant and a real Mexican cantina. Decorated with bold colors and recognizable Mexican icons, this "house" has dominoes and other games to play. It's popular with locals and foreigners for Mexi snacks and full meals. Couples and friends socialize after work at the bar, and those heading out to dance start the night here with a light meal from the endless menu and listen to the ranchero or mariachi musicians who stroll the premises. ♦ Mexican ♦ Daily, lunch and dinner. Av Diego Rivera 19 (at Paseo de los Héroes), Zona Río. 634.3065

> Between 1825 and 1831, California was a part of Mexico, with San Diego as its capital.

21 BABY ROCK

Ask architecture buffs to name the strangest building in town and they'll inevitably mention this one, designed by **Jaime Bejar**. The perennially popular disco is shaped like—you guessed it—a big brown outcropping of boulders half buried in rocks. The line winds down the boulevard on Friday and Saturday nights as a chic crowd of young adults waits to be admitted to the cavernous dance hall filled with soaring lights and the throbbing beat of the latest tunes. ♦ Th-Su, 9PM-5AM. Av Diego Rivera 1482 (at Paseo de los Héroes). 634.2406

22 CIEN AÑOS

★★$$ Dine with well-off Mexicans and tourists who've bolted from the beer-slinging bars of Avenida Revolución in this simple yet elegant, upscale eatery. Waiters are helpful and attentive yet unobtrusive and happy to explain some of their unique Mexican specialties. Innovative dishes include cactus or watercress salads, mild chilies stuffed with shrimp and vegetables, lobster crepes, and roast duck in a sauce of garlic and honey. Breakfast is served after 8AM, and the kitchen's open until midnight most Friday and Saturday nights. ♦ Mexican ♦ Daily. Calle José María Velasco 1407, between Paseo de los Héroes and Vía Rápida Poniente, Zona Río. 634.3039 or 888/534.6088 from the US. www.cien.info

23 HOTEL LUCERNA

$$ When President Miguel de la Madrid inaugurated this hotel in 1980, it was the only four-star facility in town. Today the hotel has an Old World ambience in the lobby and restaurants; it's well-situated near the Plaza Río Shopping Center and a number of popular discos. The location is probably the quietest of any hotel in town, and the heavy drapes, air conditioning, and lack of outside noise make for a superb night's sleep. Of its two restaurants, **El Acueducto** is often recommended by locals. The hotel often receives kudos for its attentive staff. ♦ Paseo de los Héroes 10902 (at Blvd Rodríguez). 633.3900, 800/LUCERNA.

24 FIESTA INN

$$$ The original Vita Spa Agua Caliente has metamorphosed several times; it's remained a Fiesta Inn since 1995. The restaurant is wedged between the lobby and the pool area, where under a Moorish-style cement canopy you can relax in the slightly sulfurous waters of the original thermal spring. Rooms are a bit more elegant than other Tijuana accommodations of this price range—with dark pink carpets, cream walls, forest green upholstery, and floral accents in the same palette. Each room has a writing desk and

HISTORY

1542 On 28 September, the Spanish ships *San Salvador* and *La Victoria* arrive in **San Diego Bay**, which the Spanish call **San Miguel**. Explorer Juan Rodríguez Cabrillo leads his men ashore, where they rest for a few days among the local Kumeyaay people and then sail north.

1602 On 10 November, Spanish explorer Sebastián Vizcaíno sails into San Miguel and officially renames the bay San Diego after the saint San Diego de Alcalá.

1769 On 11 April, the Spanish ship *San Antonio* anchors in San Diego Bay; days later, the *San Carlos* arrives. In the following months, Spanish troops arrive by land from Baja California. Led by Gaspar de Portola, the troops move north toward San Francisco, leaving behind a small group of settlers. On 16 July, Padre Junípero Serra celebrates Mass at the new settlement atop **Presidio Hill**, beginning the first of a chain of missions in Alta California. The Spaniards place the Kumeyaay and other local Native Americans under the jurisdiction of the mission and rename them the Diegueños. On 15 August, the Kumeyaay attack the settlement, killing one Spaniard. The settlers stay.

1770 Portola and his troops return from the north to the garrison on Presidio Hill.

1774 Serra and other priests move their mission up the **San Diego River** to get away from the soldiers' cruel treatment of the local Indians and to take advantage of the river valley's water supply and fertile land.

1775 On 4 November, the Kumeyaay attack and destroy the mission, which is rebuilt a few months later. Father Luis Jayme is killed in the attack.

1798 The Franciscans found the **Mission San Luis Rey** in northern San Diego near what is now **Oceanside**. The mission becomes the largest and most prosperous in California.

1800 The Presidio is enlarged and fortified, and a second fortress is built at **Point Loma**.

1807 The San Diego River is dammed to create grazing lands for cattle and sheep. About 1,600 Kumeyaay are listed as having been baptized by the priests in the previous decade. Records also show that about 9,000 of those Native Americans subsequently die from diseases brought by the Spaniards.

1821 Mexico gains independence from Spain, and the Mexican government claims Spain's territory in California. The Spanish flag continues to fly above the Presidio until 1823 or 1824, when it is replaced by the Mexican flag. The settlers begin moving from the guarded Presidio to the area now called **Old Town**.

1833 Mexico's Secularization Act places church property into private ownership and dissolves the mission system, creating vast ranches from mission lands. Mexican settlers begin arriving and creating prosperous cattle ranches.

1835 On 1 January, San Diego becomes an official civil pueblo with some 400 Mexican residents. Juan Osuna is elected the first mayor and judge.

1840 Sailor Richard Henry Dana, who arrived in San Diego 5 years earlier on the trading ship *Pilgrim* from New England, publishes his book *Two Years Before the Mast*, describing the people of California, called the Californios.

1846 The Mexican-American War begins. On 12 December, after fierce battles between the Californios and the Americans, the US Army enters and claims San Diego.

1847 On 17 January, the Californios surrender to US Colonel John Fremont.

1848 On 2 February, the Mexican-American War ends with the signing of the Treaty of Guadalupe Hidalgo; the US pays Mexico $15 million for much of what is now the southwestern US, including California.

1850 On 18 February, the San Diego region becomes a US county. On 27 March, San Diego becomes a city. On 9 September, California becomes the 31st state in the union. William Heath Davis and several partners purchase 160 acres of land facing San Diego Bay for $2,304 and begin building a new community where downtown San Diego now stands. Streets are laid, prefabricated houses are put up, and a wharf is built. But the citizens of Old Town prefer to stay where they are, and call the new settlement Davis's Folly. Davis's rising debt halts construction, and his fledgling metropolis becomes a ghost town.

1852 The city of San Diego declares bankruptcy.

1855 The **Old Point Loma Lighthouse** is lit.

1862 President Abraham Lincoln gives the mission back to the Catholic church.

1867 Alonzo Horton arrives in San Diego, intent on building a new city. A month later, he buys 960 acres in the downtown area at a land auction. Picking up where William Heath Davis left off 17 years earlier, he establishes **New Town**.

1868 William Gatewood and Edward Bushyhead found the *San Diego Union*. It begins as a weekly but becomes a daily in 1871.

1869 The population of San Diego hits 2,300 as newcomers are drawn to Horton's new city, which now includes **Horton's Wharf**, the **Horton House Hotel**, and **Horton Plaza**.

1870 Whalers from New England begin hunting the gray whales that migrate every winter from the Bering Strait to San Diego and Baja California. The whales soon learn to bypass San Diego Bay. Chinese immigrants begin settling in the **Stingaree** district of downtown in what's now called the **Gaslamp Quarter**.

Rancher Fred Coleman discovers gold in the mountains outside San Diego, and the Northern California gold rush moves south. Gold mining attracts thousands of settlers, but by 1876 many of the gold mines are closed.

1871 The cornerstone is laid for San Diego's **courthouse**.

1872 Fire destroys much of the business district of Old Town. Merchants abandon the neighborhood and move into Horton's New Town.

1885 Train tracks are laid and the first transcontinental train arrives in San Diego.

1886 The first electric lights shine over downtown's streets.

1888 Trolley tracks and telephone lines are installed in the city. The **Hotel del Coronado** opens in **Coronado**.

1890 San Diego's population reaches 16,000.

1891 The train tracks are washed away in a storm and San Diego is once again isolated, except for a small supply line to Los Angeles. The city of Coronado secedes from San Diego.

1895 The same company behind the *San Diego Union* begins publishing the *San Diego Evening Tribune*, a daily afternoon paper.

1897 Madame Katherine Tingley and the Universal Brotherhood and Theosophical Society purchase 130 acres on Point Loma and begin building **Lomaland**'s outdoor Greek theater and school buildings.

1898 The iron gunboat the USS *Pinta* enters San Diego Harbor, beginning the navy's ongoing presence in San Diego Bay.

1900 San Diego's population reaches 17,700.

1905 The USS *Bennington*'s boiler explodes in San Diego Harbor, killing 60 and injuring 47.

1908 The navy's battleship fleet visits San Diego while on a world tour to demonstrate US naval power. The ships are greeted with great fanfare, and the War Department starts planning to dredge San Diego Bay to accommodate larger ships.

1911 Aviator Glenn Curtiss lands his floating biplane beside the navy cruiser USS *Pennsylvania* in San Diego Bay, inspiring the navy to allot $25,000 to the development of naval aviation. Curtiss establishes the first military aviation school in the country at **North Island**.

1915 The **Panama-California Exposition** opens in **Balboa Park**.

1916 The Zoological Society of San Diego is formed under the direction of Dr. Harry Wegeforth.

1919 The US Marine Corps Recruit Depot opens.

1922 The San Diego Naval Training Station opens, and ground is broken for a naval hospital at **Balboa Park**.

1923 San Diego is named the headquarters of the Eleventh Naval District and the Pacific Fleet. The first known photographs of a solar eclipse are taken in San Diego.

1925 Pioneer aviator T. Claude Ryan starts Ryan Airlines, offering the first scheduled commuter flights from San Diego to Los Angeles. Ryan's company eventually becomes Teledyne Ryan Aeronautical, a leading manufacturer of military and civilian aircraft and equipment.

1927 Charles Lindbergh hires T. Claude Ryan to build a plane that can handle a solo flight across the Atlantic Ocean. Two months later, the *Spirit of St. Louis* is ready for flight. On 28 April, Lindbergh pilots the *Spirit of St. Louis* on a test flight at **Dutch Flats,** where San Diego's Midway Drive Post Office now stands. On 20 May, Lindbergh flies his new plane from New York to Paris.

1928 San Diego's airport, **Lindbergh Field**, is dedicated as 222 military planes roar in the sky. Colonel Ira C. Copley purchases the *San Diego Union* and the *San Diego Evening Tribune* as part of his Copley chain of newspapers.

1929 Archeologists from the **Museum of Man** discover the prehistoric bones of the Del Mar Man.

1932 Reuben H. Fleet moves his Consolidated Aircraft factory to San Diego. It later merges with other companies as Convair, and then General Dynamics, becoming one of the region's largest employers, along with the Ryan, Solar, and Rohr aircraft companies.

1933 San Diego weathers the Great Depression with assistance from President Franklin Roosevelt's relief programs. Workers in the Works Progress Administration build animal cages at the zoo, a fairgrounds and race track in **Del Mar**, and the first buildings for **San Diego State University**. The CCC (California Conservation Corps) is put to work in the mountains of East County, clearing trails and planting trees.

San Diego's first migrant workers' camps begin to appear. Most of the workers are homeless Dust Bowl families looking for work. Though the faces and nationalities change, migrant camps will continue to appear in the decades to come.

1935 Banking on a rise in prosperity and the imminent end of the Depression, San Diegans decide to host a second exposition in Balboa Park, using many of the buildings from the 1915–1916 Panama-California Exposition. On 29 May, the **California-Pacific Exposition** opens and runs for 2 years.

1940 San Diego's population reaches 203,000.

1941 On 7 December, loudspeakers at the San Diego Zoo broadcast a command for all military personnel to report for duty as news of the Japanese attack on Pearl Harbor, Hawaii, spreads. San Diego becomes mobilized as the US enters World War II. Balboa Park is declared off-limits to civilians, renamed **Camp Kidd**, and used as a training center and military hospital. Local aircraft factories operate around the clock, and San Diego's population swells with an influx of workers. Military units patrol the beaches; large nets are strung into the bay to prevent submarines from entering the harbor.

1942 The War Department begins detaining Japanese-Americans in inland camps; by the end of the war, approximately 2,000 San Diegans of Japanese ancestry are interred in the camps.

1945 As the war ends, San Diego switches its focus from military defense to tourism. Voters pass a bond to create an aquatic center and tourist attraction at **Mission Bay**. The post-war housing boom creates new neighborhoods throughout the county, and real estate prices soar. By the 1980s, tourism will be San Diego's third largest industry, after manufacturing and military interests.

1948 *San Diego Magazine*, the first city magazine in the nation, begins publication.

1958 Interstate Highway 8 opens in February, following ancient Indian trails through Mission Valley.

1963 Ground is broken for the city's first convention center at the downtown **Community Concourse**.

The **Salk Institute for Biological Studies,** headed by Dr. Jonas Salk, opens in an architectural masterpiece designed by **Louis I. Kahn**.

1964 **Sea World** opens on 22 acres at the edge of Mission Bay; the **University of California** opens a 1,000-acre campus in **La Jolla**.

1965 On 28 August, the Beatles perform before 18,000 adoring fans at Balboa Stadium.

1968 Old Town becomes a state historic park.

1969 The **San Diego–Coronado Bay Bridge**, which spans San Diego Bay, is completed and the ferries between downtown and Coronado cease operation.

1970 San Diego's population reaches 696,000.

1972 The **San Diego Wild Animal Park** opens in **Escondido**.

1974 The **Gaslamp Quarter Association** (now the Gaslamp Quarter Council) is founded to oversee preservation and development in the historic area of downtown.

1975 Nearly 20,000 Vietnamese immigrants are housed at **Camp Pendleton** in north San Diego County as the Vietnam War ends.

1978 On 25 September, **PSA Flight 182** from Sacramento collides with a private plane over the **North Park** neighborhood, taking 144 lives.

1983 The navy begins construction on a new hospital in **Florida Canyon** near its original hospital.

1984 The one remaining house from William Heath Davis's original community is moved to the Gaslamp Quarter to serve as the offices for the Gaslamp Quarter Council.

1985 The worst brush fire heretofore in San Diego's history destroys 116 homes in the neighborhood of **Normal Heights**.

1989 The **San Diego Convention Center** opens.

1991 On 29 January, radio station **B100** puts out a call to San Diegans to go to **Jack Murphy Stadium** to show their support for the US troops fighting in the Persian Gulf War. More than 30,000 people show up; 3,000 of them form a human American flag, which is photographed and sent to the troops.

1994 On 8 November, Californians pass Proposition 187, making illegal immigrants ineligible for public services, including education and nonemergency health care, and denying some benefits to legal immigrants as well. Lawsuits immediately follow the proposition's passage, and enforcement is stalled.

1995 In January, the **San Diego Chargers** win the AFC (American Football Conference) championship and go to the **Super Bowl**, where they are soundly defeated by the **San Francisco 49ers**.

1996 The **Republican National Convention** is held in August at the San Diego Convention Center.

1997 While the Naval Training Center at Point Loma is closed to all active military duty,

the reconstructed **House of Hospitality** reopens in Balboa Park.

1998 The **Padres** win the National League pennant but lose to the New York Yankees in the **World Series**. The **Coors Amphitheatre** opens in **Chula Vista**, and voters not only approve of the convention-center expansion in downtown and the Padres' ballpark but also green-light $1.5 billion in city school bonds.

1999 **Legoland California** opens in **Carlsbad**. The **San Diego Presidio** ruins are once again covered up for posterity to preserve them for future archeological digs.

2000 The population of San Diego hits 1,223,400. The San Diego County population is 2,813,833.

2002 US Navy aircraft carriers based in San Diego begin deployment to the Persian Gulf to prepare for war with Iraq.

A 15-foot-high steel fence rises at the border between San Diego and Tijuana.

2003 Two wildfires burn down over 2,000 homes and businesses and kill 16 people in San Diego.

2004 The Securities and Exchange Commission investigates irregularities in the city of San Diego's financial disclosures and pension system deficit.

Petco Park, the new baseball field for the San Diego Padres, opens in downtown.

Mayor Dick Murphy wins reelection after protracted legal battles over the majority vote for write-in candidate Donna Frye.

2005 On 25 April, under pressure from various groups, Mayor Dick Murphy announces his resignation seven months into his second term. On 28 November, US Congressman Randy "Duke" Cunningham from San Diego resigns over a bribery scandal.

2007 Local sports hero and ex-Padre Tony Gwynn is inducted in the National Baseball Hall of Fame.

Five wildfires rage through San Diego's backcountry for several days, destroying more than 1,700 homes in Rancho Bernardo, Poway, Jamul, and other outlying communities.

Kate O. Sessions House **79**
Kate Sessions Park **123**
Kazumi Sushi ★★★$$ **81**
Keating Hotel $$$$ **54**
Keating House $$ **89**
Kelly, Francis **109**
Kemo Sabe ★★$$$ **82**
Ken Cinema **192**
Kickers **187**
Kim, C. W. **40, 47, 75**
King Promenade **47**
Kit Carson Park **166**
K. Nathan Gallery **156**
Knott's Soak City USA **167**
Knudson, Vern D. **29**
Koalas **17**
Kona Kai Resort $$ **108**
Kono's Cafe ★★$ **126**
Krisle & Shapiro **74**

L

La Avenida Inn $$ **71**
La Casa de Estudillo **94**
La Casa del Zorro Resort **167**
La Casa de Machado y Stewart **93**
L.A. Cetto Winery **174**
La Costa ★★$$ **174**
La Costa Resort & Spa **163**
La Diferencia ★★★$$ **177**
La Especial ★★★$ **173**
La Jolla **138** (chapter), **139** (map), **149** (map)
La Jolla Beach & Tennis Club $$$ **147**
La Jolla Cove **148**
La Jolla Cove Suites $$$$ **148**
La Jolla Inn $$ **150**
La Jolla Library **158**
La Jolla Playhouse **143**
La Jolla Post Office **153**
La Jolla Recreation Center **156**
La Jolla Shores **146**
La Jolla Shores Hotel $$$ **146**
La Jolla Village Lodge $$ **156**
La Jolla Village Square **146**
La Jolla Woman's Club **155**
La Leña (Tijuana) ★★★$$ **177**
Lamb's Players Theatre **70**
La Mesa **166**
Lamont Street Grill ★★$$$ **127**
Landing, The ★★★$ **122**
Landmark's Hillcrest Cinemas **81**
Language, Tijuana **169**
La Paloma **163**
La Pensione Hotel $ **51**
La Piñata ★$ **93**
Lara, Federico **172**

Las Olas **163**
Las Rosas $$ **182**
L'Auberge Del Mar **161**
Lauren, Alfredo **176**
La Valencia $$$$ **150**
La Villa de Zaragoza Hotel $ **174**
Lawrence Welk Museum **164**
Lawrence Welk Resort **164**
Le Cousteau $$$$ **179**
Lee Palm Sportfishers **111**
Legoland **164**
Legoretta, Ricardo **167**
Lemeche-Meade House **69**
Leña, La (Tijuana) ★★★$$ **177**
Les Artistes **162**
Lestat's Coffee House **192**
Le Travel Store **55**
Leucadia **163**
Ley **172**
Liberty Station **106**
Library, South Chula Vista **167**
Liebhardt, Frederick **113**
Liebhardt, Weston and Goldman **146**
Liebhardt and Weston **143**
Lily Pond **21**
Limousines **5**
Lindbergh Field, ground transportation **5**
Lindbergh Field San Diego International Airport **5, 106**
Little Italy **33** (chapter and map), **50**
Little Italy Inn $$ **50**
Living Room Coffeehouse (La Jolla) ★★$ **152**
Living Room Coffeehouse (Shelter Island) ★$ **112**
Lodge at Torrey Pines, The $$$ **140**
Loews Coronado Bay Resort $$$$ **74**
Loma Vista Bed & Breakfast **166**
Long-Waterman House **89**
Lorimer-Case **81**
Los Arcos ★★★$$ **177**
Lou's Records **163**
Lucerna, Hotel $$ **176**
Lumpkins, William **151, 153**
Lyceum Theatre **43**
Lyon, Mark **82**

M

McP's Irish Pub ★$ **69**
Main Events, The **8**
Manchester Grand Hyatt San Diego $$$$ **46**

Manhattan ★★$$$ **156**
Map key **6**
Marine Corps Air Station Miramar **164**
Marine Room, The ★★★★$$$$ **147**
Maritime Museum **35**
Marrakesh ★★$$$ **158**
Marston House **14**
Mary Star of the Sea **157**
Mason Street School **94**
Medea, The **36**
Mercado de Artesanías **172**
Mercado Hidalgo **175**
Mesa, La **166**
Mexican Sampler, A **181**
Michele Coulon Dessertier ★★$$$ **158**
Middletown **85**
Miguel's Cocina (Coronado) ★$ **72**
Miguel's Cocina (Shelter Island) ★$ **112**
Mille Fleurs **162**
Mills Manor **137**
Mingei International Museum **24**
Mingel International Museum North County Satellite **166**
Mission Basilica San Diego de Alcalá **101**
Mission Bay and Beaches **114** (chapter), **115** (map)
Mission Bay Golf Course **116**
Mission Bay Park **115** (map), **116, 117**
Mission Bay Park, Visitors' Information Center **118**
Mission Bay Park Headquarters **123**
Mission Bay SportCenter **117**
Mission Beach **114** (chapter), **115** (map), **128, 129** (map)
Mission Beach Club **129**
Mission Brewery Plaza **84**
Mission Café ★★$ **129**
Mission Hills Nursery **79**
Mission Hills Pioneer Park **80**
Mission San Luis Rey **164**
Mission Valley **90** (chapter), **100** (map), **101**
Mission Valley Resort $$ **99**
Mistral ★★$$$$ **75**
Mixture **50**
Model Railroad Museum, San Diego **26**
Money **10**
Money, Tijuana **170**
Monkey Trails **15**

Monsoon ★★★$$$ **56**
Moonlight Beach **163**
MooTime Creamery ★$ **68**
Morely Field Sports Complex **14**
Mormon Battalion Memorial
    Visitors Center **94**
Morton's of Chicago ★★★$$$$
    48
Mosher, Drew, Watson & Ferguson
    66
Mosher, Robert **20, 154, 158**
Mountains, Day Trips **164**
Mount Laguna **167**
Mount Soledad **159**
Municipal Gymnasium **29**
Municipal Sportfishing Pier **111**
Museo de los Niños/Children's
    Museum San Diego **47**
Museum of Art, San Diego **19, 20**
    (map)
Museum of Contemporary Art San
    Diego (Downtown) **39**
Museum of Contemporary Art San
    Diego (La Jolla) **155**
Museum of History and Art **69**
Museum of Man **22**
Museum of Photographic Arts **26**
Musical Nights **109**
My Beautiful Dog-O-Mat **84**

N

Nati's Mexican Restaurant $$
    136
Natural History Museum **22**
Nature's Calendar **135**
Naval Amphibious Base **74**
NBC **43**
Neale Street **81**
Nettleship, Neil **125**
Newbreak Coffee Co. ★$ **104**
New Orleans Creole Cafe ★★$$
    96
Newport Avenue Antique Center
    136
Nick's at the Beach ★★$$ **127**
Nick's at the Pier ★$$ **134**
Nido, El $$ **179**
Night & Day Cafe ★$ **67**
Niki de Saint-Phalle Sculpture
    Garden **166**
976 Cafe **124**
Nine-Ten ★★★$$$ **153**
No. 1 Fifth Avenue **190**
North County, Coastal **160** (map)
North County, Inland **160** (map),
    164
North Island **64**

North Park Adult Video **192**
Numbers **190**

O

O. B. Donuts **137**
Obelisk—the Bookstore **188**
OB People's Organic Foods Market
    134
O'Brien, Jack **141** (bests)
Observatory, Palomar **167**
Oceanaire ★★★★$$$$ **59**
Ocean Beach **115** (map), **131,
    132** (map), **133**
Ocean Beach Antique Mall **137**
Ocean Beach International Hostel
    $ **136**
Ocean Beach Pier **133**
Ocean Beach Pier Cafe $ **133**
Ocean Boulevard and Seawall **71**
Ocean Park Inn $$$ **127**
Oceanside **164**
Olas, Las **163**
Old Adobe Chapel **97**
Old Point Loma Lighthouse **109**
Old Town **91**
Old Town and Mission Valley **90**
    (chapter and map)
Old Town Mexican Cafe and
    Cantina ★★★$ **96**
Old Town Plaza **94**
Old Town State Historic Park **94**
Old Venice ★★★$ **112**
Ole Madrid Cafe ★★$$ **55**
Omni San Diego $$$ **61**
On Broadway **42**
One American Plaza **39**
150 Grand Café **166**
Onyx Room, The **53**
Orange Avenue **67**
Orfila Vineyards and Winery **165**
Orientation **4**
Ortega's (Mission Bay and
    Beaches) ★★$$ **136**
Ortega's (South of Tijuana) **179**
Osteria Panevino ★★$$$ **56**
Our Lady of the Rosary Parish **51**
Over-the-Line **122**

P

Pacifica, Cafe ★★★★$$$$ **97**
Pacifica Del Mar **161**
Pacific Beach **123** (map)
Pacific Beach Surf Shop **128**
Pacific Coast Grill **162**
Pacific Gaslamp Stadium **15, 56**
Pacific Rim Park **108**

Pacific Shores Bar **136**
Pacific Shores Inn $$ **124**
Pacific Terrace Hotel $$$$ **124**
Padre Trail Inn $$ **91**
Palacio Frontón **174**
Palisades Building **28**
Paloma, La **163**
Palomar Mountain State Park **167**
Palomar Observatory **167**
Pannikin **45**
Pantoja Park **44**
Papas & Beer **179**
Paradise Point Resort and Spa
    $$$$ **118**
Parallel 33 ★★$$$$ **80**
Parisi, Hotel $$$ **150**
Parkhouse Eatery ★★$$$ **186**
Parking **7**
Park It on Market **57**
Park Manor Suites $$ **87**
Parque Obrero **183**
Parroquía Espíritu Santo **175**
Passports, Tijuana **170**
Patrick's, Il **53**
Pay One Sports Arena **104**
Pearl Hotel, The $$ **110**
Pecs **190**
Peirera, William **142**
Peninsula Tennis Club **133**
Pennant, The **131**
Pensione Hotel, La $ **51**
Peohe's ★★$$$$ **65**
Pepper Grove **28**
Personal Safety **11**
Personal Safety (Tijuana) **170**
Pescador Fish Market, El ★$$
    158
Petco Park **48**
Photographic Arts, Museum of **26**
Piatti, Ristorante ★★$$$ **148**
Pickering, Ernest **125**
Pieper, Norbert W. **46**
Pilar's Beach Wear **129**
Piñata, La ★$ **93**
Pine Valley **167**
Pizza Nova (Point Loma) ★★$
    111
Pizza Nova (Uptown) ★★$$ **81**
Plaza de Balboa **26**
Plaza del Pasado **93**
Plaza Río Tijuana **175**
Plums **70**
Plunge, The **130**
Point Loma Elliot Hostel $ **105**
Point Loma/Harbor Island/Shelter
    Island **102** (chapter and map)
Point Loma Nazarene University
    107

Point Loma Seafoods ★★★$ **111**
Polar Bear Plunge **17**
Poma's ★★$ **136**
Pomegranate (La Jolla) **151**
Pomegranate (Uptown) **83**
Po Pazzo ★★★$$$$ **50**
Porkyland ★$ **157**
Posada El Rey Sol $ **183**
Post Office, La Jolla **153**
Post Office, San Diego **44**
Prado Restaurant, The ★★★$$ **25**
Prego Ristorante ★★$$$ **99**
Presidio Park **92**
Primavera Ristorante ★★$$$ **67**
Princess Pub and Grille ★★$ **51**
Promenade, The **128**
Prospect Place **151**
Pt. Loma Camera **112**
Publications **11**
Public Library, San Diego **44**
Pueblo Amigo **172**
Pueblo Amigo, Hotel $$ **173**
Puerto Nuevo **180**

Q

Quail Botanical Gardens **163**
Qualcomm Stadium **101**
Quarter Kitchen ★★★$$$$ **54**
Quayle Brothers **77**
Quigley, Rob Wellington **31, 44, 47, 48**
Quigley, Rob Wellington, and Everyone Else in the Office **56** (bests)
Quince Street Bridge **87**
Quivira Basin **123**

R

Racine & Laramie **93**
Rainwater's on Kettner ★★★$$$$ **37**
Ralph's **83**
Rama ★★★$$$$ **60**
Ramada Inn & Suites $$$ **53**
Ramada Limited San Diego Airport $ **110**
Rancho Bernardo **164, 165**
Rancho Bernardo Inn **165**
Rancho California Road **164**
Rancho Santa Fe **162**
Rancho Santa Fe, Inn at **162**
Rancho Valencia Resort **163**
Rancho Valencia Restaurant **163**
Rapp Brothers **28**
RA Sushi ★★$$$ **41**
Raymond, Robert S. **79**

Real Del Mar Golf Resort and Country Club **178**
Red Pearl Kitchen ★★★$$ **59**
Red Roost and Red Rest **148**
Red Sails Inn ★$ **113**
Reid, James **67, 73, 74**
Reid, Merritt **73, 74**
Rental cars **6**
Requa, Richard **18, 28, 29, 77, 86**
Residence Inn (Real del Mar) **178**
Restaurants **11**
Restaurants, rating **6**
Reuben E. Lee **107**
Reuben H. Fleet Space Theater and Science Center **26**
Rew-Sharp Estate **68**
Rey Sol, El $$ **183**
Rhinoceros Cafe & Grille ★★$$ **70**
Rich's **188**
Ristorante Piatti ★★$$$ **148**
Ritz, Café ★★$$$ **171**
Riviera del Pacífico **183**
Robb Field **132**
Robb Field Skate Park **132**
Robbins Jorgenson Christopher **74**
Robert House **71**
Robinson-Rose House and Visitors' Center **93**
Roehrig, Frederick **69**
Rogers, Lincoln **130**
Ropería **93**
Roppongi Restaurant, Bar and Cafe ★★$$$ **154**
Rosarito Beach **178**
Rosarito Beach Hotel $$ **179**
Rosarito Tourist and Visitors Bureau **179**
Rosas, Las $$ **182**
Rose and Desert Gardens **27**
Rosen, Manuel **175**
Royal Thai Cuisine ★$$ **59**
Rubio's Deli-Mex ★★★$ **127**
Ruocco, Lloyd **143**

S

Sacred Heart Catholic Church **67**
Sadler, Tucker **39**
Safety, Personal **11**
Safety, Personal (Tijuana) **170**
Saffron Noodles and Saté ★★★$ **85**
Sail Bay **116**
St. Agnes Roman Catholic Church **111**
St. Francis, Chapel of **23**

St. James by-the-Sea Episcopalian Church **155**
Salk Institute for Biological Studies **141**
Sally's ★★$$$ **47**
Sammy's California Woodfired Pizza ★★$ **159**
Sanborn's **174**
San Diego **2** (map)
San Diego, California, Temple for the Church of Jesus Christ of Latter-Day Saints **146**
San Diego, Museum of Contemporary Art (Downtown) **39**
San Diego, Museum of Contemporary Art (La Jolla) **155**
San Diego, University of, (UCSD) **91**
San Diego Aerospace Museum **29**
San Diego Aircraft Carrier Museum **44**
San Diego and Environs *see inside front cover* (map)
San Diego Automotive Museum **29**
San Diego Bay and the Embarcadero **35**
San Diego Bay Ferry (Downtown) **38**
San Diego by Bike **119**
San Diego Chinese Historical Museum **47**
San Diego Convention Center **48, 55** (map)
San Diego-Coronado Bridge **64**
San Diego County Administration Building **35**
San Diego Day Trips **160** (chapter and map)
San Diego Eagle **192**
San Diego Ferry (Coronado) **65**
San Diego Hall of Champions **28**
San Diego Harbor Excursion **38**
San Diego Historical Society Museum **26**
San Diego International Airport, Lindbergh Field **5**
San Diego Marriott Del Mar **162**
San Diego Marriott Gaslamp Quarter $$$$ **59**
San Diego Marriott Hotel & Marina $$$$ **47**
San Diego Marriott Mission Valley $$$ **100**
San Diego Model Railroad Museum **26**

San Diego Museum of Art **19, 20** (map)
San Diego Post Office **44**
San Diego Public Library **44**
San Diego Trolley **9**, *see also inside back cover* (map)
San Diego Union Newspaper Historical Building **94**
San Diego Wild Animal Park **165**
San Diego Yacht Club **113**
San Diego Zoo **14, 15** (map)
San Elijo State Beach **163**
San Pasqual Valley **165**
Santa Fe Depot **38**
Santa Ysabel **167**
Sante ★★★$$$ **154**
San Ysidro/Tijuana, Border crossing **171**
Saska's ★★$$$ **129**
Sbicca **163**
Science Center, Reuben H. Fleet Space Theater and **26**
Scripps Aviary **17**
Scripps Inn $$$ **155**
Scripps Institution of Oceanography (SIO) **143**
SD Wine & Culinary Center **48**
Seabreeze Nautical Books and Charts **112**
Seaforth Boat Rentals **122**
Sealife Calendar **88**
Seaport Village **46**
Seau's The Restaurant ★★$$ **100**
Sea World **121**
Seeley Stables **94**
Self-Realization Fellowship **86**
Self-Realization Fellowship Retreat and Hermitage **163**
Señor Frogs ★★$ **172**
Sessions, Kate, Park **123**
Sessions, Kate O., House **79**
Sevilla, Café ★★★$ **58**
SGPA **81**
Shades ★★$$ **134**
Shakespeare Pub & Grille ★★$$ **85**
Shell Beach Guest Apartments $$$ **152**
Shelter Island **102** (chapter and map), **110** (map)
Sheraton San Diego Hotel and Marina $$$ **107**
Sheraton Suites San Diego $$$$ **37**
Sherman-Gilbert House **95**
Shopping **11**
Shopping, Tijuana **170**
Shores, The **74**

Shores Restaurant, The ★★$$ **147**
Shuttles **5**
Silver Strand State Beach **74**
Singer, David Raphael **26, 153**
SIO (Scripps Institution of Oceanography) **143**
Ski Beach **118**
Skidmore, Owings & Merrill **37, 46**
Sky Room, The ★★★★$$$$ **150**
Smoking **11**
Snyder, Robert W. **19**
Social Sciences and Humanities Library **142**
Society Billiard Cafe **126**
Sofia Hotel $$ **40**
Solamar Hotel $$$$ **59**
Solana Beach **162**
Soledad, Mount **159**
Solunto Baking Company **51**
Sommerset Suites Hotel $$ **80**
South Beach Bar & Grill ★★$ **134**
South Chula Vista Library **167**
Southcoast Surf Shop **135**
South Mission Beach Park **131**
South of Tijuana **178** (map)
South to Chula Vista **165**
Space Theater and Science Center, Reuben H. Fleet **26**
Spanish Landing **106**
Spanish Village Art Center **18**
Spa Tiki **48**
Spencer, Eldridge **118**
Splash Wearable Art **60**
Sportsmen's Seafoods ★$ **122**
Spreckels Building **70**
Spreckels Organ Pavilion **27**
Spreckels Park **67**
Spreckels Theatre **43**
Spruce Street Footbridge **86**
SRO ★$ **192**
Starlight Bowl **29**
Star of India **35**
Star Park **69**
Stephens-Terry House **67**
Stingaree **59**
Street plan **11**
Street plan, Tijuana **170**
Stretch's Cafe ★$ **67**
Stuart Collection **142**
Sun Bear Forest **16**
Sunset Cliffs **137**
Surf Diva **147**
Surf Lingo **117**
Surprise, HMS **36**
Sushi Deli Two ★★$ **40**
Sushi on the Rock ★★$$ **157**
Swami's **163**

Sweetwater Marsh National Wildlife Refuge **167**
Swings n' Things **46**
Swoozy's **136**
Sydney's Grill $ **17**
Symphony Hall, Copley **37**
Symphony Towers **37**

T

Tacos el Fénix **183**
Tapenade ★★★★$$$$ **158**
Tarasuck, Mark **86**
Tartine ★$ **65**
Tasende Gallery **154**
Taste of Szechuan ★$ **82**
Taxes **11**
Taxis **6, 7**
Teague, Walter **29**
Tea Pavilion ★$ **27**
Telephone numbers, essential **10**
Telephones, Tijuana **170**
Temecula Valley **165, 166**
Temecula Valley Winegrowers Association **166**
Temple Beth Israel **96**
Thee Bungalow ★★★$$$$ **131**
3rd Corner, The ★★★$$$ **132**
3500 Block of Seventh Avenue **86**
3162 Second Avenue **86**
Thornton Winery **166**
Thorpe and Kennedy **151**
Tickets **11**
Tidelands Park **66**
Tide Pools **109**
Tiger River **16**
Tijuana **168** (chapter), **169** (map)
Tijuana, Visitors' Information Offices **171**
Tijuana Centro Cultural **174**
Tijuana Country Club **177**
Tijuana Day Trips **178** (map)
Tijuana/San Ysidro Border Crossing **171**
Time zones **11**
Timken Art Gallery **23**
Tin Fish ★★★★$ **61**
Tipping **11**
Tired of Tramping Around? Take the Tram **27**
Todos Santos **181**
Tom Ham's Lighthouse $$$ **106**
Tony's Jacal **162**
Top of the Cove **151**
Top of the Market ★★$$$ **45**
Torrey Pines Gliderport **141**
Torrey Pines Municipal Golf Course **140**

Torrey Pines State Reserve **140, 160**
Tourist and Visitors Bureau, Rosarito **179**
Tourmaline Park **124**
Tours **8**
Tower 23 $$$$ **125**
Tower Two Beach Cafe ★$ **134**
Town and Country Hotel $$ **98**
Trader Joe's **126**
Train Station (Long-Distance) **7**
Transportation **5**
Trattoria Acqua ★★$$ **152**
Travel Store, Le **55**
Treks and Tours **87**
Trolley **9,** see also inside back cover (map)
Trolley, Tijuana **169**
Trolley Transfer Station **49**
Trophy's Sports Grill ★★$ **99**
Tucker Sadler and Associates **44**
Tuna Harbor **45**
Tunaman's Memorial **108**
Turf Club **162**
24 Hour Fitness **187**
Twiggs Coffee Shop ★★$ **79**
Twiggs Tea & Coffee **186**
222 Cafe **47**
Tye, Ben **125**

U

UCSD (University of California, San Diego) **142**
Ullrich, Edgar **154**
United Methodist Church **159**
University Bookstore **142**
University of California, San Diego (UCSD) **142**
University of San Diego **91**
Up, Up, and Away **151**
Upstart Crow and Company **46**
Uptown **76** (chapter and map)
Uptown District **81**
Urban Lighting **60**
Urban Mo's ★$ **188**
U.S. Grant Hotel $$$$ **41**
US Marine Corps Recruit Depot **105**

V

Valencia, La $$$$ **150**
Vázquez, Pedro Ramírez **175**
Vegetable Shop (Chino's) **163**
Venetian, The ★★$$ **105**
Venissimo Cheese **80**
Venturi, Robert **155**

Veterans Museum and Memorial Center **30**
Via de la Valle **162**
Villa de Zaragoza Hotel, La $ **174**
Village Grill ★$ **21**
Village Hillcrest **81**
Villa Montezuma **192**
Villa Saverios ★★★$$$ **177**
Vince's Seafood Restaurant $$ **179**
Visitor Center, Coronado **70**
Visitor Information Center, Anza-Borrego Desert State Park **167**
Visitors Center, Mormon Battalion Memorial **94**
Visitors' Center, Robinson-Rose House and **93**
Visitors' Information Center, Mission Bay Park **118**
Visitors' Information Centers **10, 11**
Visitors' Information Offices, Tijuana **171**

W

Wahrenbrock's Book House **42**
Walking **9**
Warner Springs **167**
Warwick's **155**
Waterfront Bar, The **50**
Waterman, Hazel **94**
Waters Café ★$ **21**
Wave House **130**
Wear It Again Sam **83**
Wellington, Gerald **21**
Westfield Shoppingtown Horton Plaza **44**
Westfield Shoppingtown Mission Valley Center **99**
Westfield Shoppingtown UTC **145**
Westgate $$$$ **40**
Westin Horton Plaza $$$$ **43**
Westin San Diego $$$$ **39**
West Marine **112**
Whale Overlook **109**
Whaley House **96**
Wheelchair accessibility **6**
Wheeler, Richard George **21, 25**
Wheeler, William **53**
Wheeler, Wimer, Blackman & Associates **143**
Whitmore, Douglas **70**
W Hotel $$$$ **38**
Wild Animal Park, San Diego **165**
William Heath Davis House **58**
Wimmer, Marie **20**
Windansea Beach **159**
Wine Country **166**

Wineries **182**
Wine Steals **105, 188**
Winslow, Carleton **21, 22, 23, 24, 86, 157**
WorldBeat Center **28**
World Curry ★★$ **126**
World Famous ★★$$$ **128**
Wright, John Lloyd **77, 81**

X

Xploration **180**

Y

Yacht Club, San Diego **113**
Yamada, Joseph **20**
Yee-Haw, Mary—The Rodeo Comes to Town **191**
Yokohama Friendship Bell **108**
Yoshino ★★★$ **84**
Youth Camps **117**
Yuma Building, The **57**

Z

Zarape, El ★★$ **79**
Zazen **65**
Zenbu ★★$$ **157**
Z Gallerie **57**
Zocalo Grill ★$$$ **97**
Zona Río **174**
Zoo, San Diego **14, 15** (map)
Zucchero, Café ★★$$ **51**

RESTAURANTS

Only restaurants with star ratings are listed below. All restaurants are listed alphabetically in the main (preceding) index. Always call in advance to ensure a restaurant has not closed, changed its hours, or booked its tables for a private party. The restaurant price ratings are based on the average cost of an entrée for one person, excluding tax and tip.

★★★★ An Extraordinary Experience
★★★ Excellent
★★ Very Good
★ Good

$$$$ Big Bucks ($21 and up)
$$$ Expensive ($16–$20)
$$ Reasonable ($10–$15)
$ The Price Is Right (less than $10)

INDEX

★★★★

Cafe Pacifica $$$$ **97**
Donovan's Steak & Chop House
  $$$$ **144**
Extraordinary Desserts
  (Downtown) $ **36**
George's at the Cove $$$ **151**
JRDN $$$$ **125**
The Marine Room $$$$ **147**
Oceanaire $$$$ **59**
Saffron Noodles and Saté $ **85**
The Sky Room $$$$ **150**
Tapenade $$$$ **158**
Tin Fish $ **61**

★★★

Adam's Steak 'n' Eggs and Albie's
  Beef Inn $$ **98**
Alfonso's $$ **152**
Anthology $$$ **52**
Apollonia Greek Bistro $$ **145**
Athens Market Taverna $$ **44**
Baleen Restaurant and Bar $$$
  118
Bandar $$ **53**
Barbarella $$ **147**
Bully's $$$ **100**
Busalacchi's $$$ **84**
Café Japengo $$$$ **144**
Café Sevilla $ **58**
California Cuisine $$$ **188**
Cheese Shop $ **57**
Chez Loma $$$$ **69**
Croce's Restaurant & Jazz Bar
  $$$$ **54**
El Agave Restaurant and Tequileria
  $$$$ **97**
Extraordinary Desserts (Uptown)
  $ **87**
The Field $ **58**
Fresh [er] $$$$ **153**
Grant Grill $$$$ **41**
The Guild $$ **49**
Indigo Grill $$$ **51**
Isabel's Cantina $$ **125**
Jack and Giulio's Italian
  Restaurant $$$ **97**
Jack's La Jolla $$$$ **154**
Kazumi Sushi $$ **81**
La Diferencia $$ **177**
La Especial $ **173**
La Leña (Tijuana) $$ **177**
The Landing $ **122**
Los Arcos $$ **177**
Monsoon $$$ **56**
Morton's of Chicago $$$$ **48**

Nine-Ten $$$ **153**
Old Town Mexican Cafe and
  Cantina $ **96**
Old Venice $ **112**
Point Loma Seafoods $ **111**
Po Pazzo $$$$ **50**
The Prado Restaurant $$ **25**
Quarter Kitchen $$$$ **54**
Rainwater's on Kettner $$$$ **37**
Rama $$$$ **60**
Red Pearl Kitchen $$ **59**
Rubio's Deli-Mex $ **127**
Sante $$$ **154**
Thee Bungalow $$$$ **131**
The 3rd Corner $$$ **132**
Villa Saverios $$$ **177**
Yoshino $ **84**

★★

Azul La Jolla $$$$ **152**
Barefoot Bar & Grill $$ **118**
Bertrand at Mister A's $$$ **89**
Blue Point Coastal Cuisine $$$
  57
Brigantine (Coronado) $$$ **71**
The Brigantine (Shelter Island)
  $$$ **112**
Brockton Villa Restaurant $$ **148**
Cafe Athena $ **126**
Café Cerise $$ **38**
Cafe Eleven $$ **189**
Café Ritz $$$ **171**
Cafe 222 $ **47**
Café Zucchero $$ **51**
Canes Bar and Grill $$ **131**
Casa Guadalajara $$ **93**
Chiki Jai $ **174**
Chive $$$$ **57**
Cien Años $$ **176**
Crest Cafe $ **190**
Crown Room $$ **73**
Dave & Buster's $$ **100**
Dobson's $$$$ **43**
El Indio (Uptown) $ **85**
El Zarape $ **79**
Fairouz $ **104**
1500 Ocean $$$ **73**
Filippi's Pizza Grotto $ **51**
Fish Market (Downtown) $$ **45**
Gelato Vero Caffe $ **85**
Girard Gourmet $ **154**
Greek Island Cafe $ **46**
Harry's Coffee Shop $ **158**
Hash House a Go Go $$ **84**
Hodad's $ **134**
Humphrey's $$$ **113**
Jimmy Love's $$ **56**

J-Six $$$ **60**
Kaiserhof $$ **134**
Karinya $$ **126**
Karl Strauss' Brewery &
  Restaurant $ **38**
Kemo Sabe $$$ **82**
Kono's Cafe $ **126**
La Costa $$ **174**
Lamont Street Grill $$$ **127**
Living Room Coffeehouse (La
  Jolla) $ **152**
Manhattan $$$ **156**
Marrakesh $$$ **158**
Michele Coulon Dessertier $$$
  158
Mission Café $ **129**
Mistral $$$$ **75**
New Orleans Creole Cafe $$ **96**
Nick's at the Beach $$ **127**
Ole Madrid Cafe $$ **55**
Ortega's (Mission Bay and
  Beaches) $$ **136**
Osteria Panevino $$$ **56**
Parallel 33 $$$$ **80**
Parkhouse Eatery $$$ **186**
Peohe's $$$$ **65**
Piatti, Ristorante $$$ **148**
Pizza Nova (Point Loma) $ **111**
Pizza Nova (Uptown) $$ **81**
Poma's $ **136**
Prego Ristorante $$$ **99**
Primavera Ristorante $$$ **67**
Princess Pub and Grille $ **51**
RA Sushi $$$ **41**
Rhinoceros Cafe & Grille $$ **70**
Ristorante Piatti $$$ **148**
Roppongi Restaurant, Bar and
  Cafe $$$ **154**
Sally's $$$ **47**
Sammy's California Woodfired
  Pizza $ **159**
Saska's $$$ **129**
Seau's The Restaurant $$ **100**
Señor Frogs $ **172**
Shades $$ **134**
Shakespeare Pub & Grille $$ **85**
The Shores Restaurant $$ **147**
South Beach Bar & Grill $ **134**
Sushi Deli Two $ **40**
Sushi on the Rock $$ **157**
Top of the Market $$$ **45**
Trattoria Acqua $$ **152**
Trophy's Sports Grill $ **99**
Twiggs Coffee Shop $ **79**
The Venetian $$ **105**
World Curry $ **126**
World Famous $$$ **128**
Zenbu $$ **157**

★

Adams Avenue Grill $$ **78**
Albert's $$ **17**
Baja Betty's $ **190**
Bar West $$$$ **127**
Big Kitchen Cafe $ **192**
Blarney Stone Pub & Restaurant
  $ **58**
The Boat House (Harbor Island)
  $$$ **106**
Bondi $$ **60**
Brian's American Eatery $ **187**
Bronx Pizza $ **80**
Cafe 1134 $ **70**
Cafe in the Park $ **26**
Café Lulu $ **54**
Cafe on Park $ **190**
California Pizza Kitchen $ **146**
Cass Street Bar & Grill $ **124**
City Delicatessen $ **188**
Coronado Boathouse 1887 $$$
  74
The Corvette Diner, Bar & Grill
  $$ **82**
Dakota Grill & Spirits $$ **53**
Dick's Last Resort $$ **60**
Dinosaur Café $ **22**
Downtown Johnny Brown's $ **37**
Eggery Etc. $ **128**
El Pescador Fish Market $$ **158**
French Gourmet $$$ **124**
Green Flash $ **128**
Hob Nob Hill $ **89**
Ichiban $ **83**
Il Fornaio $$$ **65**
Island Prime & C Level $$$ **107**
Jimmy Carter's Café $ **87**
Joe's Crabshack $$ **49**
Jose's Court Room $ **153**
Kansas City Barbeque $ **46**
La Piñata $ **93**
Living Room Coffeehouse (Shelter
  Island) $ **112**
McP's Irish Pub $ **69**
Miguel's Cocina (Coronado) $ **72**
Miguel's Cocina (Shelter Island)
  $ **112**
MooTime Creamery $ **68**
Newbreak Coffee Co. $ **104**
Nick's at the Pier $$ **134**
Night & Day Cafe $ **67**
Porkyland $ **157**
Red Sails Inn $ **113**
Royal Thai Cuisine $$ **59**
Sportsmen's Seafoods $ **122**
SRO $ **192**
Stretch's Cafe $ **67**

Tartine $ **65**
Taste of Szechuan $ **82**
Tea Pavilion $ **27**
Tower Two Beach Cafe $ **134**
Urban Mo's $ **188**
Village Grill $ **21**
Waters Café $ **21**
Zocalo Grill $$$ **97**

HOTELS

The hotels listed below are grouped according to their price ratings; they are also listed in the main index. The hotel price ratings reflect the base price of a standard room for two people for one night during the peak season.

$$$$ Big Bucks ($250 and up)
  $$$ Expensive ($175–250)
    $$ Reasonable ($100–175)
      $ The Price is Right (less than
        $100)

$$$$

Beach Village **74**
Casa Natalie **182**
Coronado Island Marriot Resort
  66
Courtyard by Marriott **42**
Embassy Suites (Downtown) **46**
Hard Rock Hotel **61**
Hilton San Diego Gaslamp
  Quarter **61**
Hilton San Diego Resort **119**
Hotel del Coronado **72**
Hyatt Regency Mission Bay Spa
  and Marina **122**
Ivy Hotel **54**
Keating Hotel **54**
La Jolla Cove Suites **148**
La Valencia **150**
Le Cousteau **179**
Loews Coronado Bay Resort **74**
Manchester Grand Hyatt San
  Diego **46**
Pacific Terrace Hotel **124**
Paradise Point Resort and Spa
  118
San Diego Marriott Gaslamp
  Quarter **59**
San Diego Marriott Hotel &
  Marina **47**
Sheraton Suites San Diego **37**
Solamar Hotel **59**
Tower 23 **125**

U.S. Grant Hotel **41**
Westgate **40**
Westin Horton Plaza **43**
Westin San Diego **39**
W Hotel **38**

$$$

Bahia Resort Hotel **121**
Beach Haven Inn **124**
Bed & Breakfast Inn at La Jolla
  156
Britt Scripps Inn **88**
Catamaran **128**
Courtyard San Diego Old Town **97**
Crowne Plaza San Diego **98**
Crystal Pier Hotel & Cottages **126**
The Dana On Mission Bay **121**
Doubletree Hotel **99**
Embassy Suites (La Jolla) **145**
Estancia **141**
Fiesta Inn **176**
Glorietta Bay Inn **72**
The Grande Colonial **153**
Hilton La Jolla Torrey Pines **140**
Horton Grand Hotel **58**
Hotel Parisi **150**
Humphrey's Half Moon Inn &
  Suites **113**
Hyatt Regency La Jolla at Aventine
  144
La Jolla Beach & Tennis Club **147**
La Jolla Shores Hotel **146**
The Lodge at Torrey Pines **140**
Ocean Park Inn **127**
Omni San Diego **61**
Ramada Inn & Suites **53**
San Diego Marriott Mission Valley
  100
Scripps Inn **155**
Shell Beach Guest Apartments
  152
Sheraton San Diego Hotel and
  Marina **107**

$$

Balboa Park Inn **191**
Bay Club Hotel and Marina **107**
Best Western Hacienda Suites—Old
  Town **94**
Best Western Island Palms Hotel
  107
Best Western Suites Hotel **66**
The Bristol **40**
Comfort Inn Gaslamp **45**
Crown City Inn **66**
El Cordova Hotel **71**

INDEX

Festival Plaza **179**
Grand Hotel **175**
Hacienda Bajamar Hotel **181**
Handlery Hotel & Resort **98**
Heritage Park Bed & Breakfast Inn **95**
Hilton San Diego Airport Harbor Island **106**
Holiday Inn Express **98**
Holiday Inn San Diego Bayside **111**
Hotel Lucerna **176**
Hotel Pueblo Amigo **173**
Keating House **89**
Kona Kai Resort **108**
La Avenida Inn **71**
La Jolla Inn **150**
La Jolla Village Lodge **156**
Las Rosas **182**
Little Italy Inn **50**
Mission Valley Resort **99**
Pacific Shores Inn **124**
Padre Trail Inn **91**
Park Manor Suites **87**
The Pearl Hotel **110**
Rosarito Beach Hotel **179**
Sofia Hotel **40**
Sommerset Suites Hotel **80**
Town and Country Hotel **98**

$

Coronado Village Inn **68**
Corona Plaza **176**
The Hillcrest Inn **191**
Hostelling International Downtown Hostel **57**
Island Inn **47**
J Street Inn **48**
Kasa Korbett **187**
La Pensione Hotel **51**

La Villa de Zaragoza Hotel **174**
Ocean Beach International Hostel **136**
Point Loma Elliot Hostel **105**
Posada El Rey Sol **183**
Ramada Limited San Diego Airport **110**

FEATURES

Aviation in San Diego **145**
Bird's-Eye Views **105**
Child's Play **25**
Festivals **187**
Free Tuesdays **19**
Guided Tours (Tijuana) **180**
In the Swing **142**
The Main Events **8**
A Mexican Sampler **181**
Musical Nights **109**
Nature's Calendar **135**
Over-the-Line **122**
San Diego by Bike **119**
Sealife Calendar **88**
Surf Lingo **117**
Tired of Tramping Around? Take the Tram **27**
Treks and Tours **87**
Up, Up, and Away **151**
Wineries **182**
Yee-Haw, Mary—The Rodeo Comes to Town **191**

BESTS

Davies, Hugh M. **42**
Guillas, Bernard **36**
Harris, Mike **172**
Heying, Jan **120**
Hubbell, Jim **22**
Irvine, Georgeanne **30**

O'Brien, Jack **141**
Quigley, Rob Wellington, and Everyone Else in the Office **56**

MAPS

Balboa Park **12, 31**
Coastal North County **160**
Coronado **63**
Desert Day Trips **160**
Downtown **32**
Gaslamp Quarter **32**
Gay San Diego **185, 189**
Harbor Island **102**
Inland North County **160**
La Jolla **139, 149**
Little Italy **33**
Map key **6**
Mission Bay and Beaches **115**
Mission Bay Park **115**
Mission Beach **115, 129**
Mission Valley **100**
Ocean Beach **115, 132**
Old Town **90**
Pacific Beach **123**
Point Loma **102**
San Diego **2**
San Diego and Environs see inside front cover
San Diego Convention Center **55**
San Diego Day Trips **160**
San Diego Museum of Art **20**
San Diego Trolley see inside back cover
San Diego Zoo **15**
Shelter Island **102, 110**
South of Tijuana **178**
Tijuana **169**
Tijuana Day Trips **178**
Trolley see inside back cover
Uptown **76**